"This extensively researched and passionately argued book will invariably provoke discussion in Bonhoeffer studies as it challenges misconceptions of his role as assassin and patriot. It persuasively reconciles Bonhoeffer's pacifist writings with his political activities in the Abwehr, as well as themes of pacifist obedience with political responsibility often separated by Niebuhrian 'political realist' readings. This is an invaluable study of Bonhoeffer's theological ethics that must be taken seriously."

—**David Haddorff**, St. John's University

"Those of us who have been uneasy with the too-glib assumption that Bonhoeffer gave up his commitment to pacifism to join a conspiracy against Hitler can now rejoice. This book's careful scholarship thoroughly proves that the major change in Bonhoeffer's theology happened much earlier and that he remained steadfast thereafter as a pacifist until his death at Nazi hands. This clarifying volume must be read by everyone."

—**Marva J. Dawn**, theologian, lecturer, and author of *The Sense of the Call*, *Unfettered Hope*, and *Being Well When We're Ill*

"This book's provocative title is designed to challenge the received view of Dietrich Bonhoeffer's role in the German Resistance's plans to overthrow the Nazi regime by murdering Hitler. The authors seek to show that he had no sympathy with such political violence. Instead he remained true to the teachings of the Sermon on the Mount, especially to Jesus's teachings about the ethics of peace, which he had outlined so forcefully in his book *The Cost of Discipleship*. Their careful analysis of Bonhoeffer's writings finds no evidence that he endorsed tyrannicide. They make a strong case for a re-evaluation of his legacy."

—**John S. Conway**, University of British Columbia

BONHOEFFER THE ASSASSIN?

Challenging the Myth, Recovering His Call to Peacemaking

Mark Thiessen Nation,
Anthony G. Siegrist,
and Daniel P. Umbel

Baker Academic
a division of Baker Publishing Group
Grand Rapids, Michigan

Published by Baker Academic
a division of Baker Publishing Group
P.O. Box 6287, Grand Rapids, MI 49516-6287
www.bakeracademic.com

Printed in the United States of America

Library of Congress Cataloging-in-Publication Data

Nation, Mark.
Bonhoeffer the assassin? : challenging the myth, recovering his call to peacemaking / Mark Thiessen Nation, Anthony G. Siegrist, and Daniel P. Umbel.
pages cm
Includes bibliographical references and index.
ISBN 978-0-8010-3961-4 (pbk.)
1. Bonhoeffer, Dietrich, 1906–1945. I. Title.
BX4827.B57N38 2013
230′.044092—dc23 2013015964

13 14 15 16 17 18 19 7 6 5 4 3 2 1

In memory of Franz Hildebrandt (1909–85),
Bonhoeffer's "best-informed and most like-minded friend"
(Eberhard Bethge)

Contents

Acknowledgments

This work is, we hope, a coherent monograph written by three authors. Mark has served as the overall editor to ensure coherence (with help from Anthony). Individual chapters were divided up among us. Mark wrote the introduction, the first three chapters, and the conclusion. Dan wrote chapters 4 and 5. Anthony wrote chapters 6 and 7. We are all thankful for the assistance of a variety of people. The list below is surely incomplete.

From Dan. I would like to thank both of my coauthors, without whose help my own chapters would have never reached press. Thanks are due especially to Mark for his encouragement, insight, and frequently exercised patience. Thanks are also due to my friends and family for their support, encouragement, and understanding, especially to my parents, my congregation at Mt. Olivet Church, and my beloved wife, Tonya, who came into my life when I needed her most.

From Anthony. I would like to thank Sarah, Dave, Dorothy, and Jeff. This book has been germinating for a long time. The four of you have kept me hopeful that it would one day be completed. Some twelve years ago Oz Lorentzen assigned Bonhoeffer's *Ethics* to a small class of undergraduate theology students. I am thankful for his ambition. A number of my students here at Prairie read early drafts of the project and took the argument seriously despite the fact that it went against the current of much of the secondary literature they were reading at the time. At the Toronto School of Theology Jim Reimer allowed me to explore some of the lines of argument developed here in a course he taught on War and Peace in the Christian Tradition. His comments were helpful. Finally, I am grateful to Mark for the idea of the book and for his sustained attention to the subject matter over the years that the project has been in development.

From Mark. I have been studying this set of issues for a long time. I am grateful to LeRoy Friesen, himself a Bonhoeffer scholar, who more than thirty years ago directed my master's thesis on nonviolent forms of resistance within Nazi Germany at Associated (now Anabaptist) Mennonite Biblical Seminary. I am grateful to John Howard Yoder for allowing me to write a long paper for him on the Confessing Church out of the same research. I am also grateful to have been able to attend the American commemoration of the 50th anniversary of the Barmen Conference in April 1984 in Seattle, Washington. There I had the opportunity to hear speeches from one of the original signers of the Barmen Confession, Heinrich Vogel, along with Bonhoeffer's close friends and (with the latter two) former students, Franz Hildebrandt, Eberhard Bethge, and Wolf-Dieter Zimmermann. At the beginning of the 1990s Jan Ligus, visiting Bonhoeffer scholar from the Czech Republic, offered me a directed study course on Bonhoeffer at Christian Theological Seminary. A few years later, Ray Anderson agreed to do another directed study on Bonhoeffer at Fuller Theological Seminary.

More immediately pertinent to the book, a sabbatical at Eastern Mennonite Seminary in 2009–10 allowed me to do substantial research on attempts on Hitler's life while examining the relevant facts about Bonhoeffer's biography that might or might not connect with these attempts. I am grateful for that. I am grateful to the students who have been in my Bonhoeffer classes here at Eastern Mennonite Seminary, especially in spring of 2011 when we used early versions of chapters of the present book. Esther Lanting loaned me her notes from interviews she conducted with friends and family of Dietrich Bonhoeffer in Europe in the mid-1970s. She spoke with them specifically about his pacifism and possible involvement in attempts to kill Hitler. David Graybill improved my three biographical chapters by offering his expert editorial help.

My wife, Mary, has been very supportive—as always—during my years of working on this book; thank you. She and the interesting life of our local Mennonite church, the Early Church—which is connected with and meets in a community center that serves some of the poorest people in Harrisonburg—regularly remind me that costly grace and the discipleship flowing from it are not simply words appearing in a book written in 1937, or lived only ages ago; they are still realities still being embodied.

All of us who work on Bonhoeffer's life and thought are deeply indebted to Eberhard Bethge for keeping Bonhoeffer's legacy alive until his own death in 2000. We are also now indebted to the hard-working team of scholars who have edited and translated the collected works. Clifford Green is certainly one who has worked very hard on this project as executive director of the collected works in English (as well as editor of several volumes). We dedicate this work, however, to Bonhoeffer's close friend Franz Hildebrandt. I sometimes wonder how the legacy of Bonhoeffer might have been perceived if Hildebrandt had not needed to leave Germany in 1937. From meeting him and having a brief conversation with him in 1984, I am hopeful he would be pleased with our book.

Finally, I want to thank my coauthors, Dan and Anthony. It is a great gift to have very intelligent students. These men are two of the brightest students I have ever had. They both took my Bonhoeffer course. I knew soon after I had decided to write this book that I wanted to ask them to write it with me. They graciously said yes. Each of them has done a better job on his respective chapters than I could have done.

We are all three grateful to the Baker staff, who have been great to work with. Rodney Clapp was the original acquisitions editor, and Robert Hosack, our second acquistions editor, has proved to be delightful to work with. We also express appreciation to Robert Hand and Bethany Murphy for their very professional editing, Bryan Dyer for his helpfulness with publicity, and Paula Gibson for producing a wonderful cover for the book. I'm sure there are others behind the scenes at Baker who deserve our gratitude (including my friend, Steve Ayers); thanks to all of you. And finally a thank you to Stanley Hauerwas for his ongoing friendship, his unceasingly creative and provocative writings, and the wonderful foreword he has written for our book in the midst of a very busy life.

Foreword

What about Dietrich Bonhoeffer?" I have lost track of how many times I have been asked that question after giving a lecture. The lecture may have only mentioned in passing my commitment to Christian nonviolence, but it seems the mere suggestion that Christians should be committed to nonviolence is enough to put someone on the defensive. So they ask, "What about Dietrich Bonhoeffer?" My questioner may not know a great deal about Bonhoeffer or have read deeply in his work, but they "know" he was a participant in one of the plots that allegedly sought to kill Hitler. That is quite sufficient, they seem to think, to call into question a commitment to Christian nonviolence.

In response to the question about Bonhoeffer I have always accepted the premise that Bonhoeffer was in fact part of the *Abwehr* plot to kill Hitler. But I also emphasize that Bonhoeffer was a pacifist, having been deeply influenced by Jean Lasserre during his time at Union Theological Seminary in New York. Lasserre, moreover, was not a "liberal pacifist." Lasserre's advocacy of nonviolence was based in Scripture and, in particular, on the Decalogue. In like manner, Bonhoeffer's commitment to nonviolence was not something he could or would easily abandon because that commitment was grounded in his reading of the Sermon on the Mount. In short, as Nation argues, you cannot separate Bonhoeffer's Christology and his commitment to nonviolence. They are one.

I also point out to those that use Bonhoeffer to challenge a commitment to nonviolence that there are a number of ambiguities surrounding his participation in the plot against Hitler. For example, we know from Bonhoeffer's negotiations with the British that the plotters did not originally seek to kill Hitler because they feared if they killed Hitler the German people might turn Hitler into a martyr. Moreover, Bonhoeffer's work with the *Abwehr* was first and foremost motivated by his desire to avoid being drafted into the military. I observe, therefore, we simply do not have the evidence necessary to know how deeply Bonhoeffer was involved in the plot against Hitler or what he may have thought about his alleged willingness to be engaged in an attempt to kill Hitler.

I have to acknowledge, however, that there are some passages in *Ethics* about responsibility and guilt that seem to reflect Bonhoeffer's attempt to think through his involvement in the plot to take Hitler's life. Because I have always thought Bonhoeffer's *Discipleship* to be the definitive statement of his "ethics," I confess I am not sure how some of the passages in the *Ethics* are to be read in light of what he says in his earlier book. That is complicated by my conviction that if you begin to read Bonhoeffer from the beginning, that is, with *Sanctorum Communio*, I believe you cannot help but see that the fundamental theological commitments that shaped his life and work are constant throughout his life.

I relate how I have tried to respond to the question "What about Dietrich Bonhoeffer?" to suggest the significance of this book by Nation, Umbel, and Siegrist. What they have done is nothing short of revolutionary. Through careful scholarship they have called into question the fundamental assumptions that seem to make the question about Bonhoeffer's participation in the plot against Hitler, as well as attempts such as mine to respond to that question, problematic. For example, with considerable detail they take us through the plots against Hitler in which Bonhoeffer might have had the opportunity to be involved to show that we have no evidence that he was. There is, therefore, no indication in Bonhoeffer's life or work that he ever abandoned his pacifism to join a plot to kill Hitler.

Nation, Umbel, and Siegrist are quite methodical in how they develop their argument. Though it may seem artificial, they first provide an account of his life before engaging in close reading of his theological work. Their decision to separate his life from his work proves necessary if they are to challenge the presumption—a presumption that functions for many as a given—that Bonhoeffer was involved in a plot to kill Hitler. That presumption, they show, has shaped the reception of Bonhoeffer's theology, particularly in the United States, in a problematic manner. By first treating Bonhoeffer's life, therefore, they are able to offer a persuasive reading of his theological development that challenges those that assume his later work stands in some tension with his earlier theology.

I found both parts of the book extremely helpful. In particular, their account of the relationship between *Discipleship* and *Ethics* will be profoundly significant for how Bonhoeffer is read in the future. The unfinished character of *Ethics*, of course, means we will never know how Bonhoeffer would have finally put the book together, but I think the suggestions that Nation, Umbel, and Siegrist make about how these two works are interrelated is persuasive. Their account of Bonhoffer's account of the relationship between responsibility and guilt in *Ethics* is extremely important. They have, I think, finally provided the decisive argument against those that would read Bonhoeffer on responsibility through the eyes of Reinhold Niebuhr.

I have no doubt this book will stir considerable controversy. It will do so because they challenge habits of interpretation of Bonhoeffer that have been taken for granted for many years. The "obvious" is never given up without a struggle. But Nation, Umbel, and Siegrist have done their homework. I am sure, therefore, they will be more than ready to hold their own in the debates the book will no doubt produce.

For it is not just those that use Bonhoeffer to justify violence that this book challenges, but the argument they develop means I must rethink how I have been responding to the question "What about Bonhoeffer?" No longer should the presumption behind the question be granted. Not only do we have no indication that Bonhoeffer was involved in a plot against Hitler's life, but we can now approach his work with fresh eyes in the hope of learning from him how to go on in the face of the presumption there is no alternative to war.

It would be a mistake, however, if the significance of this book is understood only to force a reinterpretation of Bonhoeffer's life and work. Far more important this book means the question "What about Bonhoeffer?" must now perform a different function. If you think Bonhoeffer not only lived a remarkable life but was a significant theologian, then his commitment to nonviolence cannot be dismissed. In short, you cannot have both Bonhoeffer and war. To entertain the question "What about Bonhoeffer?" means the assumption of the inevitability of war must now be challenged.

Those that use the question about Bonhoeffer to justify war assume that someone has to oppose the Hitlers of the world. Yet it is often forgotten that this was the same justification made by Christians—Catholic and Protestant Christians—who served in Hitler's army because they presumed there is no alternative to war. Of course that presumption will continue to operate and confuse as long as Christians fail to acknowledge that the Church is the alternative to war. "What about Bonhoeffer?" turns out, therefore, to be a question that, given the argument of this important book, makes the challenge of Christian nonviolence unavoidable.

Stanley Hauerwas
Duke Divinity School
May 2013

Introduction

> Here alone lies the force that can blow all this hocus-pocus sky-high—like fireworks, leaving only a few burnt-out shells behind.
>
> Dietrich Bonhoeffer

Dietrich Bonhoeffer (1906–45), a pastor and theologian, is perhaps best known today for his involvement in the conspiracy to topple the Hitler government, which included involvement in efforts to kill Hitler, leading to Bonhoeffer's subsequent execution at the hands of the Third Reich. That Bonhoeffer's resistance to the Nazis has captured the imagination of both the public and scholars is not surprising. But what if the nature of that resistance was different than what is commonly supposed? Would that change our view of Bonhoeffer? Would it make him less admirable? Would we see his theology, his ethics, and his example in a different light?

Early in my work on this book, my wife and I watched the film *Valkyrie*, starring Tom Cruise.[1] This is a cinematic version of the best-known attempt to kill Hitler. It is a powerful and moving story. Here we see a number of military officers and government officials who are willing—at great potential cost to themselves—to attempt to overthrow the Hitler government (of which they are, at this point, very much a part). Cruise plays one of the central characters in this unfolding story: Claus Schenk von Stauffenberg (1907–44).[2] On April

1. *Valkyrie*, directed by Bryan Singer (Beverly Hills: MGM, 2008), DVD.

2. For two brief accounts of Stauffenberg, see Joachim Fest, *Plotting Hitler's Death: The Story of the German Resistance*, trans. Bruce Little (New York: Metropolitan Books, 1996), 202–36; and Roger Moorhouse, *Killing Hitler: The Plots, the Assassins, and the Dictator Who Cheated Death* (New York: Bantam Books, 2006), 251–68. For the definitive account of Stauffenberg's

7, 1943, while in Africa under Rommel's command, Stauffenberg had been seriously wounded in combat, losing an eye, his right hand, and two fingers of his left hand. The film shows Hitler personally commending Stauffenberg for his bravery. What Hitler doesn't know is that his chief of staff to the commander of the reserve army was by June of 1944—at the very moment Hitler commends him as a model officer—involved in an unfolding plot to kill the Führer. In fact Stauffenberg is, by this point, committed to carrying out the assassination himself. He is one of the few conspirators involved in Hitler's military briefing conferences—one of the rare places where someone has guaranteed access not only to Hitler but also to Himmler and other top officials. Thus on July 20, 1944, Stauffenberg carried a bomb with him into the briefing room at Hitler's headquarters, the Wolf's Lair, near Rastenburg, East Prussia. As planned, he exited the room before the bomb exploded. As an eyewitness recalled, "In a flash the map room became a scene of stampede and destruction. . . . There was nothing but wounded men groaning, the acrid smell of burning and charred fragments of maps and papers fluttering in the wind."[3] From a safe distance Stauffenberg heard the explosion. He assumed the attempt was successful. Hitler was dead! Stauffenberg flew back to Berlin and began to implement the takeover of the Hitler government, with the Führer himself safely out of the way—or so he believed. As it happened, Hitler suffered only minor injuries. By 1:00 a.m. the German people were reassured by Hitler himself that he was alive and still the Reichsführer of Germany. Thousands of executions followed this attempt on Hitler's life. Stauffenberg himself was executed close to midnight on July 20.

I wonder how a film director might create a film centered not on Stauffenberg but rather on another significant figure in the resistance, Helmuth James Count von Moltke (1907–45).[4] Such a film might well focus on Moltke's work

---

life in English, see Peter Hoffman, *Stauffenberg: A Family History*, 3rd ed. (Montreal: McGill-Queen's University Press, 2009). For a fuller account of the many attempts on Hitler's life, with some of the most relevant documents, see Ian Kershaw, *Luck of the Devil: The Story of Operation Valkyrie* (New York: Penguin Books, 2009). For a thorough, easy to follow, chronological account, see Nigel Jones, *Countdown to Valkyrie: The July Plot to Assassinate Hitler* (London: Frontline Books, 2008). For the most thorough account of the resistance movements in English, see Peter Hoffman, *The History of the German Resistance 1933–1945*, 3rd ed. (Montreal: McGill-Queen's University Press, 1996). The brief narrative that follows draws upon details from these accounts.

3. As quoted in Moorhouse, *Killing Hitler*, 263.

4. For brief accounts of Moltke, see Beate Ruhm von Oppen, introduction to *Letters to Freya, 1939–1945*, by Helmuth James von Moltke, ed. and trans. Beate Ruhm von Oppen (New York: Alfred A. Knopf, 1990), 3–25; and Hans Mommsen, "The Kreisau Circle and the Future Reorganization of Germany and Europe," in *Alternatives to Hitler: German Resistance Under the Third Reich* (London: I. B. Tauris, 2003), 134–51. For a full account, see Ger van Roon, *German Resistance to Hitler: Count von Moltke and the Kreisau Circle*, trans. Peter Ludlow

for the *Abwehr*, the military intelligence agency for which he began work in the fall of 1939 (about a year before Dietrich Bonhoeffer).[5] Moltke seemed perfect for the job. He came from a prominent military family and was a lawyer, specializing in international law. His job description said that he was to gather military intelligence for the *Wehrmacht*, the Armed Forces, using his expertise to assist Germany in its war efforts. This entailed reading reports regarding German military efforts as well as those of other nations; it also involved extensive travel. However, what he actually did differed significantly from his job description. Admiral Wilhelm Canaris, who headed the Abwehr, and Hans Oster, his right-hand man, facilitated what came to be referred to as a "nest of resistance" within this military organization.[6] A number of the resisters who later came to be well known worked within the Abwehr. Moltke was one. Thus Moltke used his position in the Abwehr—and used knowledge gained through his work—to resist Hitler.

Through his travels and access to documents, Moltke came to know much about the war that Germany was waging. A letter to his wife on October 21, 1941, gives us an important glimpse into the war and how Moltke reflected on it, important enough that we quote him at length:

> The day is so full of gruesome news that I cannot write in peace, although I retired at 5 and have just had some tea. But my head aches all the same. What affects me most at the moment is the inadequacy of the reactions of the military. [Officers] Falkenhausen and Stülpnagel have returned to their posts instead of resigning after the latest incidents [i.e., the shootings of hostages on September 3], dreadful new orders are being issued, and nobody seems to see anything wrong in it all. How is one to bear the burden of complicity?
>
> In one area in Serbia two villages have been reduced to ashes, 1,700 men and 240 women from among the inhabitants have been executed. That is the "punishment" for an attack on three German soldiers. In Greece 220 men of one village have been shot. The village was burnt down, women and children were left there to weep for their husbands and fathers and homes. In France

(London: Van Nostrand Reinhold, 1971); and Michael Balfour and Julian Frisby, *Helmuth von Moltke: A Leader Against Hitler* (London: Macmillan, 1972).

5. *Abwehr* literally means "defense." Abwehr is the name used for the central military intelligence agency within Germany, the center of espionage and counter-espionage activities for the German Supreme Command (OKW).

6. Sabine Dramm, in her recent book on Bonhoeffer, challenges some tendencies to exaggerate the numbers of resisters in the Abwehr. According to Dramm, at its peak the Abwehr had thirteen thousand employees working at all levels. Only about fifty of these could be counted as "supporters of the resistance," which amounts to 0.4 percent of the whole workforce. See Sabine Dramm, *Dietrich Bonhoeffer and the Resistance*, trans. Margaret Kohl (Minneapolis: Fortress, 2009), 33.

> there are extensive shootings while I write. Certainly more than a thousand people are murdered in this way every day and another thousand German men are habituated to murder. And all this is child's play compared with what is happening in Poland and Russia. May I know this and yet sit at my table in my heated flat and have tea? Don't I thereby become guilty too? What shall I say when I am asked: And what did you do during that time?
>
> Since Saturday the Berlin Jews are being rounded up. They are picked up at 9.15 in the evening and locked into a synagogue overnight. Then they are sent off, with what they can carry, to Litzmannstadt [Lodz] and Smolensk. We are to be spared the sight of them being simply left to perish in hunger and cold, and that is why it is done in Litzmannstadt and Smolensk. . . .
>
> How can anyone know these things and still walk around free? With what right? Is it not inevitable that his turn will come too one day, and that he too will be rolled into the gutter?—All this is only summer-lightning, for the storm is still ahead.—If only I could get rid of the terrible feeling that I have let myself be corrupted, that I do not react keenly enough to such things, that they torment me without producing a spontaneous reaction. I have mistrained myself, for in such things, too, I react with my head. I think about a possible reaction instead of acting.[7]

With such overwhelming suffering before him, Moltke may have, quite understandably, felt that he didn't do enough. But Moltke was indeed *acting* in his role with the Abwehr—though not, as most Germans at the time would have perceived it, on behalf of Germany. Making allies where he could, he attempted to work against the escalation of the war as well as to mitigate atrocities masquerading as legitimate war tactics, such as those described above. These efforts involved gathering specific data and communicating with relevant German officials, attempting to convince them of the need to obey international laws, sometimes utilizing arguments of self-interest—such as mutual, respectful treatment of political prisoners—in order to be convincing. He improved local conditions for people where he could through invoking legal principles. After he knew that Jews were being deported, he attempted to get them rerouted to countries that would be a safe haven for them. When possible, he personally helped Jews escape to safe territories.[8] Armed with his extensive information and his connections with the German resistance movement, he communicated especially with his friends in England. He wanted them to be apprised of what was happening.

7. Moltke, *Letters to Freya*, 174–75.

8. This was true, for example, in two 1943 cases when he intervened at great personal risk to help Danish Jews in one instance and Norwegian Jews in another to escape to Sweden (Dramm, *Dietrich Bonhoeffer and the Resistance*, 139–40).

And he wanted them to know that there were Germans, like himself, who wanted to see the Hitler government defeated and wanted a different German society to emerge.

Moltke's position in the Abwehr enabled him to do the practical work of an international lawyer. However, the particulars of what he did—engaging in risky acts of compassion—were motivated, shaped, and sustained by his Christian faith. As he put it to his English friend Lionel Curtis in a letter in 1942:

> Today it is beginning to dawn on a not too numerous but active part of the population not that they have been misled, not that they are in for a hard time, not that they might lose the war, but that what is done is sinful, and that they are personally responsible for every savage act that has been done, not of course in a mortal way, but as Christians. Perhaps you will remember that, in discussions before the war, I maintained that belief in God was not essential for coming to the results you arrive at. Today I know I was wrong, completely wrong. You know that I have fought the Nazis from the first day, but the amount of risk and readiness for sacrifice which is asked from us now, and that which may be asked from us tomorrow require more than right ethical principles, especially as we know that the success of our fight will probably mean a total collapse as a national unit. But we are ready to face this. The second great danger which confronts us as soon as we get rid of the NS [National Socialist] force is to visualize Europe after the war. We can only expect to get our people to overthrow this reign of terror and horror if we are able to show a picture beyond the terrifying and hopeless immediate future.[9]

This letter reflects Moltke's central passions and convictions. These convictions led him not only to do his difficult work through the Abwehr; they also led him to organize a resistance group that came to be known as the "Kreisau Circle," named for his family estate on which some of the meetings were held. As Joachim Fest has put it, "What brought the Kreisau group together was not principally a determination to overthrow the Nazi regime but rather the common project of planning, through their preparatory discussions, what a modern, post-Hitler Germany would look like."[10]

The members of the Kreisau Circle disagreed among themselves on a variety of issues, including the use of violence to topple the Hitler government, although Fest is probably right that "most members of the Kreisau Circle rejected

9. Helmuth James von Moltke, "Letter in English from Moltke to an English Friend," in Roon, *German Resistance to Hitler*, 376–77. Though this book is mostly a secondary account written by Ger van Roon, it also contains one hundred pages of letters and documents from the Kreisau Circle.

10. Fest, *Plotting Hitler's Death*, 158.

any sort of violence."[11] What becomes obvious to anyone who reads about this resistance group is that they believed that the problems in Nazi Germany were not just Hitler and a few of his henchmen. There were fundamental problems in Germany that could not be resolved merely through a few changes in the top leadership. Knowing of the atrocities of the Nazi war effort, some within this group believed that the only way that Germany could become a healthy contributor to Europe or the world was to be brought to its knees through utter defeat. Not all agreed. But at least within the context of this group, the primary focus was that of envisioning a new post-Hitler Germany. This was a clear enough emphasis that Peter Hoffman, one of the foremost authorities on the resistance movements, has said of the Kreisau Circle: "They had little or no confidence in the prospects of a military coup, and they pursued what might be described as a pacifist option of resistance."[12]

But in the meantime, before there was a "post-Hitler Germany," Moltke did what he could to express his Christian convictions in tangible ways—as strange as it may seem at first glance—through a military intelligence agency within Germany. His work in the Abwehr allowed him to be relieved of military duty on the front lines and thus killing in the name of Hitler. It also gave him opportunities to mitigate some of the worst destructiveness of the German armed forces. And it afforded him opportunities to give aid to those very people who were potential victims of the German nation at the time. As one summary statement has it: "By wielding his legal expertise like a bureaucratic monkey wrench to counter the deportation and murder of Jews and the execution of captured soldiers, he saved untold lives."[13] However, it was the Kreisau Circle to which Moltke devoted his free time and energy.[14] And by all accounts he was its central force and leading light. It gave him hope and sustained him spiritually to be among a group of resisters who were envisioning another world for the future. Such a world had to be envisioned from the ground up and in specific terms. For as he said to his friend Lionel Curtis, "We need a revolution, not a coup d'état."[15] Some historians believe that in the end Moltke approved of

11. Ibid., 160. He does not mean most were pacifist; he means they were unwilling to assassinate leaders.

12. Peter Hoffman, introduction to *The Power of Solitude: My Life in the German Resistance*, by Marion Yorck von Wartenburg (Lincoln: University of Nebraska Press, 2000), xx.

13. From the dust jacket of Moltke, *Letters to Freya*, inside front flap. Sabine Dramm refers to Moltke as one of "the two most important regime-critical civilians in the Military Intelligence Foreign Office," Bonhoeffer's brother-in-law, Hans von Dohnanyi, being the other (Dramm, *Dietrich Bonhoeffer and the Resistance*, 102).

14. The first small but formal gathering of those who came to be called the Kreisau Circle took place at least as early as August 1940 (Roon, *German Resistance to Hitler*, 141).

15. As quoted in Mommsen, "Kreisau Circle," 139.

the assassination of Hitler. However, no one of whom I am aware believes that we have really understood Moltke or the Kreisau Circle that gathered around him if we focus primarily on his possible links to attempts on Hitler's life. Beate Ruhm von Oppen paraphrases and quotes from a farewell letter that Moltke wrote to his two sons on October 11, 1944, after nearly nine months in jail. He wanted them to know from him what the cause of his execution was:

> "Throughout an entire life, even at school, I have fought against a spirit of narrowness and unfreedom, of arrogance and lack of respect for others, of intolerance and the absolute, the merciless consistency among the Germans, which found its expression in the National Socialist state. I exerted myself to help to overcome this spirit with its evil consequences, such as excessive nationalism, racial persecution, lack of faith, and materialism." He continued that from their point of view the Nazis were therefore right in killing him. But they were wrong to kill him inasmuch as he had always opposed acts of violence, like the attempted coup of 20 July 1944, for a number of reasons, but chiefly because it would not change the mentality behind the Third Reich.[16]

In his last letter to his wife, on January 11, 1945, Moltke said the following:

> The decisive phrase of the trial was: "Herr Graf, one thing Christianity and we National Socialists have in common, and only one: we demand the whole man." I wonder if he realized what he was saying? Just think how wonderfully God prepared this, his unworthy vessel. At the very moment when there was danger I might be drawn into active preparations of a putsch—it was the evening of the 19th that Stauffenberg came to Peter [Yorck]—I was taken away, so that I should be and remain free from all connection with the use of violence.[17]

Let us consider a few questions. If Moltke were to become well known, would his name mostly be associated with the "plots to kill Hitler"? Would his contemporary importance mostly be seen in relation to those clearly willing to assassinate the Führer, such as Stauffenberg? After all, Moltke worked with the Abwehr and was executed precisely because his name was linked to conspirators, some of whom did attempt to kill Hitler. Would we ignore what seems to be his expressed desire, in some of his last words, that he not be associated with the assassination attempt of July 20, 1944? And would we

16. Von Oppen, introduction to *Letters to Freya*, 3. Moltke's widow in an interview confirms that he was opposed to the attempts to kill Hitler. See Dorothee von Meding, "Freya von Moltke," in *Courageous Hearts: Women and the Anti-Hitler Plot of 1944*, trans. Michael Balfour and Volker R. Berghahn (Providence, RI: Berghahn Books, 1997), 70, 73.

17. Moltke, *Letters to Freya*, 410. Also see Freya von Moltke, *Memories of Kreisau and the German Resistance*, trans. Julie M. Winter (Lincoln: University of Nebraska Press, 2003).

mostly ignore the central focus of his short life, including his work to save the lives of Jews and his work to curb German military abuses? Including the fact that his clearest and deepest commitments and convictions seemed to be expressed in the context of the organization that he founded, the Kreisau Circle, which by all accounts was centrally about envisioning a new German society that valued the Christian faith, small communities, individual responsibility, and so on—not on mounting a violent coup?

And would we imply that somehow Stauffenberg's life and commitments were more important than Moltke's—because he engaged in the ultimately "responsible" act of attempting to assassinate Hitler? Even though Moltke was probably responsible for the saving of thousands of lives? Even though Stauffenberg, as a military officer, was probably responsible for the killing of hundreds, if not thousands, of people as part of the German military?[18] Even though Stauffenberg not only failed in his attempt to kill Hitler but, precisely because of this obvious attempt, provoked the eventual execution of thousands of people, including Moltke?[19]

I ask these questions because it seems that something very much like this has happened to the legacy of Dietrich Bonhoeffer. Of course, the particulars of their two lives differ. However, it should be obvious that Bonhoeffer's daily life, linked with his theological writings, from the fall of 1940 until his arrest in April of 1943, as an agent of the Abwehr, comes much closer to the life and legacy of Moltke than of Stauffenberg.[20]

I have watched the fine 1982 documentary film *Dietrich Bonhoeffer: Memories and Perspectives* many times. It is mostly composed of interviews with Bonhoeffer's family members and former students. I am always quite moved when I watch the interview with Emmi Bonhoeffer, the widow of Klaus Bonhoeffer,

18. However, it should also be said about Stauffenberg that, according to Peter Hoffman, he attempted "throughout 1942 . . . singlehandedly and against overwhelming odds . . . to convince senior commanders on the eastern front to overthrow Hitler." Peter Hoffman, introduction to *To the Bitter End: An Insider's Account of the Plot to Kill Hitler 1933–1944*, by Hans Bernd Gisevius, trans. Richard and Clara Winston (original German 1946; New York: DaCapo Press, 1998), xvii.

19. See Anton Gill, *An Honorable Defeat: A History of German Resistance to Hitler, 1933–1945* (New York: Henry Holt, 1994), viii.

20. On Moltke and Bonhoeffer, see Dramm, *Dietrich Bonhoeffer and the Resistance*, 133–53. Dramm is, to some extent, in this chapter specifically focusing on distinctions between the two. It seems that Bonhoeffer's work in the Abwehr mostly consisted of continuing his ecumenical contacts throughout Europe and Scandinavia, to inform his friends of activities and progress of the German resistance movements, and to solicit assistance where possible from others. Additionally, the Abwehr gave him an exemption from military service, time to study theology and meet with theologians, and the opportunity to do some writing both on *Ethics* and otherwise. He also did some of the other things Moltke did, but he wasn't an expert in international or military law like Moltke and thus couldn't begin to accomplish as much.

Dietrich's brother, who was also executed for being tied to the conspiracy. At one point in the film she is speaking of one of her last conversations with her husband, when he was convinced his arrest was imminent.

> I forgot if it was on this occasion or later when [my husband] came in August to see the children for the last time, when I asked him: "When you will be arrested what can I do?" And he said: "You can't do anything. It will be as if I fell into a lion's den. Try to save your life for the children. And you will get help from friends." I have to go my way. But I feel [she pauses, apparently holding back tears] at least my children will never have to be ashamed of their father. That he had known about [all the horrible things going on] and hadn't done anything.[21]

Having studied the Nazi era, World War II, and the Holocaust of the Jews fairly extensively, I empathize with her. I hear the quite understandable, if sad, pride in her voice. Unlike the overwhelming majority of Germans at the time, her husband *did something* to try to stop Hitler. Unlike many others, their children "will never have to be ashamed of their father." He acted "responsibly." Who would not be moved? But her husband was not a theologian. More importantly, unlike his brother Dietrich, he was not a theologian who had committed a significant portion of his life to a serious study of the Sermon on the Mount and to teaching about and living costly discipleship based upon that study.

On January 14, 1935, Dietrich Bonhoeffer wrote a letter to his brother Karl-Friedrich. He was expressing his excitement about his ongoing discoveries as he prepared sermons for the congregation he was pastoring in London, England—especially what he was learning through his engagement with the Scriptures:

> Perhaps I seem to you rather fanatical and mad about a number of things. I myself am sometimes afraid of that. But I know that the day I became more "reasonable," to be honest, I should have to chuck my entire theology. When I first started in theology, my idea of it was quite different—rather more academic, probably. Now it has turned to something else altogether. But I do believe that at last I am on the right track, for the first time in my life. I often feel quite happy about it. I only worry about being so afraid of what other people will think as to get bogged down instead of going forward. I think I am right in saying that I would only achieve true inner clarity and honesty by really starting to take the Sermon on the Mount seriously. Here alone lies the force that can blow all this

21. Emmi Bonhoeffer, excerpts from interview in *Dietrich Bonhoeffer: Memories and Perspectives*, directed by Bain Boehlke (Lansdale, PA: Trinity Films, 1983), DVD. Transcription has been amended slightly to improve Emmi Bonhoeffer's English.

> hocus-pocus sky-high—like fireworks, leaving only a few burnt out shells behind. The restoration of the church must surely depend on a new kind of monasticism, which has nothing in common with the old but a life of uncompromising discipleship, following Christ according to the Sermon on the Mount. I believe the time has come to gather people together and do this.[22]

By referring to a force that can "blow all this hocus-pocus sky-high—like fireworks," it does not appear that Bonhoeffer imagines that what he is discovering through living with the Sermon on the Mount is either a kind of safe, individually tailored pietism or some pure idealism with little relevance for daily living in the midst of the Third Reich. No, he believes he is grasping something simultaneously relevant for the restoration of the church and explosive of normal existence. He will name his discovery more fully through the manifesto that will in book form be titled *Nachfolge*, or in the first English translation, *The Cost of Discipleship*, and now simply *Discipleship*.[23]

In a little more than three months Bonhoeffer will start a seminary for the Confessing Church at Zingst and then move it to Finkenwalde less than two months later. The training in a "new kind of monasticism," Bonhoeffer's attempts at the "restoration of the church," will begin. It is interesting to hear the impressions left on a student at the Finkenwalde seminary, Joachim Kanitz:

> That semester we worked on the exegesis of the Sermon on the Mount; later on he worked this into his book, *The Cost of Discipleship*. It became clear to us on the basis of this Bible study that it is not possible for Christians to justify killing or to justify war. So, of course, we also had to talk about the very immediate question of what we would do if it came to war or even if it didn't come to war, what we would do if we were drafted, since the draft had been introduced. We were just the age that would be taken first. We worried because we didn't think this through all that carefully because there was so much else to be concerned about—there was the question of the church and the Jews and our work in the parish. When it came to the point when we were in fact drafted—I was called

22. Dietrich Bonhoeffer, *London: 1933–1935*, ed. Keith W. Clements, trans. Isabel Best, vol. 13 of *Dietrich Bonhoeffer Works* (Minneapolis: Fortress, 2007), 284–85.

23. According to Eberhard Bethge, this book has its roots in 1932 (after Bonhoeffer's year in New York City). Its more obvious textual roots are in sermons Bonhoeffer preached during his eighteen-month pastorate in London. Unfortunately, the manuscripts from his sermons on the Sermon on the Mount, in London, are lost. However, we have other sermons—some of which I will quote in chapter 2—which clearly are similar in wording and passion to his book *Discipleship*. Most directly Bonhoeffer presented lectures to his students at the seminary that would become the book *Nachfolge*, first published in 1937. It was first published in English as *The Cost of Discipleship* in 1948. The critical English edition, published in 2001, reflects the German title, and thus is simply *Discipleship*.

up on May 15, 1939—we went in with a bad conscience. It was against our convictions. But the alternative was being lined up against a wall and shot. I remember that when it came to the outbreak of war on September 1st 1939, I was still hoping that the Confessing Church would come out with a loud "no," but by then it was no longer in a position to act at all.[24]

So far Kanitz's reflections might be expected. Yes, this is the Bonhoeffer of *Discipleship*. But this, for some, is still overly concerned with moral purity, about the identity of Christians, a sort of monasticism. Kanitz continues:

"Being for others": this is something Bonhoeffer is particularly known for. Above all, being there for those who otherwise have no one to be with them. To cry out for all the disadvantaged people in the world. To be the church, not in such a way that it fights primarily for its own survival; but unfortunately this is what we in the Confessing Church did almost exclusively. But Bonhoeffer was one of the few in the Confessing Church who always saw the whole picture. Above all, he saw Christ as the brother of all persecuted human beings, of all people tortured and made victims of others.

Kanitz entered military service, as noted above, in May 1939. Several years later, as an officer in the military, he spoke with Bonhoeffer while on leave:

The last time I saw [Dietrich] was in the summer of 1943 [*sic*], shortly before his arrest.[25] I visited him in his home in Berlin while I was on leave from the Russian front. I was wearing an officer's uniform since I was just on my way back. I was wearing the Iron Cross; I was terribly ashamed, because I had an idea of what he was involved with here in Berlin. I knew nothing for sure; he didn't even tell his closest friends anything about the conspiracy activities. Then he asked me, in utter sincerity, without any judgment, how I had earned my medal. And all I could do was mumble that I didn't know, that it was merely routine. It was then that my wish, my desire was strengthened to will only one thing: to survive the war and see to it that such a thing never happened again. The reason I tell about this is that through the pacifism that Bonhoeffer had taught us, that we had come to by reading the Bible, the will to resist fascism and dictatorship had been planted so firmly in me that these seven years as a soldier were utter hell for me. Sometimes I was close to insanity because of it. At any rate, the only thing I could conclude for the rest of my life was: never again.

24. Joachim Kanitz, excerpts from interviews in *Dietrich Bonhoeffer: Memories and Perspectives*. The two following quotes from Kanitz are also from this documentary film.

25. Bonhoeffer was arrested on April 5, 1943. Kanitz is likely remembering his visit on August 2, 1942. See *Conspiracy and Imprisonment: 1940–1945*, ed. Mark Brocker, trans. Lisa E. Dahill and Douglas W. Stott, vol. 16 of *Dietrich Bonhoeffer Works* (Minneapolis: Fortress, 2006), 689.

Discipleship, the vital importance of the Christian community, being for others, crying out for the disadvantaged, resisting fascism, loving enemies (including refusing to kill in wars): all of these commitments, for Bonhoeffer, came out of a serious theological engagement with the Scriptures—especially the Sermon on the Mount—with Jesus Christ at the center. These teachings were still remembered by his former student quite powerfully in the summer of 1942. Did Bonhoeffer himself still believe them at that point?

It has struck me for many years that among numerous Christians, academics, and others, typically a three-step move is made in relation to Bonhoeffer. First, we "know" that Bonhoeffer was involved in one or more plots to kill Hitler. Second, this "knowledge" then becomes the lens through which his theological and ethical legacy is understood. Third, then, we can of course see that what we thought might be true is indeed true, that *Discipleship* and *Life Together* are works from Bonhoeffer's less mature period before he truly confronted the hard realities of a world war and the Holocaust. These early books may still be useful as expressions of piety and devotion. But for hard, real life we need the realism captured in the language of *Ethics* and *Letters and Papers from Prison*. Thus words and phrases like "responsibility," "this-worldliness," "vicarious representative action," "guilt," "living unreservedly in life's duties," or "living in the realities of this world"—terms found in these later writings—are seen quintessentially as expressions that reflect and warrant his realism that led to his involvement in the plots to kill Hitler. Therefore Bonhoeffer's life and legacy are seen much more in light of these latter two works. And whatever significance these earlier works have, they too are seen in light of Bonhoeffer's later involvements in assassination attempts and key passages from these later works.

What then follows from this? Of course, there are the moves that strike typical North American Christian ethicists as bizarre, such as invoking the name of Bonhoeffer to justify killing a doctor who performs abortions or a dictator in Latin America.[26] There is also the move—by respectable Christian ethicists and Bonhoeffer scholars—of employing Bonhoeffer to justify the (mostly) US wars in Iraq and Afghanistan.[27] Of course, there is often the implicit justification of the Allied efforts in World War II. And then there is

26. Despite his disagreement with such logic, Rob Arner does a good job of showing the logic of justifying killing a doctor who performs abortions. See Rob Arner, *Consistently Pro-Life: The Ethics of Bloodshed in Ancient Christianity* (Eugene, OR: Pickwick, 2010), 13–23. The reference to Latin American dictators is an allusion to a statement made by George W. Bush.

27. See Jean Bethke Elshtain, *Just War Against Terror: The Burden of American Power in a Violent World* (New York: Basic Books, 2004), where Bonhoeffer's name is invoked several times to justify her argument. It should be mentioned that Elshtain has also written a handful of academic essays on Bonhoeffer. On Afghanistan, see Geffrey B. Kelly and F. Burton Nelson,

the statement I received by email. It came from a Christian educator who was a visiting scholar on our campus. Before he came he had apparently read an essay written by me on Bonhoeffer. Thus he sent me a message, saying he would like to discuss Bonhoeffer with me. Among other things, in his email he said: "If it were not for Bonhoeffer I would be a pacifist." At first I was taken aback by this. But then I thought, this is simply a bold and candid statement that follows from what seems to me to be the standard Niebuhrian reading of Bonhoeffer and follows from the moves named in the previous paragraph.[28]

This book will challenge that reading. Or rather it will argue not only that Joachim Kanitz is accurately remembering what he had been taught by his teacher in 1935, but that the evidence suggests that Bonhoeffer continued to believe these things in 1942 and beyond. Without question, his contexts and involvements—of necessity—changed from, say, 1935 to 1942 or 1939 to 1944. But we will argue for fundamental continuities in Bonhoeffer's theology and life from 1932 until the end of his life. And specifically we will argue that it is highly unlikely that Bonhoeffer was involved in any assassination attempts. And since he was not involved in such attempts, there is no textual evidence that he attempted ethically to justify such attempts.

The argument will be made through the discussion that unfolds in seven chapters and a conclusion. The first three chapters will offer an overview of Bonhoeffer's life. The first chapter will cover his life up through his involvement in helping to draft the Bethel Confession in August 1933, for what was becoming the Confessing Church. The second chapter will cover the period from his move to London, England, in October 1933 until the eve of his second trip to New York City in the summer of 1939. The third chapter will begin with the trip back to Germany, continue through Bonhoeffer's involvement in the Abwehr and connections with the resistance movements, and end with his execution on April 9, 1945. This third chapter is less ordered by chronology, but it does cover the period from 1939 to 1945.

Since Bonhoeffer was a theologian, writings conveying theological thought were very much a part of his life. Thus the first three chapters will offer

The Cost of Moral Leadership: The Spirituality of Dietrich Bonhoeffer (Grand Rapids: Eerdmans, 2003), 115–20.

28. An early reader of this essay questioned this claim about how Bonhoeffer is understood. However, I have encountered this interpretation many times. While this is not the place to document the claim extensively, let me simply point to one source from two respected Bonhoeffer scholars who are giving what seems to me to be at least one, brief version of the standard account of Bonhoeffer's shift from pacifism and the approach of *Discipleship* to the real, harsh world of involvement in conspiracies: Kelly and Nelson, *Cost of Moral Leadership*, 112–15. (This is not to say that there is little that is valuable in this book; there is indeed much that is useful and important.)

some significant exposure to Bonhoeffer's theology and theological ethics. However, it is chapters 4 through 7 that look in more depth at Bonhoeffer's formal writings.

Specifically, chapter 4 will deal with a lecture Bonhoeffer presented in Barcelona in 1929 on Christian ethics. This chapter will point to a formal approach to ethics that remains constant throughout Bonhoeffer's life, while also suggesting major points of disruption between 1929 and 1932 that came to affect the rest of Bonhoeffer's short life. Chapter 5 will discuss and contextualize the book *Discipleship*. It will both discuss the vital importance of this book as an expression of Bonhoeffer's mature substantive commitments and show its links to his previous and subsequent thought.

Chapters 6 and 7 will discuss Bonhoeffer's "book" *Ethics*. This will involve linking this set of originally unpublished manuscripts especially to his earlier thought. There will also be an engagement of two of the most important concepts often drawn on in discussions related to the subject of this book—namely, Bonhoeffer's understanding of responsibility and guilt. The conclusion will then summarize the main points of the book as well as look toward a future legacy for Bonhoeffer's witness, free of the myth of his involvement in assassination attempts.

Part 1

Bonhoeffer's Biography Reconsidered

This book wrestles with theological ethics and the central question of the applicability of Jesus's teaching in a sinful, violent world, but the main argument is inescapably biographical. We are exploring how one human being, a twentieth-century German theologian and church leader named Dietrich Bonhoeffer, reflected on these issues in the context of the Third Reich, one of the most oppressive and destructive regimes in human history. The first section, the next three chapters, provides a sketch of the whole of Bonhoeffer's short life. Like any such account, this one will emphasize some elements and events more than others. Every effort has been made, however, not only to be fair in this portrayal but also to avoid distortion by omission.

1

"Pacifist and Enemy of the State"

On March 7, 1936, when Bonhoeffer was thirty years old and Hitler had been in power for a little more than three years, Bishop Theodor Heckel, director of the Church Foreign Office for the German Evangelical Church, expressed concern about Bonhoeffer's influence.[1] He wrote to church authorities that Bonhoeffer could "be accused of being a pacifist and enemy of the state" and that the Prussian church committee should "disassociate itself from him" and not allow him to provide theological training.[2] Heckel's twin accusations provide one way of framing this biographical narrative, for they point to two dimensions of Bonhoeffer that, if true, make him virtually unique among pastors and theologians in Germany in the 1930s and '40s. Here was a man who, by 1936, had come to embrace what he himself referred to as pacifism, and yet already was being perceived by authorities as a threat to the state. By most accounts, it should be noted, the two accusations—pacifist

1. Like all of us who write about Bonhoeffer, I am deeply indebted to Eberhard Bethge's very detailed *Dietrich Bonhoeffer: A Biography*, rev. ed., ed. Victoria J. Barnett (Minneapolis: Fortress, 2000). Additionally, I have read the following biographies: Mary Bosanquet, *The Life and Death of Dietrich Bonhoeffer* (New York: Harper & Row, 1968); Renate Wind, *A Spoke in the Wheel*, trans. John Bowden (Grand Rapids: Eerdmans, 1991); Ferdinand Schlingensiepen, *Dietrich Bonhoeffer 1906–1945: Martyr, Thinker, Man of Resistance*, trans. Isabel Best (London: T&T Clark, 2010); and Eric Metaxas, *Bonhoeffer: Pastor, Martyr, Prophet, Spy* (Nashville: Thomas Nelson, 2010).

2. As quoted in Bethge, *Dietrich Bonhoeffer*, 511–12.

and enemy of the state—are mutually exclusive. So who was this man who came to be identified in this way?

On February 4, 1906, Bonhoeffer was born into a tight-knit, upper-middle-class family, the sixth of eight children. Both parents were from influential, well-established families. Indeed, his father became one of the most respected psychiatrists in Germany.

Bonhoeffer's family was patriotic but not militaristic. When World War I broke out, in 1914, and one of Bonhoeffer's sisters "dashed into the house shouting 'Hurrah, there's a war,' her face was slapped."[3] The Bonhoeffers did not celebrate war. On the other hand, a conflict undertaken by one's own nation normally required assent and doing one's patriotic duty. Thus it appears that the family did not hesitate to send all three of Dietrich's older brothers to serve in the First World War, a conflict of unprecedented violence and loss. Speaking in November of 1930, in New York City, Bonhoeffer recalled that during World War I "death stood at the door of almost every house and called for entrance." Germany, he said, "was made a house of mourning."[4]

The Bonhoeffer home was not spared. Three of Dietrich's first cousins died at the front. His brother Walter, born in 1899, was killed on the battlefield in April of 1918. According to Bethge, Walter's death "seemed to break his mother's spirit."[5] The loss of Walter "and his mother's desperate grief left an indelible mark on Bonhoeffer." Three years later, at Dietrich's confirmation, his mother "gave him the Bible that Walter had received at his confirmation in 1914. Bonhoeffer used it throughout his life for his personal meditations and in worship."[6]

When the Nazis came to power, Bonhoeffer's immediate family saw the regime very early on for what it was. In fact, by the end of the Third Reich, two brothers and two brothers-in-law had been executed for being involved in the resistance movement.[7] Nonetheless, we should not imagine that the household in which Dietrich grew up questioned the German patriotism of the day. As a child, Bonhoeffer responded enthusiastically to the early German

3. Bethge, *Dietrich Bonhoeffer*, 26.

4. Bonhoeffer, "Sermon on 1 John 4:16, New York, Armistice Day Sunday, November 9, 1930," in *Barcelona, Berlin, New York: 1928–1931*, ed. Clifford Green, trans. Douglas W. Stott , vol. 10 of *Dietrich Bonhoeffer Works* (Minneapolis: Fortress, 2008), 582; cf. 411–18.

5. Bethge, *Dietrich Bonhoeffer*, 27.

6. Ibid., 28. See also Bonhoeffer's reflections on the war in *Barcelona, Berlin, New York*, 411–18, and reflections on the impact of the death of his brother offered by his twin sister, quoted by his cousin Hans Christoph von Hase, "'Turning Away from the Phraseological to the Real': A Personal Reflection," in *Barcelona, Berlin, New York*, 594.

7. See, for instance, Eberhard Bethge and Renate Bethge, eds., *Last Letters of Resistance: Farewells from the Bonhoeffer Family*, trans. Dennis Slabaugh (Philadelphia: Fortress, 1986).

successes in World War I.[8] Indeed, through the late 1920s he seemed to be a fairly typical young German male. For instance, while a theological student at Tübingen, he took it in stride that he would join the Hedgehogs, the same patriotic fraternity his father had joined when he was a student. In November of 1923, as a member of this fraternity, Dietrich did two weeks of military training with the Ulm Rifles Troop, learning to use various weapons. He wrote to his parents, with apparent pride: "Today I am a soldier."[9]

Just over five years later, in February 1929, as an assistant pastor of a German-speaking congregation in Barcelona, Spain, Bonhoeffer lectured on Christian ethics. In this lecture he spoke against applying the Sermon on the Mount to the present, because to do so was to violate the spirit of Christ and freedom from the law.[10] He went on, in this lecture, to provide a rationale for killing enemies to protect one's family and one's fellow Germans. He said:

> I will take up arms with the terrible knowledge of doing something horrible, and yet knowing I can do no other. I will defend my brother, my mother, my people, and yet I know that I can do so only by spilling blood; but love for my people will sanctify murder, will sanctify war.[11]

Eberhard Bethge notes that "neither in his sermons nor in his letters did [Bonhoeffer] ever make any such statements again." Referring to such statements as "excessively nationalist," Bethge goes on to say that such words "never crossed his lips again, for he now saw them transformed into nationalistic slogans and interwoven with anti-Semitic agitation."[12] It is important to be informed that Bonhoeffer *never* speaks like this again. However, is it possible that Bethge's interpretive comments could be misleading? First, relative to typical German theologians in the late 1920s, Bonhoeffer's statements, though couched in his own peculiar theology, would not have been perceived to be "excessively nationalist." They would have been common ethical fare.[13]

8. Bethge, *Dietrich Bonhoeffer*, 26.

9. Dietrich Bonhoeffer, *The Young Bonhoeffer: 1918–1927*, ed. Paul D. Matheny, Clifford J. Green, and Marshall D. Johnson, trans. Mary Nebelsick and Douglas W. Stott, vol. 9 of *Dietrich Bonhoeffer Works* (Minneapolis: Fortress, 2003), 70. See also Metaxas, *Bonhoeffer*, 45–46; and Bethge, *Dietrich Bonhoeffer*, 51–53.

10. Bonhoeffer, *Barcelona, Berlin, New York*, 367.

11. Ibid., 372. He goes on to say, on this same page, that he must love his enemies, yet will kill them because of love and gratitude toward his own people.

12. Bethge, *Dietrich Bonhoeffer*, 119, 127.

13. See John A. Moses, "Dietrich Bonhoeffer's Repudiation of Protestant German War Theology," *Journal of Religious History* 30 (2006): 354–70. Also see Eberhard Busch, *Karl Barth: His Life from Letters and Autobiographical Texts*, trans. John Bowden (Philadelphia: Fortress, 1975), 81–83.

Second, Bethge seems to be suggesting that Bonhoeffer dropped such language primarily because it could be co-opted by others, transforming his language "into nationalistic slogans and interwoven with anti-Semitic agitation." Thus it is implied that clear shifts, obvious by 1932, are because of such practical, contextual concerns. However, the evidence suggests that in 1929 Bonhoeffer was on a serious theological (and spiritual) journey, a journey upon which he will be transformed during the 1930–31 school year, when he is in New York City. It is a journey that will come to mature expression theologically between 1935 and 1938. And the shifts in convictions that happen within this journey are shifts made through theological deliberation, in the context of transforming spiritual experiences, not because of the pragmatic concerns Bethge named.

Bonhoeffer departed Barcelona on February 17, 1929, upon completion of his one-year pastoral assistantship there. His return signaled his reentry into the academic world. He had done doctoral work in theology at the University of Tübingen and the University of Berlin between the summer of 1923 and the end of 1927. He defended his doctoral thesis, *Sanctorum Communio*, in December. In the summer of 1929, Bonhoeffer became an academic assistant in systematic theology for Wilhelm Lütgert, at the University of Berlin. During that term and the 1929–30 winter term, Bonhoeffer wrote his second (*Habilitation*) dissertation, *Act and Being*, in order to be qualified to teach in German universities. His thesis was accepted on July 12, 1930; he successfully completed his oral *Habilitation* examination that summer and thus was qualified to become a formal lecturer in the universities. On July 31 Bonhoeffer gave his inaugural lecture at the University of Berlin, "The Anthropological Question in Contemporary Philosophy and Theology."[14] In September of 1930, three years after it was originally written, a revised version of his doctoral thesis, *Sanctorum Communio*, was published.

Becoming a theologian was a goal Bonhoeffer had had since he was fifteen years old. Yet his father had reservations. Many years later his father expressed the concerns that he had felt at the time. Ironically, he feared that Dietrich would live "'a quiet, uneventful minister's life,' which 'would really almost be a pity'" for someone with his son's obvious abilities.[15] However, given the combination of Bonhoeffer's own theological trajectory and the political events that would unfold within Germany over the next fifteen years, "uneventful" is far from describing his life.

During the process of qualifying to be a university professor, Bonhoeffer had applied for and secured a one-year fellowship to study at Union Theological

14. Bonhoeffer, *Barcelona, Berlin, New York*, 389–408.
15. Bethge, *Dietrich Bonhoeffer*, 37.

Seminary in New York City. Bonhoeffer anticipated this time with eagerness. However, he could not have imagined the transformation he would undergo because of his year in the United States.

"A Grand Liberation"

As it happens, we know from Bonhoeffer himself about a transformation that occurred in his life sometime prior to 1933. He wrote about it in a letter to his girlfriend, Elizabeth Zinn, on January 27, 1936. It is so vital to our understanding of Bonhoeffer that we must quote it at length:

> I threw myself into the work in a very unchristian and rather arrogant manner. A mind-boggling ambition, which many have noticed about me, made my life difficult and separated me from the love and trust of my fellow human beings. At that time I was terribly alone and left to my own devices. That was really a terrible time. Then something different happened, something that has changed my life, turned it around to this very day. I came to the Bible for the first time. It is terribly difficult for me to say that. I had already preached several times, had seen a lot of the church, had given speeches about it and written about it—but I still had not become a Christian, I was very much an untamed child, my own master. I know, at that time I had turned this whole business about Jesus Christ into an advantage for myself, a kind of crazy vanity. I pray God, it will never be so again. I had also never prayed, or at least not much and not really. With all my loneliness, I was still quite pleased with myself. It was from this that the Bible—especially the Sermon on the Mount—freed me. Since then everything is different. I am clearly aware of it myself; and even those around me have noticed it. That was a grand liberation. There it became clear to me that the life of a servant of Jesus Christ must belong to the church, and gradually it became clearer how far this has to go. Then came the troubles of 1933. They only strengthened me in this. At this time I also found people who looked with me toward the same goal. I now saw that everything depended on the renewal of the church and of the ministry. . . . Christian pacifism [*christliche Pazifismus*], which I had previously fought against with passion, all at once seemed perfectly obvious [*Selbstverständlichkeit*]. And so it went further, step by step. I saw and thought of nothing else. . . . My calling is quite clear to me. What God will make of it I do not know. . . . I must follow the path. Perhaps it will not be such a long one. Sometimes we wish it were so (Philippians 1:23). But it is a fine thing to have realized my calling. . . . I believe the nobility of this calling will become plain to us only in the times and events to come. If only we can hold out![16]

16. Dietrich Bonhoeffer, *Reflections on the Bible: Human Word and Word of God*, ed. Manfred Weber, trans. M. Eugene Boring (Peabody, MA: Hendrickson, 2004), 9–10. Beginning with

Given some of the language Bonhoeffer uses, he appears to have in mind some specific experiences within a specifiable period of time that brought about this "grand liberation." In fact, partly because of his reference to coming to see Christian pacifism as "perfectly obvious," we can set chronological parameters for the transforming experiences he underwent. In February of 1929, when the lecture in Barcelona was given, we know that Bonhoeffer was still against pacifism. By the summer of 1932 he is giving lectures that passionately communicate his opposition to war, in theological terms, and sometimes specifically affirming pacifism. Between the Barcelona lecture and his 1932 lectures was Bonhoeffer's time at Union Theological Seminary in 1930–31.[17] So, it is not difficult to see his experiences in the United States as crucial to his transformation.

Yet it is also true that Bonhoeffer was already on a journey that led him to connect with experiences in New York City. Bonhoeffer, for instance, already had some experiences that led him to empathize with those who suffer. In a lecture in New York City on November 9, 1930, he noted: "I have been accustomed once in every year since my boyhood to wander on foot through our country and so I happen to know many classes of German people very well. Many evenings I have sat with the families of peasants around the big stove talking about past and future, about the next generation and their chances."[18] Dietrich informs family members of the varied people he interacts with regularly in his role as assistant pastor in Barcelona (1928–29), including those who are poor and those who are criminals.[19] Specifically, on August 7, 1928, he writes to his friend Helmut Rossler:

"My calling is quite clear," the quote is taken from Bethge, *Dietrich Bonhoeffer*, 205. Compare the translations given in "Editor's Afterword," in Bonhoeffer, *Discipleship*, 291–92, and Bethge, *Dietrich Bonhoeffer*, 204–5. Cf. Dietrich Bonhoeffer, *Illegale Theologenausbildung: Finkenwalde 1935–1937*, ed. Otto Dudzus et al., vol. 14 of *Dietrich Bonhoeffer Werke* (Munich: Chr. Kaiser Verlag, 1996), 112–14.

17. We can possibly set the parameters even more closely around 1930–31. Bonhoeffer edited and abridged *Sanctorum Communio* probably in the first half of 1930. In it he has a sentence regarding war that sounds more like his lecture in Barcelona in 1929 than like lectures he presented in 1932. Dietrich Bonhoeffer, *Sanctorum Communio: A Theological Study of the Sociology of the Church*, ed. Clifford J. Green, trans. Reinhard Krauss and Nancy Lukens, vol. 1 of *Dietrich Bonhoeffer Works* (Minneapolis: Fortress, 1998), 119. So, before he goes to New York, in September of 1930, he appears to still be thinking in terms similar to what he articulated in his lecture in February of 1929. On the other end, Bonhoeffer and Jean Lasserre lectured on peace in Mexico to an audience of more than three hundred students in June of 1931. Lasserre said in an interview that "on that occasion Dietrich spoke as firmly as I, if not more strongly, on the meaning of pacifism." Lasserre said he was at the time surprised because "I didn't think he had understood the pacifist vision of things so well as that." However, together they said essentially "the same thing . . . , condemning war and violence." Geffrey B. Kelly, "An Interview with Jean Lasserre," *Union Seminary Quarterly Review* 27 (1972): 152.

18. Bonhoeffer, "Sermon on 1 John 4:16," in *Barcelona, Berlin, New York*, 583.

19. See, for instance, his letter to his brother Karl-Friedrich on July 7, 1928 (Bonhoeffer, *Barcelona, Berlin, New York*, 109–12).

> I'm getting to know new people each day, at least their life stories. Sometimes one can also peer through their portrayals to the person—and in the process one thing is always striking; one encounters people here the way they are, far from the masquerade of the "Christian world"; people with passions, criminal types, small people with small goals, small drives, and who thaw a bit when you speak to them in a friendly manner—real people. I can only say I have the impression that precisely these people stand more under grace than under wrath, but that it is precisely the Christian world that stands more under wrath than under grace. "I am sought out by those who did not ask; . . . to those who did not call on my name I said, 'Here I am' (Isa. 65:1)."[20]

Bonhoeffer had prepared for such encounters, had hoped for them. Thus, in his doctoral thesis, *Sanctorum Communio*, finished in July 1927, Bonhoeffer critiques the church, saying, "Our present church is 'bourgeois.' The best proof remains . . . that the proletariat has turned its back on the church, while the bourgeois (civil servant, skilled worker, merchant) stayed. . . . Sermons are thus aimed at people who live relatively securely and relatively stable morally."[21] In *Sanctorum Communio* Bonhoeffer attempts to give an account of the Christian community that is not captive to normal bourgeois sensibilities. To the average reader Bonhoeffer's doctoral thesis may seem overly abstract and far removed from what will become his central concerns. And certainly it is a sophisticated piece of scholarship that attempts to integrate sociology and theology in a way that takes full advantage of the insights of the former while allowing the latter to be decisive in shaping the argument. Bonhoeffer is, after all, an academic theologian. Yet we will not appreciate this work if we fail to note his desire to articulate the social dimensions of the church in a way that has theological integrity—a way that is captive not to the status quo but to the Word of God that frees the church to be faithful in its life together while engaging the larger world through faithful witness.

This work was Bonhoeffer's first effort to reflect his indebtedness to the theology of Karl Barth. When three years later Bonhoeffer wrote his second thesis, *Act and Being*, Barth's theology was again in focus. However, in this second thesis Bonhoeffer engaged Barth more critically. This time, employing philosophy, Bonhoeffer wrestled, albeit indirectly, with the connections between theology and ethics. How is it that the Word of God—including the command of God—can have continuity across time? Bonhoeffer's answer: the Word of God made flesh in the person of Jesus Christ and held before us by the church.[22]

20. Ibid., 127.

21. Bonhoeffer, *Sanctorum Communio*, 273n430.

22. On the importance of *Act and Being*, see Michael P. DeJonge, "The Fact of the Person of Jesus Christ: Dietrich Bonhoeffer's *Act and Being*" (PhD diss., Emory University, 2009). Revised

But this would only be given full, clear theological expression after Bonhoeffer's year in New York and after several years of living with the Sermon on the Mount. All of this served as a backdrop for the life-changing experiences he would have in America.[23]

As for Union Seminary itself, Bonhoeffer didn't like it very much. Nor did he like the preaching he heard in the white congregations he visited. He saw both as dominated by liberal theology.[24] This is not to say that Bonhoeffer did not take his courses at Union seriously. He did. Nor is it to say that he did not learn from them in important ways. It appears, for instance, that he likely acquired a commitment to the social dimensions of the gospel partly through the social teachings of some of his teachers at Union, despite his serious misgivings about the theology of the "social gospel" as such. As Bonhoeffer put it:

> The impressions I got of contemporary representatives of the social gospel will remain determinative for me for a long time to come. The sobriety and seriousness of a book such as that of H. Ward, *Which Way Religion?* is irrefutable; and yet the entire protest must repeatedly be raised if that is preached as *real* Christianity while abbreviating all the crucial Christian ideas. In many discussions and lectures I tried to show that Reformation Christianity does indeed include

---

and published as Michael P. DeJonge, *Bonhoeffer's Theological Formation: Berlin, Barth and Protestant Theology* (Oxford: Oxford University Press, 2012).

23. On this year, see Clifford Green, "Bonhoeffer at Union. Critical Turning Points: 1931 and 1939," *Union Seminary Quarterly Review* 62 (2010): 1–16; Clifford Green, "Editor's Introduction to the English Edition," in Dietrich Bonhoeffer, *Barcelona, Berlin, New York*, 1–50, esp. 17–43; Hans Pfeifer, "Learning Faith and Ethical Commitment in the Context of Spiritual Training Groups: Consequences of Dietrich Bonhoeffer's Post Doctoral Year in New York City 1930/31," *Beiträge zur Dietrich Bonhoeffer-Forschung* 3 (2008): 251–79; Charles Marsh, "Bonhoeffer on the Road to King: 'Turning from the Phraseological to the Real,'" in *Bonhoeffer and King: Their Legacies and Import for Christian Social Thought*, ed. Willis Jenkins and Jennifer M. McBride (Minneapolis: Fortress, 2010), 123–38, 278–80; Ruth Zerner, "Dietrich Bonhoeffer's American Experiences: People, Letters, and Papers from Union Seminary," *Union Seminary Quarterly Review* 31 (Summer 1976): 261–82; Heinz Eduard Tödt, "Dietrich Bonhoeffer's Decisions in the Crisis Years 1929–33," *Studies in Christian Ethics* 18, no. 3 (2005): 107–23; and Scott Holland, "First We Take Manhattan, Then We Take Berlin: Bonhoeffer's New York," *Cross Currents* (2000): 369–82. And for the most thorough treatments, see Josiah Ulysses Young III, *No Difference in the Fare: Dietrich Bonhoeffer and the Problem of Racism* (Grand Rapids: Eerdmans, 1998); and Reggie Williams, "Christ-Centered Empathic Resistance: The Influence of Harlem Renaissance Theology on the Incarnational Ethics of Dietrich Bonhoeffer" (PhD diss., Fuller Theological Seminary, 2011).

24. See his quite critical reports on both semesters: Bonhoeffer, *Barcelona, Berlin, New York*, 305–22. See his parallel comments on his brief time in New York in 1939: Bonhoeffer, "Protestantism Without Reformation," in *Theological Education Underground: 1937–1940*, ed. Victoria J. Barnett, trans. Claudia D. Bergmann, Scott A. Moore, and Peter Frick, vol. 15 of *Dietrich Bonhoeffer Works* (Minneapolis: Fortress, 2011), 438–62. See also Bonhoeffer, letters to Max Diestel, *Barcelona, Berlin, New York*, 265–66, 296–97.

> rather than exclude all these things, but that their assessment is different. But people basically just didn't want to believe that.[25]

In 1932 Bonhoeffer wrote a memorandum in which he expressed both appreciation and critique of the social gospel, elaborating on the points made above. After a number of pages of nuanced appreciation, Bonhoeffer offers a list of seven critiques. Two overarching criticisms are especially significant. The fourth point he makes is that in the social gospel "the biblical message is not clearly imparted." Under this point he briefly mentions the deficient ways in which the social gospel deals with eschatology, history, sin, Christ, and God. His seventh point really serves as a summary: "The contempt for theology is outrageous. Rauschenbusch's own 'theology for the social gospel' clearly shows, like its successors, that a lack of obedience to Scripture is characteristic for the teaching of the social gospel."[26] For anyone who knows Bonhoeffer's theology, his seven points of critique, taken together, are quite devastating. No one should confuse his own approach with that of the social gospel.

However much Bonhoeffer's classes at Union affected him, it appears to have been primarily four friendships with fellow students that served to connect him to transformative experiences during his year in America. Paul Lehman, an American but one fluent in German, would stay connected to Bonhoeffer over much of the rest of his life. Erwin Sutz, a Swiss national and a serious student of Barth, would keep Bonhoeffer tied to Barth's influence while at Union and remain a regular and important connection throughout most of the rest of Dietrich's life.

Jean Lasserre was a French Reformed pastor. Meeting him was Bonhoeffer's "first encounter with a Christian pacifist of his generation." Thus, "Lasserre confronted him with an acceptance of Jesus' peace commandment that he had never encountered before."[27] His influence on Bonhoeffer was clearly life changing.[28] As Bethge puts it, "In Jean Lasserre [Bonhoeffer] found a man who shared his longing for the concretion of divine grace and

25. Bonhoeffer, *Barcelona, Berlin, New York*, 318–19. The translations of Bonhoeffer's work in the *Dietrich Bonhoeffer Works* series regularly use italics to relate various marks of emphasis in Bonhoeffer's original work. When we quote from these translations throughout this volume, we will preserve the italics without comment in the notes. We will indicate when we add emphasis of our own.

26. Bonhoeffer, "Memorandum: 'The "Social Gospel,"'" in *Berlin: 1932–1933*, ed. Larry L. Rasmussen, trans. Douglas W. Stott, Isabel Best, and David Higgins, vol. 12 of *Dietrich Bonhoeffer Works* (Minneapolis: Fortress, 2009), 241–42.

27. Bethge, *Dietrich Bonhoeffer*, 153.

28. On this see F. Burton Nelson, "The Relationship of Jean Lasserre to Dietrich Bonhoeffer's Peace Concerns in the Struggle of Church and Culture," *Union Seminary Quarterly Review* 40 (1985): 71–84; and Kelly, "Interview with Jean Lasserre," 149–60.

his alertness to the danger of intellectually rejecting that proximity of grace. His friend confronted him with the question of the relationship between God's word and those who uphold it as individuals and citizens of the contemporary world. This soon led Bonhoeffer to a new understanding of the Sermon on the Mount." "It was also Lasserre," says Bethge, "who provided the initial impulse for Bonhoeffer's great book *Discipleship*."[29] The two men traveled to Mexico together in the early summer of 1931 and—unheard of for a Frenchman and German at the time—spoke publicly together in Mexico on peace.

Of equal transformative import was Bonhoeffer's friendship with Frank Fisher, an African American who would, very importantly, connect Bonhoeffer to the African American experience, especially as expressed through a particular Christian community. As Clifford Green has said, "It is not too much to say that studying the black community and involvement in it was Bonhoeffer's major extracurricular activity in 1930–31."[30] Within a month after arriving in New York City, Bonhoeffer took a guided trip to acquaint himself with "Negro" life and culture in Harlem. He secured reading lists, books, and articles and read voraciously to familiarize himself with issues related to such topics as race, racism, and civil rights. Bonhoeffer was deeply moved by what he read. Green writes:

> In February 1931, going beyond the assigned literature, he read about "the first lynching in 1931," a horrible crime on January 12 in Maryville, Missouri. An African American accused of rape was chained to a schoolhouse roof and burned to death by a lynch mob. Anyone who saw the photograph of the burning schoolhouse and the lynch mob would never forget it. Two months later Bonhoeffer learned about the infamous Scottsboro case, in which nine young black men were hastily convicted and condemned to death, after being accused "of raping a white girl of dubious reputation," as Bonhoeffer described it. This "terrible miscarriage of justice" prompted him to ask a German church leader to join the international protest—he declined. The Scottsboro case was still fresh in Bonhoeffer's mind when he wrote about the ethics of office and vocation over a decade later.[31]

Bonhoeffer spent considerable time with Frank Fisher, including traveling with him to Washington, DC. But Fisher was especially important to Bonhoeffer because he connected him to the Abyssinian Baptist Church, a large

29. Bethge, *Dietrich Bonhoeffer*, 153–54.
30. Green, "Editor's Introduction," 28.
31. Ibid., 29–30.

congregation in Harlem, not far from Union Seminary. Bonhoeffer would be intimately involved in the life of this church for six months. During this time Bonhoeffer taught Sunday school, helped in weekday classes once a week, led a Bible study for women, worked in a boys' club, and was in the homes of a number of families from the church. In summarizing his experiences, Bonhoeffer said, "This personal acquaintance with Negroes was one of the most important and gratifying events of my stay in America."[32] The congregation's pastor was the dynamic Dr. Adam Clayton Powell Sr. Born within weeks after the end of the Civil War, in 1865, Powell was quite conscious of his heritage. His mother was African-Choctaw-German, and his stepfather was a former slave. Having himself experienced a dramatic conversion to the Christian faith, he was a dynamic preacher.[33] Here is the way Eric Metaxas attempts to convey Bonhoeffer's experience of Abyssinian Baptist Church:

> Starving from the skim milk at Union, Bonhoeffer found a theological feast that spared nothing. Powell combined the fire of a revivalist preacher with great intellect and social vision. He was active in combating racism and minced no words about the saving power of Jesus Christ. He didn't fall for the Hobson's choice of one or the other; he believed that without both, one had neither, but with both, one had everything and more. When the two were combined, and only then, God came into the equation. Then and only then was life poured out. For the first time Bonhoeffer saw the gospel preached and lived in obedience to God's commands. He was entirely captivated, and for the rest of his time in New York, he was there every Sunday to worship and to teach a Sunday school class of boys; he was active in a number of groups in the church; and he gained the trust of many members and was invited into their homes. Bonhoeffer realized that the older people at Abyssinian had been born when slavery was legal in the United States. Surely some of them were born into the horrid institution.[34]

This rich description, it seems to me, captures something of Bonhoeffer's transformative experience through Powell's preaching and the congregation's life.[35] Here is Bonhoeffer's own description:

32. Bonhoeffer, *Barcelona, Berlin, New York*, 315.

33. See Ralph Garlin Clingan, *Against Cheap Grace in a World Come of Age: An Intellectual Biography of Clayton Powell, 1865–1953* (New York: Peter Lang, 2002).

34. Metaxas, *Bonhoeffer*, 108–9.

35. This description also fits with what I read in the helpful chapter on Powell, the Abyssinian Baptist Church, and Bonhoeffer in Williams, "Christ-Centered Empathic Resistance," 125–77. This thesis, in general, provides a rich context for understanding early 1930s black experience in Harlem and Bonhoeffer's empathetic connections to the black Christians of Abyssinian Baptist Church. Also see Young, *No Difference in the Fare*.

> In a Negro church it is not difficult to observe where the interest of the congregation awakens and where it does not, since the enormous intensity of feeling among the Negroes repeatedly finds expression in their outcries and interrupting shouts. But it is clear that whenever the gospel itself really is mentioned, their participation peaks. Here one really could still hear someone talk in a Christian sense about sin and grace and the love of God and ultimate hope, albeit in a form different from that to which we are accustomed. In contrast to the often lecture-like character of the "white" sermon, the "black Christ" is preached with captivating passion and vividness.[36]

Bonhoeffer's ten months in the United States in some ways foreshadows the commitments that will be given expression in his life and writings. Or to put it differently, it is not difficult to imagine that the Spirit working through this congregation, combined with the influences of Lehman, Sutz, Lasserre, and Fisher, led to what Bonhoeffer referred to as his "grand liberation"—to truly becoming a Christian (with all the specific changes this brought into his life). Only a few months before he left for New York City, he had referred in a paper to Hebrews 12:1 and "the cloud of witnesses."[37] As Clifford Green suggests, "The Spirit-filled preaching and the passionate worship at Abyssinian helped bring home to Bonhoeffer personally the conversations about the Sermon on the Mount and following Jesus that we know he was having with Jean Lasserre and his other friends at that time. Here Bonhoeffer found his 'cloud of witnesses.'"[38] Still, more than ten years later, on November 5, 1942, Bonhoeffer said that his year in New York City "has been of the greatest significance for me up to the present day."[39]

On June 20, 1931, Bonhoeffer left New York by ship for Europe. Beginning on July 10 he would spend three weeks in Bonn, to attend lectures by Karl Barth. On July 23 Barth invited Bonhoeffer to dinner and conversation. The next day Bonhoeffer wrote to Erwin Sutz: "I have, I believe, seldom regretted not having done something in my theological past as much as I now regret that I did not go to hear Barth sooner." He continued, "There is [in Barth] an openness, a willingness to listen to a critical comment directed to the topic at hand, and with this such concentration and with a vehement insistence on the topic at hand, for the sake of which he can speak proudly or humbly,

36. Bonhoeffer, "Report on My Year of Study at Union Theological Seminary in New York, 1930/1931," in *Barcelona, Berlin, New York*, 315.

37. Bonhoeffer, *Barcelona, Berlin, New York*, 385.

38. Green, "Editor's Introduction," 31.

39. Bonhoeffer, *Conspiracy and Imprisonment: 1940–1945*, ed. Mark Brocker, trans. Lisa E. Dahill and Douglas W. Stott, vol. 16 of *Dietrich Bonhoeffer Works* (Minneapolis: Fortress, 2006), 367–68.

dogmatically or with utter uncertainty, in a way that is certainly not intended primarily to advance his own theology."[40] Bonhoeffer was elated that he not only could hear Barth's lectures but that he could also have this personal exchange. As he put it, "I am impressed by his discussion even more than by his writing and lectures. He is really fully present. I have never seen anything like it nor thought it possible." Perhaps importantly for Bonhoeffer's future book *Discipleship*, Barth challenged him that he "was making grace into a principle and bludgeoning everything else to death with it."[41] Until Bonhoeffer's departure for England in October of 1933, he visited Barth in Bonn frequently. Much later, in a letter to Barth on May 17, 1942, Bonhoeffer indicated that his high level of interest in Barth and his theology had not waned: "In my Swiss trips I have looked forward to nothing more than to these visits with you."[42]

At the beginning of August 1931, Bonhoeffer began serving as a lecturer at the University of Berlin. Though he would give a number of courses of lectures and these would be appreciated by many of his students, his career in the university would be short-lived. This was at least partly by choice. In September 1934, in a letter to Erwin Sutz, he said, "I no longer believe in the university; in fact I never really have believed in it."[43] On October 1 he was appointed chaplain at the Technical College in Berlin-Charlottenburg. In this role Bonhoeffer preached and gave varied talks. But, according to Bethge, his chaplaincy work was really not very fruitful.

On November 15, 1931, Bonhoeffer was ordained and appointed city synodal vicar at the Zion Church, Berlin-Wedding. From November of 1931 until the following March he would conduct a confirmation class in Berlin-Wedding, a poor area of the German capital. In a letter to Sutz on December 25, 1931, Bonhoeffer says:

> What keeps me busier at the moment is the confirmation class that I am teaching for fifty boys in the north of Berlin. That is about the toughest neighborhood of Berlin, with the most difficult socioeconomic and political conditions. At the beginning the boys were acting wild, so for the first time I really had discipline

40. Bonhoeffer, letter to Erwin Sutz, July 24, 1931, in *Ecumenical, Academic, and Pastoral Work: 1931–1932*, ed. Victoria J. Barnett, Mark Brocker, and Michael B. Lukens, trans. Isabel Best, Nicholas S. Humphrey, Marion Pauck, Anne Schmidte-Lange, and Douglas W. Stott, vol. 11 of *Dietrich Bonhoeffer Works* (Minneapolis: Fortress, 2012), 37.

41. Ibid., 37–38.

42. Bonhoeffer, *Conspiracy and Imprisonment*, 278. In this same letter he expresses his loyalty to Barth. Bonhoeffer also seeks to secure page-proof copies of volumes of the *Church Dogmatics* as soon as they are ready, in order to continue to learn from Barth.

43. Dietrich Bonhoeffer, *London: 1933–1935*, ed. Keith W. Clements, trans. Isabel Best, vol. 13 of *Dietrich Bonhoeffer Works* (Minneapolis: Fortress, 2007), 217.

> problems. But here too one thing helped, namely, just simply telling the boys Bible stories in massive quantity, and especially the eschatological passages. . . . Recently I took several of them out of the city for two days; tomorrow it's another group's turn. This time together was very enjoyable for us. Since I will be keeping the boys until confirmation, I'll have to visit all fifty parents, and for this purpose I will move to that area for two months. I'm looking forward to this time very much. It's really work. Most of the home conditions are indescribable, poverty, disorder, immorality. Yet the children are still open. I am often speechless at how it is possible that a boy is not completely ruined under these conditions, and, of course, you ask yourself at the same time how you would react to an environment like that. These people must have a very strong capacity for resilience—probably morally as well.[44]

His success with these boys showed how well he had learned to relate to teenagers and also how comfortable he had become working with children from a lower social class.

Particularly important for his future, however, were his new and ever-increasing connections with formal ecumenical circles. One of these connections came through his position as youth secretary for the World Alliance, an appointment made while at its conference in Cambridge in September of 1931. In fact it was in ecumenical contexts where Bonhoeffer first articulated some of his strongest statements on peace. Three lectures in 1932 warrant special mention.

Lecturing on Peace in 1932

On July 26, 1932, Bonhoeffer presented a lecture at the ecumenical Youth Peace Conference in Czechoslovakia, entitled "On the Theological Foundation of the Work of the World Alliance."[45] Bonhoeffer opens his lecture by reflecting on the fact that there is no theology for the ecumenical movement. This is no accident, he says. For some leaders of the ecumenical movement express disdain for theology. For what they want is simply practical work, Christian action—not theology. Bonhoeffer, on the other hand, believes that articulating theology for the movement is urgent. "Because the ecumenical movement has no theology," says Bonhoeffer, "the ecumenical concept, for

44. Bonhoeffer, *Ecumenical, Academic, and Pastoral Work*, 76–77. On his work, see Bethge, *Dietrich Bonhoeffer*, 226–29; and Richard Rother, "A Confirmation Class in Wedding," in *I Knew Dietrich Bonhoeffer*, ed. Wolf-Dieter Zimmermann and Ronald Gregor Smith (1966; repr., London: Fontana Books, 1973), 57–58.

45. Bonhoeffer, "On the Theological Foundation of the Work of the World Alliance," in *Ecumenical, Academic, and Pastoral Work*, 356–69.

example, has currently become powerless and meaningless through the political wave of nationalism among the youth." He continues: "We lack a theological anchorage against which the waves from left and right would batter in vain. Our helplessness is at present profound, and the confusion of concepts knows no bounds. Whoever is involved in ecumenical work must allow himself to be chided as unpatriotic and untruthful, and every attempt to counter this is easily shouted down."[46]

As he moves on in this lecture we see some continuity in *form* with what he said in his lecture on ethics in Barcelona in 1929. Here, as there, Bonhoeffer speaks against biblical law—such as the Ten Commandments or the Sermon on the Mount—serving in and of itself as commandment for the present. In even stronger terms he speaks against the orders of creation as a basis for knowing God's commands for today. His alternative is a word spoken *now* from the living God—a word authorized because it is "the authority of the Christ who is present and living in [the church]":

> The word of the church is the word of the present Christ; it is gospel and commandment. It is not one thing alone, and it can be understood as the one only when it is also understood as the other. The church would revert back to the synagogue if its proclamation were only command; it would be a falling away of the church into Enthusiasm if it were to deny the command of God for the sake of the Gospel.
>
> As the word out of the authority of the present Christ, the word of the church today must be considered as the valid, binding word. I can be spoken to with full authority only when a word from the deepest knowledge of my humanity hits me in my full reality, here and now. Every other word is powerlessness. The word of the church to the world must therefore touch it out of the deepest knowledge of the world in its complete present if it wishes to be authoritative. The church must here and now be able to speak the word of God, of authority, out of its own knowledge in the most concrete way, or it says something entirely different, something human, a word of powerlessness. The church therefore can proclaim not principles that are always true but rather only commandments that are true today. For that which is "always" true is precisely not true "today": God is for us "always" *God* precisely "today."[47]

Bonhoeffer then proceeds to speak more concretely—in a way that is in *content* significantly different from what he said in Barcelona in 1929. He discerns that the churches represented at this meeting of the World Alliance in fact are hearing a specific command from God. "The order of *international peace* is

46. Ibid., 357.
47. Ibid., 359–60.

God's commandment for us today." To clarify this commandment of God, Bonhoeffer distinguishes it from teachings that undermine this word from God. It ought not to be confused with "pacifist humanitarianism" or with static ideals that make "peace" into a value good in itself and "preserved unconditionally." Rather, the commandment to pursue peace in the world is "an order of the preservation of the world toward Christ."[48] Bonhoeffer elaborates:

> International peace is therefore also not an absolutely ideal condition but rather an order that is aimed at something else and that is not valuable in and of itself. Naturally, the establishment of such an order of preservation can have absolute urgency, although never for its own sake, but rather for the sake of its goal, namely, for the sake of the hearing of revelation.[49]

And though the hearing of revelation is the ultimate goal, Bonhoeffer also wants his Christian auditors to know that it is also possible that we may say "peace, peace" when there is no peace. That is to say, "peace" may be a false order:

> The broken character of the order of peace is expressed in the fact that the peace demanded by God has two boundaries: first, the truth; second, justice [Recht]. A community of peace can exist only when it does not rest on a *lie* or on *injustice*. Wherever a community of peace endangers or suffocates truth and justice, the community of peace must be broken and the battle must be declared. If the battle from both sides is really about truth and justice, then the community of peace, even when externally, broken, will be realized more deeply and strongly in the battle for this very cause. . . . The sole reason that Christians have a community of peace is because the one wishes to forgive the sins of the other. Even where the order of external peace in truth and justice remains secure, forgiveness of sins remains the only basis for all peace. It is therefore also the last foundation upon which all ecumenical work rests, particularly where the brokenness seems hopeless.
>
> . . . Neither the external order of peace nor of the peace struggling for the same cause, but only the peace of God who creates the forgiveness of sins is the reality of the gospel in which truth and justice are preserved together.[50]

Thus the true peace desired by God should not be confused with tranquility, for such peace may simply mask falsehood and injustice. True peace may require struggle:

48. Ibid., 365.
49. Ibid.
50. Ibid., 365–66.

> *Struggle* as possible action with respect to Christ becomes understandable if the order of external peace is not timelessly valid but can be disrupted at any moment, precisely because the complete violation of truth and justice would threaten to make hearing about revelation in Christ impossible. Struggle is not an order of creation, but it can be an order of preservation for the future of Christ, toward the new creation.[51]

However, Bonhoeffer was also aware that many would justify war because of this potential need for struggle to secure justice and truth. Thus he felt compelled to offer clarity.

> Today, however, there is a widespread and extremely dangerous error that says that in the *justification of struggle* there is already the justification for war, that this contains the *fundamental Yes to war*. The right to wage war can be derived from the right to struggle no more than the right to inflict torture can be derived from the necessity of legal process in human society. . . . Our contemporary war does not fall under the concept of battle because it means certain self-destruction of both warring sides. For that reason today it is utterly impossible to characterize it as an order of preservation toward revelation, simply because it is absolutely destructive. . . . Today's war destroys soul and body. Because there is no way for us to understand war as God's order of preservation and therefore as God's commandment, and because war needs to be idealized and idolatrized in order to live, today's war, the next war, must be *condemned* by the church. . . . We must face the next war with all the power of resistance, rejection, condemnation. . . . We should not balk here at using the word "pacifism." Just as certainly as we submit the ultimate *pacem facere* to God, we too must *pacem facere* to overcome war.[52]

On August 29, 1932, Bonhoeffer presented another lecture, "The Church Is Dead," to the International Youth Conference of the Universal Christian Council on Life and Work and the World Alliance for Promoting International Friendship in Gland, Switzerland.[53] Much of it was similar to what he had said in July. However, there are also other accents. Early in the address Bonhoeffer anticipates emphases of later writings: "We prefer our own thoughts to those of the Bible. We no longer read the Bible seriously. We read it no longer against ourselves but only for ourselves."[54] But the presenting issue in the lecture is peace: "It is as though all the powers of the earth had sworn themselves against peace; money, the economy, the drive to power, yes, even love for the fatherland—all

51. Ibid., 366.

52. Ibid., 366–67.

53. Bonhoeffer, "The Church Is Dead," in *Ecumenical, Academic, and Pastoral Work*, 375–81. The title is taken from the first four words of this untitled address.

54. Ibid., 377–78.

have been pulled into the service of hate, the hatred of the peoples, the hate of compatriots toward their own compatriots."[55] He continues:

> Things are coming to a crisis more horribly than ever before—*millions of starving people* whose wishes have been put off or unfulfilled, desperate people who have nothing to lose but their lives and who with their lives lose nothing—*humiliated and degraded nations*, who are not able to recover from their dishonor—*political extremes against political extremes, fanaticized against fanaticized*, false gods against false gods—and behind all this, a world bristling with weapons as never before, a world that is feverishly mobilizing for war, in order to guarantee peace through armaments, a world whose false gods have become the word "security," *sécurité*—a world without sacrifice, full of distrust and suspicion, because it still feels the terrors of the past in its bones . . . —how can one think that, with a little bit of education toward international understanding and a bit of "good will," these demons can be exorcized, these forced be banished. . . . What are so-called international attempts at reconciliation, all these attempts to understand one another, all so-called international friendship—as necessary as they are in themselves—in light of this reality?[56]

So what is the way forward in light of the detailed and incredibly bleak scenario Bonhoeffer has presented? "Christ must again become present among us in preaching and sacrament, just as Christ as the crucified one made peace with God and humanity. The crucified Christ is our peace. Christ alone abjures the false gods and the demons. Only before the cross does the world tremble, not before us."[57] And to be perfectly clear, he continues:

> War in its present-day form lays waste to God's creation and obscures the view of revelation. As little as one can justify torture as a means of justice out of the necessity of justice, one can just as little justify war as a means of strife out of the necessity of strife. The church forsakes obedience whenever it sanctions war. The church of Christ stands against war in favor of peace among the peoples, between nations, classes and races.
>
> However, the church also knows that there is no peace unless justice and truth are preserved. A peace that violates justice and truth is no peace, and the church of Christ must protest against such peace. There can be a peace that is worse than struggle. Yet it must be a struggle out of love for another, a battle that comes from the Spirit, not from the flesh.[58]

55. Ibid., 378.
56. Ibid., 378–79.
57. Ibid., 379.
58. Ibid., 380. The word "spirit" has been capitalized in the quote to reflect Bonhoeffer's theology.

Finally, in December of 1932 Bonhoeffer spoke on "Christ and Peace" to the German Student Christian Movement. He begins this lecture by saying:

> Once again, the human authorities who sought to build peace upon a political foundation find themselves shipwrecked. It would be good to reflect, and not to be too amazed, for *worldly authorities* are set up by human beings and thus do not constitute absolute authority.
>
> There is only one *authority* who has spoken definitively on this question, and that is *Jesus Christ*.
>
> It is true that Christ has not given us specific rules for our conduct in every possible complex, political, economic, or other situation that may arise in human life. However, this does not mean that the gospel of Jesus Christ does not give a clear answer to the problems that confront us. To the simple reader of the Sermon on the Mount, what it says is unmistakable.[59]

And what is that? "The command, 'you shall not kill,' the word that says, 'Love your enemies,' is given to us simply to be obeyed. For Christians, any military service, except in the ambulance corps, and any preparation for war, is forbidden."[60] He would repeat these convictions conveyed in these lectures from 1932 in various ways, publicly, over the next number of years.

Peace Is More than Not Preparing for War

But, of course, Bonhoeffer knew that Christian discipleship involved more than refusing to prepare for war. It involved the whole person in the whole body of Christ as Christians discerned what it meant to live faithfully in the Germany of the 1930s. For instance, in an eerily prescient sermon on January 15, 1933, Bonhoeffer preached on Matthew 8:23–27; he focused on fear. He wanted his listeners to know that "the Bible, the gospel, Christ, the church, the faith—all are one great battle cry against fear in the lives of human beings." Later in the sermon he beckoned them:

> Learn to recognize and understand the hour of the storm, when you were perishing. This is the time when God is incredibly close to you, not far away. Right there, when everything else that keeps us safe is breaking and falling down, when one after another all the things our life depends on are being taken away or destroyed, where we have to learn to give them up, all this is happening because God is coming near to us, because God wants to be our only support and certainty.[61]

59. Bonhoeffer, "Christ and Peace," in *Berlin*, 258–59.
60. Ibid., 260.
61. Bonhoeffer, *Berlin*, 455, 459.

Two weeks later, on January 30, Adolf Hitler was appointed the Reich Chancellor of Germany. On February 1 Bonhoeffer gave a radio address he was previously scheduled to give entitled "The Younger Generation's Altered View of the Concept of Führer." He repeated this address, in expanded form, twice over the next month. Immediately upon assuming power as Chancellor, Hitler began to exert significant influence. But it was upon the death of President Hindenberg, on August 2, 1934, that Hitler, as Reich Chancellor and Führer, would come to have virtual dictatorial control of the public (and, through intimidation, private) affairs of Germany.[62] It would not be long into Hitler's rule that the last two sentences of Bonhoeffer's address on the concept of leader would have particular poignancy: "Leader and office that turn themselves into gods mock God and the solitary individual before him who is becoming the individual, and must collapse. Only the leader who is in service of the penultimate and ultimate authority merits loyalty."[63]

Because of his close relationship with his brother-in-law Hans von Dohnanyi, who worked for the ministry of justice from early in 1933 and became personal consultant to the Reich Minister of Justice beginning in May of that year, Bonhoeffer was regularly apprised of the Hitler regime's merciless pursuit of its vision.[64]

It was not long into the rule of the Nazis before anti-Jewish measures were being taken. On April 1, 1933, Jewish businesses were boycotted throughout Germany. Six days later the "Law for the Reconstitution of the Professional Civil Service" was passed. This contained what came to be called the "Aryan paragraph," an article of the law that excluded "non-Aryans" (i.e., Jews) from civil service jobs.[65] This law had wide-ranging effects. This was but the first of many measures intended initially to curb the influence of Jews, with the

62. For nuanced discussion of the daily realities, see Eric Johnson and Karl-Heinz Reuband, *What We Knew: Terror, Mass Murder and Everyday Life in Nazi Germany* (London: John Murray, 2005); Eric A. Johnson, *Nazi Terror: The Gestapo, Jews, and Ordinary Germans* (New York: Basic Books, 1999); and Robert Gellately, *Backing Hitler: Consent and Coercion in Nazi Germany* (Oxford: Oxford University Press, 2001).

63. Bonhoeffer, *Berlin*, 282.

64. Two laws that would make much of Hitler's relatively totalitarian rule possible happened very early in his time in power. The first, on February 28, 1933, was a "Decree for the Protection of the People and State," popularly known as "The Reichstag Fire Decree," following as it did immediately after the Reichstag building was damaged by fire. This decree curtailed constitutional rights, such as freedom of the press and freedom to assemble. The second was "the enabling act," passed by the Reichstag on March 24, 1933. This act gave Hitler virtually unlimited power, circumventing the process of parliamentary democracy. See Benjamin Sax and Dieter Kuntz, eds., *Inside Hitler's Germany: A Documentary History of Life in the Third Reich* (Lexington, MA: D. C. Heath, 1992), 134–37.

65. Sax and Kuntz, *Inside Hitler's Germany*, 140.

ultimate goal of eliminating the Jews altogether. This law directly affected the church, because clergy were civil servants. Thus any clergy who were baptized Jews were subject to dismissal.

Victoria Barnett is undoubtedly right that, for the most part, "Protestant leaders were ominously silent" in relation to this law.[66] When leaders did speak up, it was mostly to protect the independence of the church; they did not want the government telling them who could be pastors. Again Barnett is right to say that church leaders should have seen "the deeper question posed" by the church's founder, "a Jew, [who] had told his followers to love their neighbors."[67]

Bonhoeffer was an exception to this relative silence.[68] He responded almost immediately. The "Jewish Question" was, for Bonhoeffer, a personal matter. As Bethge reminds us, "his brother-in-law Gerhard Leibholz and his friend Franz Hildebrandt [both of whom were Jewish] were constant reminders of the consequences of the state's and church's treatments of the Jews."[69] By mid-April he had finished an essay on "The Church and the Jewish Question"; it would be published in June.[70] In this theological essay Bonhoeffer names three ways in which Christians should act in relation to the present situation. First, for Christians there are legitimate reasons to challenge the state if it is not acting properly in its role as state. This can happen either through promoting too much or too little law and order. Certainly, depriving individuals of their rights fits within these concerns. Second, the church has an "unconditional" obligation to aid victims of the state. And third, if the church observes that the state is careening in a fundamentally destructive direction, it may "seize the wheel" of the state itself. That is, it may engage in specific and "direct political action."[71] Bonhoeffer went on to say that if the state were to exclude baptized Jews from Christian congregations, then this would be extremely serious. In fact the church would find itself in *statu confessionis*, that is, in

66. Victoria Barnett, *For the Soul of the People: Protestant Protest Against Hitler* (Oxford: Oxford University Press, 1992), 35. For details see Wolfgang Gerlach, *And the Witnesses Were Silent: The Confessing Church and the Persecution of the Jews*, trans. Victoria J. Barnett (Lincoln: University of Nebraska Press, 2000). See also Richard Gutteridge, *Open Thy Mouth for the Dumb: The German Evangelical Church and the Jews 1879–1950* (Oxford: Basil Blackwell, 1976).

67. Barnett, *For the Soul of the People*, 35.

68. I am well aware of the large volume of literature on Bonhoeffer and the Jews. I will not in this book enter into this thorny set of issues. For an overview of the discussion, see Stephen R. Haynes, *The Bonhoeffer Legacy: Post-Holocaust Perspectives* (Minneapolis: Fortress, 2006).

69. Bethge, *Dietrich Bonhoeffer*, 275. Franz Hildebrandt was a baptized Jew and, to my knowledge, Gerhard Leibholz was not. This difference matters in various ways. However, so far as many Nazis and Nazi policies were concerned, the difference was of no significance. In any event, Bonhoeffer had personal connections with and acted on behalf of both.

70. Bonhoeffer, "The Church and the Jewish Question," in *Berlin*, 361–70.

71. On these specific three points see Bonhoeffer, *Berlin*, 365–66.

a formal state of confessional protest, because the truth and freedom of the gospel itself are at stake.[72]

The question of the treatment of the Jews was a theological question for Bonhoeffer in the sense alluded to by Victoria Barnett. That is, it related to what it meant to be faithful to Christ in loving our neighbors as ourselves. This was not at all unimportant. In fact it animated many of Bonhoeffer's actions. However, even more abhorrent to Bonhoeffer—and thus invoking the term *statu confessionis*—was the matter of redefining the church so that it is composed only of a pure race of Aryans. That so many others in the German Protestant church did not see this led him to say in an April 14 letter to his friend Erwin Sutz that "the most intelligent people have totally lost both their heads and their Bible."[73]

As noted before, for Bonhoeffer, the issue of how Jews were treated was a personal one. On April 11, 1933, the father of his brother-in-law Gerhard Leibholz—the Jewish husband of his twin sister, Sabine—died. Gerhard wanted Dietrich to conduct the funeral. Bonhoeffer was advised to consult his general superintendent, who then strongly counseled him against conducting the funeral of a Jew. Bonhoeffer complied. Later he felt ashamed of his action. In a letter to Gerhard and Sabine on November 23, 1933, he wrote: "I am tormented even now by the thought that I didn't do as you asked me as a matter of course. To be frank, I can't think what made me behave as I did. How could I have been so horribly afraid at the time? It must have seemed equally incomprehensible to you both, and yet you said nothing. But it preys on my mind, because it's the kind of thing one can never make up for. So all I can do is ask you to forgive my weakness then. I know for certain I ought to have behaved differently."[74] Perhaps it was this shame-filled experience that strengthened Bonhoeffer's resolve to act and speak with fearlessness in relation to the Jews who, he knew, were increasingly in danger in Germany.

Working through the volumes of the collected works of Bonhoeffer's writings, one is struck by how frequently he is engaged in actions that relate to Jews. Certainly as a theologian who cares deeply about the identity and integrity of the church, he speaks most often against the Aryan paragraph. But, in the midst of a usually very busy life, he is also vigilant on behalf of various Jews in precarious situations. For example, he writes to Friedrich Siegmund-Schultze on May 17, 1933, to try to protect the job of a Jewish sociologist named Landshut, whose job in the university is threatened because he is Jewish.[75] While in London, Bonhoeffer frequently writes letters on behalf of vulnerable

72. Bonhoeffer, *Berlin*, 366. He wrote a memorandum specifically on this; see *Berlin*, 371–73.
73. Ibid., 101.
74. Bonhoeffer, *London*, 42.
75. Ibid., 112.

Jews as well as in relation to the Aryan paragraph. Later, when he is working for the military intelligence agency, the Abwehr, he gathers data to inform military officers of the mass deportation of Jews that begins in October of 1941. In April of 1943 he is arrested because he is linked to an effort, "Operation 7," to save the lives of first seven and then fourteen Jews by helping them escape from Germany. All of these efforts are deeply a part of Bonhoeffer's Christian identity. In a letter to Erwin Sutz on September 11, 1934, he quotes Proverbs 31:8: "Speak out for those who cannot speak." He follows this with the rhetorical question, "Who in the church today still remembers that this is the very least the Bible asks of us in such times as these?"[76]

From 1933 forward, Bonhoeffer was well aware of the atrocities committed by the men in charge of the Third Reich. Through his brother-in-law Hans von Dohnanyi, Bonhoeffer received inside information many Germans would have been unaware of. Therefore, as he continued to ponder theological and ethical matters, he did so in the context of broad knowledge and deep engagement.

But, of course, Bonhoeffer was a theologian. More than that, he was one who by 1932 had come to believe that "everything depended on the renewal of the church and of the ministry." Therefore he had a particularly keen eye on what had been happening within the Protestant church in Germany since Hitler came to power.

It is tempting to be anachronistic in our reading of Hitler's rise to power, as if the anti-Christian nature of his rule would have been or should have been obvious to everyone. However, this was not the case. On February 16, 1933, slightly more than two weeks after becoming Chancellor, Hitler, in a speech at Stuttgart, declared.

> Today Christians and no international atheists stand at the head of Germany. I speak not just of Christianity; no, I also pledge that I never will tie myself to parties who want to destroy Christianity. . . . We want to fill our culture again with the Christian spirit, not just theoretically. No, we want to burn out the rotten developments in literature, in the theater, in the press—in short, burn out this poison which has entered our whole life and culture during these past fourteen years.[77]

Hearing words like these, most people within Germany, nearly all of whom would have considered themselves Christians, saw Hitler as an ally of the church.

76. Ibid., 217.

77. As quoted in Ernest Christian Helmreich, *The German Churches Under Hitler: Background, Struggle, and Epilogue* (Detroit: Wayne State University Press, 1979), 128–29.

As early as April 1933 a large segment of the Protestant church was formally calling for a "synchronization of church and state" (*Gleichschaltung*), which effectively would bring Christian identity in line with Nazi ideology.[78] Before the month was out, Hitler was attempting to maneuver *his* man, Ludwig Müller, into a position of power, so that he could significantly influence the shape of the Protestant church. He appointed him "confidential adviser and plenipotentiary in questions concerning the Protestant church."[79]

By May 6 "Ten Principles" were articulated that called for the Protestant church to be a fellowship of "German Christians" of only the "Aryan Race." Ten days later this language was softened a bit. Yet the document still firmly anchored the nurture and morality of "German Christians" in "our race and our cultural heritage."[80]

On May 27 Friedrich von Bodelschwingh, a well-respected church leader, was elected by regional delegates to be Reich Bishop. However, Bodelschwingh resigned less than a month later, after vicious campaigns had been mounted against him. Church elections were set for July 23, to elect delegates to the national synod. After significant campaigning—including a speech by Hitler the previous day—approximately two-thirds of the delegates elected were "German Christians." In August, Ludwig Müller was elected regional bishop of the Old Prussian Union, and on September 27 he was elected Reich Bishop. Additionally, at the same church synod meeting in which Müller was unanimously elected Reich Bishop, it was also ordered that only those who could give "'unconditional support for the National Socialist State and the German Protestant Church'—and were also of Aryan descent" could, in the future, serve as clergy.[81]

78. I have deliberately chosen the phrase "segment of the Protestant church" rather than "German Christians." I first came to a more nuanced understanding of the relationship between the "Confessing Church" and "German Christians" by reading James A. Zabel, *Nazism and the Pastors: A Study of the Ideas of Three Deutsche Christian Groups* (Missoula, MT: Scholars Press, 1976) not long after it came out. This more complex view is deepened and clarified by newer studies, such as Doris L. Bergen, *Twisted Cross: The German Christian Movement in the Third Reich* (Chapel Hill: University of North Carolina Press, 1996); and Richard Steigmann-Gall, *The Holy Reich: Nazi Conceptions of Christianity, 1919–1945* (Cambridge: Cambridge University Press, 2003). Of course these should be read in conjunction with books by John S. Conway, Arthur C. Cochrane, Ernst Christian Helmreich, Klaus Scholder, Eberhard Bethge, and Victoria Barnett, along with the church documents collected by Peter Matheson.

79. Bethge, *Dietrich Bonhoeffer*, 270.

80. "New Guiding Principles of the German Christians, 16 May 1933," in Peter Matheson, ed., *The Third Reich and the Christian Churches: Documentary Account of Christian Resistance and Complicity During the Nazi Era* (Grand Rapids: Eerdmans, 1981), 23.

81. Bethge, *Dietrich Bonhoeffer*, 307. For a longer, but still brief account, see Barnett, *For the Soul of the People*, 30–36. For a bit more detail, see Helmreich, *German Churches Under Hitler*,

There was a variety of immediate responses by those who questioned the acts of the German Christians. In May, eleven Westphalian pastors "issued a declaration similar to Bonhoeffer's, rejecting the exclusion of Christians of Jewish descent from the church as heretical and schismatic." This objection was also expressed by Heinrich Vogel's "Eight Articles of Evangelical Doctrine."[82] Also emerging at the beginning of May was what was called "the Young Reformation Movement." This loose configuration of individuals and groups was fairly weak and diffuse—but it at least served as a reminder that chief emphases of the German Christians were diluting or distorting doctrines considered central by those within the Reformation tradition. Students and church leaders affiliated with the Young Reformation Movement made public statements and tried to elect candidates in key positions to counter the moves that were being made to synchronize the church with Nazi ideology.[83] Members of the movement—on occasion including Bonhoeffer—sometimes walked out of meetings dominated by German Christians. But as the July 23 church elections neared, Bonhoeffer saw where the power lay. As he said in a letter to Erwin Sutz on July 17: "There is no doubt in my mind that the victory will go to the German Christians, and this will very quickly bring into view the contours of the new church, and the question will be whether we can even support it as the church."[84]

Yet this sober assessment did not cause Bonhoeffer or others in the Young Reformation Movement to stay silent. Quite the opposite. Following the defeats in the church elections, members of the movement held a July 24–25 meeting at which Martin Niemöller, a respected church leader, assumed a significant role in moving the group to articulate a confession of faith. In another meeting of the inner circle of the Young Reformation Movement, Niemöller articulated sixteen theses following from the meeting a week earlier. Among other things, he said that the group needed to "'confront the new church leadership and the movement of the German Christians—the latter of which is determinative for the former—with the confessional question' and to clear up the situation with a 'confession suitable for the times.'"[85]

133–56. For a full account, see Klaus Scholder, *Preliminary History and the Time of Illusions, 1918–1934*, vol. 1 of *The Churches and the Third Reich*, trans. John Bowden (Philadelphia: Fortress, 1988), 219–492.

82. Bethge, *Dietrich Bonhoeffer*, 280–81.

83. See, for example, "Appeal from the Young Reformation Movement," "Theses by the Student Members of the Young Reformation Movement at the University of Berlin," and "Declaration of the Pastors of Greater Berlin," in Bonhoeffer, *Berlin*, 107–9, 135–37, 137–39.

84. Bonhoeffer, *Berlin*, 140.

85. Carsten Nicolaisen, "Concerning the History of the Bethel Confession," in Bonhoeffer, *Berlin*, 509.

The "Bethel Confession"

After a preliminary meeting on August 5, work on a first draft of a confession began on August 15 and ended on August 25; there were six men, theologians and pastors, who wrote it, with Bonhoeffer having a large role in the composition.[86] In the midst of his work on the confession, Bonhoeffer wrote to his grandmother: "It is becoming increasingly clear to me that what we are going to get is a big, *völkisch* national church that in its essence can no longer be reconciled with Christianity, and that we must make up our minds to take entirely new paths and follow where they lead. The issue is really Germanism or Christianity, and the sooner the conflict comes out in the open, the better. The greatest danger of all would be in trying to conceal this."[87]

The "Bethel Confession" was the first confession formulated as a formal, communally composed response to the German Christians. And it is the only confession that Bonhoeffer helped to formulate. For both of these reasons it is important, despite the fact that it was never formally adopted. In fact, the substantially edited version that emerged by November—after passing through the hands of perhaps twenty theological editors—was a confession Bonhoeffer himself was unwilling to sign. Nevertheless, it is worth looking in some detail at the version Bonhoeffer helped to write in August.

In terms of understanding Bonhoeffer, it is important to examine this confession because it challenges any notion that he cared only about social ethics and not theology as such. There is much about his life that would challenge such a notion; his work on this confession serves as a specific example.

The confession had six articles: on the Holy Scriptures; the Reformation; the trinitarian nature of God; creation and sin; Christ; and the Holy Spirit and the church. As these topics indicate, this is intended as a full-blown doctrinal confession, in the lineage of other orthodox confessions and confessions stemming from the Reformation. Each of the main points of the confession names what one might expect within such a document in the Reformation tradition. Specific attention will be drawn to formulations

86. It appears that Bonhoeffer was the author or coauthor of articles one and three through six, subsection two (on justification and faith; out of seven subsections). But the committee worked together on the whole confession. See Bonhoeffer, *Berlin*, 374, notes 1 and 2. On the confession more generally, for a brief account, see Nicolaisen, "Concerning the History of the Bethel Confession," 509–13. For a detailed discussion of background, history, and the text itself, see Guy Christopher Carter, "Confession at Bethel, August 1933—Enduring Witness: The Formation, Revision and Significance of the First Full Theological Confession of the Evangelical Church Struggle in Nazi Germany" (PhD diss., Marquette University, 1987).

87. Bonhoeffer, *Berlin*, 159.

that are intentionally worded to distinguish the emerging Confessing Church from the German Christians.[88]

(1) In the section on Scripture, the authors wanted to make it clear that "the Holy Scriptures constitute a whole. They have their unity in Jesus Christ, the Crucified and Risen One, who speaks throughout the Scriptures" (376). Moreover, two emphases are present in several places under this first doctrine. First, one cannot claim to have revelation from God through the Holy Spirit separate from the word in Scripture. Though this point is in itself vital theologically for Bonhoeffer, the point is contextually intended to stave off the claims to some special revelation regarding the place of Hitler and Germany in God's redemptive work. Second, in various ways, the authors want to make it clear that the Old Testament is fully a part of the Christian canon of Scripture. To suggest otherwise is to engage in "religious anti-Semitism" (379).

(2) Under the brief article "What is Reformation?" the authors are clearly trying to distinguish an emphasis on Luther as "the teacher who is obedient to the Holy Scriptures" from the claim that in Luther there is "the birth of the German spirit" (381).

(3) The third article, on the Trinity, is less combative than most of the articles. Nonetheless, it stakes out similar ground, rejecting "any attempt to dismember the revelation of the Trinitarian God, to claim to understand the creation or reconciliation or redemption as a concept on its own. Instead, we have in Christ alone the whole revelation of God as Three in One, Creator, Reconciler, and Redeemer" (383).

(4) Similar notes are sounded through article four, "On Creation and Sin." In this article the authors seek to make clear that because of sin—because of the fall—human knowledge alone cannot grasp the revelation of God. We need redemption; "we are entirely dependent on God's self-revelation, as witnessed to us by the Scriptures and proclaimed through the preaching of the church. Only in obedience to the word of God in the Scriptures can we know the Creator, and not through any interpretation of events in the world" (384–85). This is joined to a rejection of "the false doctrine that this world, just as it is, corresponds to the original creation according to the will of God and must therefore be fully affirmed" (385). The next few paragraphs are particularly provocative:

> We reject the false doctrine that struggle [*Kampf*] is the fundamental law of the original creation, and that an aggressive attitude is therefore God's commandment

88. I will refer to the "August version" in what follows. This text appears in the right column of pages 374–424 in Bonhoeffer, *Berlin*. In the following pages I will include page numbers in parentheses that refer to this version of the Confession.

> arising from the original creation. Struggle presupposes the condition of being friend or foe. This condition arises only from the existence of good and evil. The goal of this struggle, to annihilate one another, is a consequence of the fall, according to which good and evil are no longer separate in a human being. Therefore, no struggle with evil, that is, with sin, may ever be aimed at the person who carries the evil, for evil is at work on both sides. The fight must be against evil as such. (385–86)

Finally, in this first subsection the authors say they reject "the false doctrine that the voice of the people [*Volk*] could be the voice of God. It is the voice of the people that cries both 'Hosanna!' and 'Crucify him!' They shouted in reply: 'Not this man, but Barabbas!'"(386–87).

Under the second subsection, on "The Orders," the authors discuss race, conflict, and obedience to the state. Having argued that race is a modern, not a biblical concept, the authors state: "To speak of the Creator God who made the entire human race, is to speak of the humanity that exists over and above the distinct peoples. That means, 'the stranger that dwelleth with you shall be unto you as one born among you, and thou shalt love him as thyself . . . I am the Lord your God' (Lev. 19:34)" (389). Two paragraphs later, the authors say, "We know that besides the resolution of conflicts by the state, to which we bow in obedience, the church's proclamation assures us of the ultimate resolution of all conflicts through redemption in Christ" (389).

Also, in relation to obedience to the state, in the second to last paragraph the authors quote the Augsburg Confession, knowing it has key phrases that add vital qualifiers. "'Christians therefore are obliged to be subject to political authority and to obey its commands and laws in all that may be done without sin. But if a command of the political authority cannot be followed without sin, we must obey God rather than any human beings' (Acts 5:29; C.A. Art. 16)" (391). And lest Christians in Germany be tempted to attach too much significance to the power of the state, this subsection concludes: "Only in Christ can the world be restored" (392).

In the third subsection, on the law, again we see the clear commitment to Scripture at work:

> The law is revealed in the Bible in numerous particular demands; these do not have the meaning for us of principles to be applied but rather carry the authority of true witness to the Lord who commands us freely. (The Ten Commandments and the Sermon on the Mount are in agreement on this.) The church therefore proclaims the law of the Scriptures, not as a principle for us each to apply in different ways, but as the concrete claim made on us by God as our Lord, which binds us again and again to the one Lord revealed in the Bible. A Christian

> receives God's law only as it is proclaimed in the church according to the Scriptures. Only through the Holy Scriptures does the Christian also understand the orders, within which he lives, as God's law. The Old Testament law differs from the laws for living and the orders of other peoples in that it is given to Israel as the people chosen to be the church. Therefore, it is to be made the subject not of comparisons but only of proclamation. (302–3)

The fourth and final subsection of this article is on sin. Basically in this subsection the authors are challenging the claim that having a German or Aryan identity is inherently good. No, the authors say, we are all fallen, sinful, and in need of redemption through Christ—all of us, whether Aryan or not.

(5) Christ has certainly already been named in most, if not all, the articles; the Confession is thoroughly christological. However, article 5 is specifically "On Christ." The article first begins with a clear affirmation: "The church teaches that Jesus Christ is Son of God and Son of David, true God and true human being, the Sinless One in the sinful flesh, and the sole salvation of humankind; that the world without Christ is lost before the wrath of God" (396). But here as clearly as anywhere, the authors must denounce current affirmations: "We reject the false doctrine that Jesus appeared as a 'flare of Nordic light' in the midst of a world tormented by signs of decay" (397). "We reject the false doctrine that says we confess Jesus as our Lord because of his heroic devotion" (397). "With the confession we hereby reject the error of the new Arians, 'that Christ is not true, essential God by nature of one eternal divine essence with God the Father and the Holy Spirit, but that he is merely adorned with divine majesty under and alongside God the Father'" (397). "We reject the false doctrine that the cross of Jesus Christ may be regarded as a symbol for a generalized religious or human truth, as expressed in the sentence, 'The public interest comes before private interest'" (397–98). "The cross of Jesus Christ is not at all a symbol for anything; it is rather the unique revelatory act of God, in which the fulfillment of the law, the judgment of death on all flesh, and the reconciliation of the world with God are carried out for all people" (398). Finally, in the last paragraph, the authors challenge the idea that the Jews are uniquely responsible for the death of Jesus. Instead, Jesus died for the sins of all.

(6) The sixth and final article is divided into seven subsections on the larger topic "On the Holy Spirit and the Church." The introduction of this article, repeating earlier emphases, again connects the Holy Spirit to the Trinity, as well as "the external Word" and the sacraments. More specifically it states that "rebellion against this teaching about the Holy Spirit is an ethno-nationalist [*völkisch*] rebellion against the church of Jesus Christ" (389). The subsection

"On Justification and Faith" is clearly trying to counter German Christian emphases, which must have included a superficial way of speaking of "trust in God." Thus, the authors aver: "Heathen trust in God sees God as a nameless power to which one must submit, as destiny. Christian faith recognizes God, revealed in Christ alone, as the living, holy, just, and merciful Father and Lord. For a Christian, to trust in God means to accept this world obediently from the hand of the God who is revealed in Christ, to take Christ's cross upon oneself and to carry it in the power of the promise that at the end of all things God will create a new heaven and a new earth" (401).

Trusting in the true, living God—and understanding justification properly—is not to be confused with simply being "decent folk." Rather, we know of our need for salvation, our need to have faith in Jesus Christ. We acknowledge that even "this faith is the work of God, and it bears fruit in the good works for which God prepared us beforehand" (402).

The third subsection is on the church, ministry, and confession. In the midst of various affirmations, the authors say that "no body of knowledge, and no statesman or government, can comprehend what the church is, except through faith in Jesus Christ the Lord, the faith that he gives" (404). "The only marks by which it is recognized are the purity with which it teaches the gospel and its correct administration of the sacraments, not the particular religious or moral status of its members" (405).

> As service to the Word of reconciliation, ministry lives by the word of the Holy Scriptures alone and can only be performed by taking this word as its source. The office of the ministry receives its mission neither from the nation, nor from the state, nor from any political and spiritual movement. The office of bishop is not by its nature set above that of the preaching ministry. Its superior position is that of the authority within the church-community. It is subject to the law of the Scriptures and of the confessions, and therefore it cannot ordain that the tie that binds the community to the confession be loosened or undone. (411)

In the fourth subsection the authors turn to the church and nation (*Volk*). "The message of the gospel is equally accessible, or equally inaccessible, to all peoples. For it is only God's Holy Spirit who can bring about faith in human beings and awaken consensus on the true confession. The communion of the confessing church extends across the borders between peoples. The boundaries of the *Volk* and church are never the same" (412).

In relation to matters of church and state, in the fifth subsection, the authors say, "All worldly government, whether good or bad, stands not within the realm of salvation but rather within the realm of death. The church enters into this realm of death with its proclamation of Christ's resurrection and of salvation only through Christ. Only in Christ does the human being receive salvation and life before God. Thus the Word proclaimed by the church has a total claim on each person" (413). Later in the discussion the authors bluntly say: "We reject the false doctrine of the Christian state in any form. . . . The state cannot presume to bring salvation to human beings. It cannot misuse the church as its moral and religious foundation. It is false doctrine to think of the church as the soul or the conscience of the state" (415–16).

The sixth subsection is on the church and the Jews. The authors begin: "The church teaches that God elected Israel, from among all the earth's peoples, to be the people of God. Israel was chosen solely by the power of God's word and in God's mercy, not because of any natural merit of its own. . . . The place of the Old Testament people of the covenant has been taken not by another nation but rather by the Christian church, called out of, and within, all nations" (416–17). "God glorifies his overflowing faithfulness in remaining true to Israel according to the flesh, from which Christ was born in the flesh, despite all Israel's unfaithfulness and even after the crucifixion" (417–18). "The sacred remnant has the character *indelebilis* [indelible] of the chosen people" (418). "The fellowship of those belonging to the church is determined not by blood nor, therefore, by race, but by the Holy Spirit and baptism" (419). "It can never in any case be the mission of any nation to take revenge on the Jews for the murder committed on Golgotha. 'Vengeance is mine,' says the Lord (Deut. 32:35; Heb. 10:30)" (419). "We object to the assertion that the faith of a Jewish Christian would, unlike that of a Gentile Christian, be a matter of race or blood, as a form of Judaistic enthusiasm" (420). "We object to the attempt to make the German Protestant church into a Reich church for Christians of the Aryan race, thus robbing it of its promise" (420). "The Christians who are of Gentile descent must be prepared to expose themselves to persecution before they are ready to betray even in a single case, voluntarily or under compulsion, the church's fellowship with Jewish Christians that is instituted in Word and sacrament" (421).

Finally we come to the seventh subsection, "On the End of All Things." This section challenges otherworldliness on the one hand and the self-glorification of the Third Reich on the other. "We reject the false doctrine that would seek to tear the world of hope apart from our world, so that the first has nothing to do with the second. We see this as an attempt to escape from the recognition that the present world is 'now' already threatened and judged by the end time, and that Jesus Christ, the end of the world, already speaks his word to the world and demands our obedience" (423). Equally, "we reject the false doctrine that would see within the world a gradual development taking place that will culminate in the new world." And "we reject any version of the doctrine of the thousand-year reign [*Reich*] that clearly seeks to interpret certain historical events as the beginning of Christ's visible reign on earth" (424).

This, in summary form, is the Bethel Confession. We have spent so much time on it because it gives us a significant window into Bonhoeffer's theology. Also, it provides an example—a contextually provocative one—of a confession that could have served as a rallying point for what came to be the Confessing Church.

Almost immediately after finishing the Bethel Confession, Bonhoeffer returned to the vital topic of the Aryan paragraph and its implications for the church as a discrete topic. Thus, even though he had written an essay on the Jewish question in April, even though he had issued a memorandum on the Aryan paragraph and its crucial significance for the church, even though Jewish concerns are addressed throughout the Bethel Confession, by the end of August, only a few days after the Bethel Confession was finished, Bonhoeffer issued a pamphlet entitled "Theses on 'The Aryan Paragraph in the Church.'"[89] As he puts it in a summary statement:

> The church is the congregation of those who are called, where the gospel is rightly taught and the sacraments rightly administered, and it does not establish any law for membership therein. The Aryan paragraph is therefore a false doctrine for the church and destroys its substance. Therefore, there is only one way to serve the truth in a church that implements the Aryan paragraph in this radical form, and that is to withdraw. This is the ultimate act of solidarity with my church. I can never serve my church in any other way than by adhering to the whole truth and all its consequences.[90]

Only a few days later—on September 5 and 6—there was a meeting of the General Synod of the Old Prussian Union of the Protestant Church in Berlin. Many of the delegates wore brown National Socialist uniforms; thus the synod is often referred to as "the Brown Synod." It was decided at this meeting "that clergy could only come from the ranks of those who stood in 'unconditional support for the National Socialist State and the German Protestant Church'—and were also of Aryan descent."[91] Bonhoeffer and his good friend Franz Hildebrandt, who was Jewish, made passionate pleas for widespread resignations from church offices. The call went unheeded. However, as a direct response to the Brown Synod, the Pastor's Emergency League was founded by

89. Bonhoeffer, *Berlin*, 425–32.
90. Ibid., 428.
91. Bethge, *Dietrich Bonhoeffer*, 307.

Bonhoeffer, Hildebrandt, Martin Niemöller, and seventeen other pastors on September 12. "The members of the Emergency League were, first of all, to commit themselves anew to the Scriptures and Confessions; secondly, to resist any violation of these; third, to give financial help to those affected by Nazi laws or by violence; and fourth, to reject the Aryan paragraph."[92] Within a short time two thousand pastors had signed on to the Emergency League. By the end of the year that number had tripled; it would later grow by another thousand. Thus the Confessing Church was essentially launched, though it would await its own formal confession until the following May.

Three days after the formation of the Pastor's Emergency League, Bonhoeffer was in Sofia, Bulgaria, attending a five-day meeting of the World Alliance for Promoting International Friendship through the Churches. It was probably because of Bonhoeffer's presence at this ecumenical gathering that the executive committee made a formal statement against "racial discrimination in any part of the world." In fact, the committee specifically said it was "deeply concerned by the treatment inflicted upon persons of Jewish origin and connection in Germany."[93]

October 14, slightly more than a month after the Pastor's Emergency League was formed, Germany left the League of Nations. Most pastors within the Emergency League—not to mention "German Christians"—applauded this act; Bonhoeffer and Franz Hildebrandt were not among them. This gap, especially on issues related to nationalism, will continue to widen between Bonhoeffer and Hildebrandt and most other leaders in the Emergency League and the Confessing Church that grows out of it.

92. Schlingensiepen, *Dietrich Bonhoeffer*, 137–38.
93. Statement by the executive committee in Bonhoeffer, *Berlin*, 174, 175.

2

Seeking a "Legitimate Christian Means" of Fighting Hitler

Bonhoeffer had the opportunity to pastor a church in Berlin, but under the circumstances he felt he could not accept it. As Franz Hildebrandt said: "He reasoned, in view of the so-called 'Aryanization' of the clergy under the Nazi laws, that he could not be in a ministry which had become a racial privilege." "I cannot recall or imagine," says Hildebrandt, "any other man to have taken this line of solidarity with those of us who had to resign their pastorates under that legislation."[1] Therefore, instead, on October 17, Bonhoeffer began an eighteen-month pastorate of two German-speaking congregations in London.

Ministry in London

We will certainly never know all the reasons Bonhoeffer went to London to pastor. However, he gives us some hints in a vulnerable letter he wrote to Karl Barth on October 24, 1933, a week after arriving in London:

1. Franz Hildebrandt, "An Oasis of Freedom," in *I Knew Dietrich Bonhoeffer*, ed. Wolf-Dieter Zimmermann and Ronald Gregor Smith (1966; repr., London: Fontana Books, 1973), 39.

> If it is at all desirable, after such a decision, to find well-defined reasons for [coming to London], I think one of the strongest was that I no longer felt inwardly equal to the questions and demands that I was facing. I felt that, in some way I don't understand, I found myself in radical opposition to all my friends. I was becoming increasingly isolated with my views of the matter, even though I was and remain close to these people. All this frightened me and shook my confidence, so that I began to fear that dogmatism might be leading me astray—since there seemed no particular reason why my own view in these matters should be any better, any more right, than the views of many really good and able pastors whom I sincerely respect. And so I thought it was about time to go into the wilderness for a spell, and simply work as a pastor, as unobtrusively as possible. At the time it seemed to me more dangerous to make a gesture than to retreat into silence.[2]

Barth fires back a strong response. He fears that Bonhoeffer's move is an escapist one—just at the very time when the German church so desperately needs him. "Under no circumstances should you now be playing Elijah under the juniper tree or Jonah under the gourd; you need to be here with all guns blazing! . . . You belong in Berlin and not in London."[3] Bonhoeffer had indicated in his letter that he probably should have consulted Barth earlier, before he made the decision to move. But perhaps, in light of Barth's response, Bonhoeffer's instinct to write Barth *after* the fact was right. Given his respect for Barth, he would have found it difficult not to take Barth's strongly worded admonitions seriously—and in fact abide by them. But it seems clear, in retrospect, that Bonhoeffer's decision was wise. He needed to be away from Berlin for these eighteen months, just as he needed the ten months away from Germany in 1930–31. In fact, the two seem closely connected.

Bonhoeffer was not so arrogant as to assume he was right in all the ways he differed with other church leaders within the Young Reformation Movement or the Pastor's Emergency League. On the other hand, he could not easily abandon convictions that were becoming clearer and clearer to him. He was extremely busy in his life in Berlin. He needed time and space away for self-evaluation. The chance to go to London afforded him this opportunity—not to escape, but to gain clarity for the difficult road ahead. In England, as in the United States earlier, there was deliberateness in his concentrated discernment. In fact, Bonhoeffer seems precisely to be clarifying the convictions that grew out of the "grand liberation" that he experienced during his time in New York.

2. Dietrich Bonhoeffer, *London: 1933–1935*, ed. Keith W. Clements, trans. Isabel Best, vol. 13 of *Dietrich Bonhoeffer Works* (Minneapolis: Fortress, 2007), 23.

3. Barth, in Bonhoeffer, *London*, 39, 41.

Beginning in November 1933, Franz Hildebrandt shared Bonhoeffer's London parsonage with him, staying for a couple of months. Hildebrandt was perhaps Bonhoeffer's only friend who agreed with him on all major issues. And yet it is intriguing to note Wolf-Dieter Zimmermann's observation that, when he spent some weeks with them in London, "Bonhoeffer and Hildebrandt were in a state of permanent dispute."[4] These lively theological discussions appear to have been one of Bonhoeffer's ways of clarifying his own convictions. There would be many other visitors who would share a few days or weeks with Bonhoeffer during his eighteen months in London. Many of their conversations with Bonhoeffer were undoubtedly lively as well.

We don't know the specific content of these discussions. More than likely they ventured far and wide, including events in Germany, events in the German church, theology, and discipleship. Bethge is undoubtedly right that "during this period [Bonhoeffer] devoted much time to reflecting on the Sermon on the Mount and on 'discipleship.'"[5] And I'm sure Bethge is right that many people perceived Bonhoeffer's engagement with the Sermon on the Mount as a "constant concern."[6] However, it is probably more precise to say that Bonhoeffer's concern during his time in London was to be able to articulate, and live, a holistic, contextually appropriate, and potentially quite costly discipleship—which certainly included living with the challenges of God's word spoken powerfully through the Sermon on the Mount.

From his first sermon in London, delivered on October 22, 1933, on 2 Corinthians 5:20, we hear resonances of Barth, along with hints of movement toward Bonhoeffer's own understanding of grace-filled, costly discipleship. Bonhoeffer here is reflecting on why it is that so many thousands find the church so boring, why it is that the cinema seems so much more interesting than the church.

> It is because we ourselves have made the church, and keep on making it, into something which it is not. It is because we talk too much about false, trivial human things and ideas in the church and too little about God. It is because we make the church into a playground for all sorts of feelings of ours, instead of a place where God's word is obediently received and believed. It is because we prefer quiet and edification to the holy restlessness of the powerful Lord God, because we keep thinking we have God in our power instead of allowing God to have power over us, instead of recognizing that God is truth and that over against God the whole world is in the wrong. It is because we like too much to talk and think about a

4. Wolf-Dieter Zimmermann, "Some Weeks in London," in *I Knew Dietrich Bonhoeffer*, 78.
5. Eberhard Bethge, *Dietrich Bonhoeffer: A Biography*, rev. ed., ed. Victoria J. Barnett (Minneapolis: Fortress, 2000), 327.
6. Ibid., 372.

> cozy, comfortable God instead of letting ourselves be disturbed and disquieted by the presence of God—because in the end we ourselves do not want to believe that God is really here among us, right now, demanding that we hand ourselves over, in life and death, in heart and soul and body. And finally, it is because we pastors keep talking too much about passing things, perhaps about whatever we ourselves have thought out or experienced, instead of knowing that we are no more than the messengers of the great truth of the eternal Christ.[7]

He ends this inaugural sermon with the following prayer: "O Lord, give all of us new hearts, open and obedient to you: hearts that love our neighbor and pray to you for our church. Lord, give us a good beginning: open your fatherly heart to us and lead us, one day, home to your kingdom of eternal reconciliation, through Christ the Lord! Amen."[8]

A couple of months later, in an advent sermon on December 17, 1933, Bonhoeffer challenges the typical, sentimental, Christmas-pageant approach to the season.

> If we want to be a part of this event of Advent and Christmas, we cannot just sit there like a theater audience and enjoy all the lovely pictures. We ourselves will be caught up in this action, this reversal of all things; we will become actors on this stage. For this is a play in which each spectator has a part to play, and we cannot hold back. . . . The judgment and redemption of the world—that is what is happening here. For it is the Christ Child in the manger himself who will bring that judgment and redemption. It is he who pushes away the great and mighty of the world, who topples the thrones of the powerful, who humbles the haughty, whose arm exercises power against all who are highly placed and strong, and whose mercy lifts up what was lowly and makes it great and glorious. . . . Something will happen to each of us who decides to come to Christ's manger. Each of us will have been judged or redeemed before we go away. Each of us will either break down or come to know that God's mercy is turned toward us.[9]

He asks, "Might this Christmas help us learn to see this point in a radically different way, to rethink it entirely, to know that if we want to find the way to God, we have to go, not up to the heights, but really down to the depths among the least of all, and that every life that only wants to stay up high will come to a fearful end?"[10] And he concludes: "Who will take their place among the lowly and let God alone be high? Who will see the glory of God in the lowliness of the child in the manger? Who will say with Mary: The Lord has

7. Bonhoeffer, *London*, 323–24.
8. Ibid., 326.
9. Ibid., 344–45.
10. Ibid., 346.

looked with favor on my lowliness. My soul magnifies the Lord, and my spirit rejoices in God my Savior. Amen."[11]

In 1934, perhaps in July, Bonhoeffer preached a sermon on 2 Corinthians 12:19. In this sermon Bonhoeffer's central point is that our God, in embodying weakness, suffers with us and calls us to be like Christ—being strong through weakness and embracing the suffering of the world. "Christianity stands or falls," he says, "with its revolutionary protest against violence, arbitrariness and pride of power and with its apologia for the weak.—I feel that Christianity is rather doing too little in showing these points than doing too much. Christianity has adjusted itself much too easily to the worship of power. It should give much more offence, more shock to the world, than it is doing. Christianity should . . . take a much more definite stand for the weak than to consider the potential moral right of the strong."[12]

Bonhoeffer also gave a series of sermons on 1 Corinthians 13. At the opening of the first of these, on October 14, 1934, Bonhoeffer gives three reasons for preaching a sermon series on this text. First, he says, it is vital to be reminded that Christians are to love one another. Christians are to live in such a way that "estranged brothers suddenly [are] no longer against each other but rather with and for each other."[13] These reconciled relationships provide a powerful witness to the gospel. Bonhoeffer goes on to say:

> The second reason I had for choosing this text is the particular situation of our German churches. Whether or not we want to see it, whether or not we think it is right, the churches are caught up in a struggle for their faith such as we have not seen for hundreds of years. This is a struggle—whether or not we agree—over our confession of Jesus Christ alone as Lord and Redeemer of this world. But anyone who inwardly and outwardly joins in this struggle for this confession knows that such a struggle for faith carries a great temptation with it—the temptation of being too sure of oneself, of self-righteousness and dogmatism, which also means the temptation to be unloving toward one's opponent. And yet this opponent can never truly be overcome if not through love, since no opponent is ever overcome, except by love. . . . Even of the most passionate battle for the faith it could well be said: ". . . *but had it not love, it would be nothing.*"[14]

Third, Bonhoeffer expresses hope that the world will "hear again the message of the Bible in its purity." That is to say, "that God is to be *loved* above all."[15]

11. Ibid., 347.
12. Ibid., 402–3.
13. Ibid., 376.
14. Ibid.
15. Ibid., 376, 377.

> To love God does not just mean that when things are going badly for us, we say: God will help us again! That truly amounts to a feeble and puny faith. To love God means to rejoice in God, to think and pray gladly to God, to love being alone in God's presence, to wait impatiently for God, for every word and every request; it means not causing God sorrow but rejoicing simply that there is God, that we can know and have and speak with and live with God. To love God—and for love of God, to love our brethren as well—in our disillusioned Protestant church do we still understand this?[16]

These sermons give us windows into Bonhoeffer the pastor as he proclaims the gospel to his German-speaking congregations in London, with a vivid consciousness of what is happening in Germany at the time. One of the particulars regarding discipleship that was a "constant concern" of Bonhoeffer was peace. There are elements of this concern contained in the sermons referenced above. We are also given a window into this from an observer in London, Lawrence B. Whitburn, who was one of Bonhoeffer's parishioners. Whitburn says that he and his wife had many conversations with Bonhoeffer about "all the subjects one can imagine. If one really wanted to raise a lively discussion, one had only to touch on the subject of divorce or pacifism. His opinion against the former and in favor of the latter was so marked and clear in his mind that the discussion soon developed into an argument, presumably as we thought the opposite. Nevertheless we still remained good friends."[17]

During his time in London, Bonhoeffer continued actively to monitor the situation in Germany. For instance, Julius Rieger, a co-pastor with Bonhoeffer in London, reported in his diary: "Bonhoeffer has found out from the Ministry of Justice that on June 30 and July 1 [1934], 207 people were shot."[18] In fact, Bonhoeffer spoke by phone regularly—often daily and at great length—with friends and family in Germany; indeed, his phone bill was so high that on at least one occasion the post office personnel who charged for the phone service felt sorry for him and reduced the bill. In addition to phoning, Bonhoeffer took trips to Germany every several weeks.

While in London, Bonhoeffer on several occasions worked in personal ways to try to help Jews who came to England to escape the ever-increasing dangers in Germany. He also continued to work against the implementation of the Aryan paragraph by the German church.

16. Ibid., 377.
17. Lawrence B. Whitburn, "Bonhoeffer without His Cassock," in *I Knew Dietrich Bonhoeffer*, 80.
18. Bonhoeffer, *London*, 216.

Meanwhile, Bonhoeffer remained actively involved in ecumenical meetings and contacts. In particular, he deepened his friendship with Anglican Bishop George Bell of Chichester, a connection that would continue to be important to him.

As he did in July 1932 in Czechoslovakia and December 1932 at the Student Christian Movement meeting in Berlin, Bonhoeffer again spoke most provocatively about his convictions regarding peace at an ecumenical gathering.[19] In August 1934 he addressed the Ecumenical Council of Churches gathering in Fanø, Denmark, on the topic "The Church and the Peoples of the World."[20]

> Nationalism and internationalism have to do with political necessities and possibilities. The ecumenical Church, however, does not concern itself with these things, but with the commandments of God, and regardless of consequences it transmits these commandments to the world.
>
> Our task as theologians, accordingly, consists only in accepting this commandment as a binding one, not as a question open to discussion. Peace on earth is not a problem, but a commandment given at Christ's coming. There are two ways of reacting to this command from God: the unconditional, blind obedience of action, or the hypocritical question of the Serpent: "Yea, hath God said . . . ?" This question is the mortal enemy of obedience, and therefore the mortal enemy of all real peace. . . . "Must God not have meant that we should talk about peace, to be sure, but that it is not to be literally translated into action? Must God not really have said that we should work for peace, of course, but also make ready tanks and poison gas for security?" And then perhaps the most serious question: "Did God say you should not protect your own people? Did God say you should leave your own a prey to the enemy?"
>
> No, God did not say all that. What He has said is that there shall be peace among men—that we shall obey Him without further question, that is what He means. He who questions the commandment of God before obeying has already denied Him. . . . For the members of the ecumenical Church, in so far as they hold to Christ, His word, His commandment of peace is more holy, more inviolable than the most revered words and works of the natural world. For they know that whoso is not able to hate father and mother for His sake is not worthy of Him, and lies if he calls himself after Christ's name. These

19. Bethge tells us that Bonhoeffer had significant theological differences with the World Alliance (and probably most of the formal ecumenical organizations). What assured his involvement in them was "the peace question" (Bethge, *Dietrich Bonhoeffer*, 194).

20. Bethge says that the text we have is not Bonhoeffer's speech at the conference but rather a morning homily (Bethge, *Dietrich Bonhoeffer*, 387). Keith Clements, editor of the English translation of the thirteenth volume of the collected works, in which this document appears, says that further research has confirmed that the document being discussed here was Bonhoeffer's speech. Keith Clements, "Editor's Introduction to the English Edition," in Bonhoeffer, *London*, 12.

> brothers in Christ obey His word; they do not doubt or question, but keep His commandment of peace. They are not ashamed, in defiance of the world, even to speak of eternal peace. They cannot take up arms against Christ himself—yet this is what they do if they take up arms against one another! Even in anguish and distress of conscience there is for them no escape from the commandment of Christ that there shall be peace.
>
> How does peace come about? Through a system of political treaties? Through the investment of international capital in different countries? Through the big banks, through money? Or through universal peaceful rearmament in order to guarantee peace? Through none of these, for the single reason that in all of them peace is confused with safety. There is no way to peace along the way of safety. For peace must be dared. It is the great venture. It can never be made safe. Peace is the opposite of security. To demand guarantees is to mistrust, and this mistrust in turn brings forth war. To look for guarantees is to want to protect oneself. Peace means to give oneself altogether to the law of God, wanting no security, but in faith and obedience laying the destiny of the nations in the hand of Almighty God, not trying to direct it for selfish purposes. Battles are won, not with weapons, but with God. They are won where the way leads to the cross. Which of us can say he knows what it might mean for the world if one nation should meet the aggressor, not with weapons in hand, but praying defenseless, and for that very reason protected by "a bulwark never failing"?[21]

This last sentence, in particular, probably reflects Bonhoeffer's keen interest in the nonviolent resistance activities of Mahatma Gandhi. Bonhoeffer had been interested in Gandhi since late 1924 or early 1925.[22] His interest had intensified in recent years, and it was during his time in London that he came closest to realizing his desire to live and study with Gandhi in India. This was in fact the third time Bonhoeffer had seriously considered visiting India. Eberhard Bethge notes a variety of reasons India had intrigued Bonhoeffer over the years. But, says Bethge, by

> 1934 Bonhoeffer was motivated by the desire to witness Gandhi's exemplification of the Sermon on the Mount—in the spiritual exercises aimed toward a certain goal, and the Indian ways of resistance against tyrannical power. . . . [He] sought a prototype for passive resistance that could induce changes without violence. His quest concealed his private fear that the church struggle might become an end in itself, remaining satisfied with reiterated confessions

21. Bonhoeffer, "The Church and the Peoples of the World," in *London*, 307–9. Bonhoeffer also composed a set of theses to be discussed at this conference, theses that were every bit as provocative as his speech. See Bonhoeffer, "Theses Paper for the Fanø Conference," in *London*, 304–6.

22. Bethge, *Dietrich Bonhoeffer*, 105.

> and ceaseless activity. He sought a means of fighting Hitler that went beyond the aims and methods of the church struggle while remaining legitimate from a Christian standpoint. While he supported the church struggle with all his might, at a deeper level he was looking for a different form of commitment that would be legitimate.[23]

Some leaders in the church discouraged such a trip. During 1933 and 1934 Gerhard Jacobi, a leader in what was becoming the Confessing Church, repeatedly warned Bonhoeffer not to go to India; he was urgently needed by the German church.[24] In June of 1934 Bonhoeffer had been invited to direct a seminary for the Pastor's Emergency League.[25] By mid-September he had decided to say yes to directing the seminary. Yet on November 1 Bonhoeffer secured a personal invitation from Gandhi to come to India to live in his ashram and study with him.[26] Bonhoeffer did not, in principle, see going to India and directing the seminary as alternatives. In fact, as Bethge says, "Bonhoeffer had been trying to avoid having to choose between India and the seminary, seeing the first as a necessary preparation for the second."[27] However, it appears that Bonhoeffer decided he did not have time for an extended visit to India; thus he did not go. To address his desire to experience a more serious form of community life, since he was not to live in an ashram in India, he visited various monastic communities during his remaining time in England.[28]

Experiment in a "New Form of Monasticism"

There is no question but that Bonhoeffer's time in London was good preparation for the next step in his life. He added to his limited pastoral experience. From afar he still managed to closely monitor the situation in Germany. He continued to nurture ecumenical relationships. And he grasped more fully what the "grand liberation" he had begun to undergo several years earlier meant for his life and ministry. In a letter to his brother Karl-Friedrich on January 14, 1935, he acknowledged that he could be perceived as "rather fanatical." Yet, he said, he was achieving "true inner clarity and honesty by really starting to

23. Ibid., 409.
24. Gerhard Jacobi, "Drawn Towards Suffering," in *I Knew Dietrich Bonhoeffer*, 73–74.
25. Diary entry by Julius Rieger, in Bonhoeffer, *London*, 155–56.
26. The letter from Gandhi is in Bonhoeffer, *London*, 229–30.
27. Bethge, *Dietrich Bonhoeffer*, 409.
28. See, e.g., Julius Rieger, "Contacts with London," in *I Knew Dietrich Bonhoeffer*, 95–103.

take the Sermon on the Mount seriously." "Things do exist," he wrote, "that are worth standing for without compromise. To me it seems that peace and social justice are such things, as is Christ himself."[29]

But perhaps offering the most direct window into Bonhoeffer's own perceptions of the next stage of his life is the letter he wrote to his good friend Erwin Sutz on September 11, 1934:

> The next generation of pastors, these days, ought to be trained entirely in church-monastic schools, where the pure doctrine, the Sermon on the Mount, and worship are taken seriously. . . . It is also time for a final break with our theologically grounded reserve about whatever is being done by the state—which really only comes down to fear. "Speak out for those who cannot speak." [Prov. 31.8]—who in the church today still remembers that this is the very least the Bible asks of us in such times as these? And then there's the matter of military service, war, etc., etc.[30]

When Bonhoeffer left for London, there was a loose configuration of protest within the Protestant church—the Pastor's Emergency League. He was now returning to a Germany in which there was a clearer identity for a Confessing Church, with its identity bolstered by the Barmen Confession, written mostly by Barth and ratified by leaders in the church at the end of May 1934 and clarified in several successive synods.[31] Bonhoeffer was excited at the prospect of training ministers for this church. Franz Hildebrandt, Bonhoeffer's close friend, says that Dietrich "viewed these years in the cause of underground ministerial training as the most fruitful period of his life."[32] Though this statement might refer to the whole period of ministerial training—that is, from 1935 to 1940—it would seem especially true for the two-and-a-half-year period from the spring of 1935 until the fall of 1937, during which Bonhoeffer and his seminarians enjoyed community life at Finkenwalde. The initial class consisted of twenty-three candidates. By the end, 150 students had been trained by Bonhoeffer.

29. Bonhoeffer, *London*, 284–85.

30. Ibid., 217.

31. For a brief account of the Barmen Synod, see Victoria J. Barnett, *For the Soul of the People: Protestant Protest Against Hitler* (Oxford: Oxford University Press, 1992), 53–60. For a fuller discussion, see Klaus Scholder, *The Year of Disillusionment 1934—Barmen and Rome*, vol. 2 of *The Churches and the Third Reich*, trans. John Bowden (Philadelphia: Fortress, 1988), 122–71. The Barmen Confession itself is published in English in various places. A recent publication of it is as the first appendix in Ferdinand Schlingensiepen, *Dietrich Bonhoeffer, 1906–1945: Martyr, Thinker, Man of Resistance*, trans. Isabel Best (London: T&T Clark, 2010), 407–11.

32. Hildebrandt, "An Oasis of Freedom," 39–40.

Taking cues from monastic communities he had visited, Bonhoeffer instituted strict practices for this learning community.[33] Each day was begun in silence, until the group met together in worship, for "God's Word was to be the first word spoken each day."[34] The daily worship consisted of Psalms and random hymn verses. As in monasteries, the whole Psalter was to be prayed every week. Additionally, whole chapters from the Old Testament and long sections from the New Testament were read within the service. Only on Saturdays would Bonhoeffer offer a commentary on the texts. Every day he offered an extemporaneous prayer during the service, which was concluded with a benediction. The service was followed by a modest breakfast and then by a half-hour meditation on a biblical text. During this time of meditation there was to be no movement or sound; no phone calls were accepted. The meditation was centered on a single biblical text chosen for each week.

After the meditation, the students engaged in the theological work normally expected in a seminary. The first course Bonhoeffer offered was on discipleship. Apart from this class, which was unheard of, the rest of the courses were relatively standard and included such subjects as homiletics and pastoral care (albeit with Bonhoeffer's distinctive emphases). A half hour before lunch there was the singing of hymns, in unison. During the noon meal there were often oral readings. Following lunch was further class work. The evenings were filled with games and music. The day concluded with worship, with the same pattern as the morning worship. Each month there was a celebration of the Lord's Supper. The seminarians were encouraged to make personal confessions to one another. Bonhoeffer himself practiced this with Eberhard Bethge. There was also what was referred to as the "Finkenwalde Rule," which was the pledge not to speak about a brother when he was absent.

A number of ministerial candidates found the community disciplines to be quite onerous. There were varied complaints. However, many students came greatly to appreciate the practices.[35] Bonhoeffer had clearly put careful deliberation into the structure of the community's life. In fact, in order to provide greater coherence and consistency for the community, he invited some students to stay in the community after their training was over, to form what

33. The following is taken from Gerhard Ludwig Müller and Albrecht Schönherr, "Editors' Afterword to the German Edition," in Dietrich Bonhoeffer, *Life Together and Prayerbook of the Bible: An Introduction to the Psalms*, ed. Geffrey B. Kelly, trans. Daniel W. Bloesch and James H. Burtness, vol. 5 of *Dietrich Bonhoeffer Works* (Minneapolis: Fortress, 1996), 123–24. See also Bethge, *Dietrich Bonhoeffer*, 424–72.

34. Müller and Schönherr, "Editors' Afterword to the German Edition," *Life Together*, 123.

35. For testimonies to this effect, in addition to Joachim Kanitz, quoted in the introduction to this book, and Eberhard Bethge, see *I Knew Dietrich Bonhoeffer*, esp. in section 4, 107–61.

he referred to as "The House of Brothers." Six volunteered to do this initially, including Joachim Kanitz and Eberhard Bethge.

Critiques from the outside often included the accusations that the theology and practices inculcated by the seminary were legalistic and a new form of monasticism. Even Barth, in a letter of October 14, 1936, when he read about the life of the seminary, retorted that he sensed "an almost indefinable odor of a monastic eros and pathos."[36]

There is no question that Bonhoeffer had come to believe that strict forms of discipline—drawn from rich monastic traditions in the history of the church—were needed to form the deep moral and theological convictions that would enable pastors to navigate the treacherous world being created by the Third Reich. Though Bonhoeffer, as a still-convinced Lutheran, was teaching a robust understanding of grace, he did so with a clear realization that a true understanding of God's redemptive love could not equal "cheap grace."

At the same time, Bonhoeffer never imagined that this seminary community was to be a "cloistered monastery," if what one means by that is a community divorced from the daily realities of the larger world. In his proposal for the House of Brothers that he sent to the Old Prussian Union on September 6, 1935, Bonhoeffer said:

> There is a need for a group of completely free, trained pastors to preach the Word of God for decision and for discerning the spirits, in the present church struggle and in others to come, and to be immediately ready to serve as preachers at the outbreak of any new emergency. . . . They will find their home and all the fellowship they need for their service in the community from which they come and to which they return continually. *The aim is not the seclusion of a monastery, but a place of the deepest inward concentration for service outside.*[37]

In *Life Together*, his book that offers theological reflections on the experiment at Finkenwalde, Bonhoeffer reflects on the need for Christian community to be a place of equipping, not of escape:

> Every day brings the Christian many hours of being alone in an unchristian environment. These are times of *testing*. This is the proving ground of a genuine time of meditation and genuine Christian community. Has the community served to make individuals free, strong, and mature, or has it made them insecure and dependent? Has it taken them by the hand for a while so that they would learn again to walk by themselves, or has it made them anxious and unsure? This

36. Karl Barth, in Dietrich Bonhoeffer, *The Way to Freedom: Letters, Lectures and Notes 1935–1939*, trans. Edwin H. Robertson and John Bowden (London: Fount Paperbacks, 1972), 121.

37. Bonhoeffer, *Way to Freedom*, 30–31, emphasis added.

> is one of the toughest and most serious questions that can be put to any form of everyday Christian life in community. Moreover, we will see at this point whether Christians' time of meditation has led them into an unreal world from which they awaken with a fright when they step out into the workaday world, or whether it has led them into the real world of God from which they enter into the day's activities strengthened and purified. Has it transported them for a few short moments into a spiritual ecstasy that vanishes when everyday life returns, or has it planted the Word of God so soberly and so deeply in their heart that it holds and strengthens them all day long, leading them to active love, to obedience, to good works?[38]

At the seminary, one evening per week was devoted to a discussion of current issues; in the midst of the quickly unfolding events of the Third Reich, it was not difficult to find subjects for discussion. One of the early topics was military service. Conscription was introduced in Nazi Germany on March 16, 1935; a new law affecting military service went into effect on May 1. Most Christians in Germany, including those in the Confessing Church, saw military service as a patriotic duty. For virtually everyone, that conviction remained, even with the rise of Hitler. In fact, for many men in the Confessing Church, serving in the military was a way to show that they were indeed patriotic Germans—despite the assumptions of German Christian critics. This positive view of military service was shared by the ordinands studying with Bonhoeffer. According to Bethge, "the number of conscientious objectors in the Evangelical church at that time could have been counted on the fingers of one hand."[39] Bonhoeffer's students must have been shocked to learn that he was among the handful.[40] He pressed them to consider conscientious objection as an option. He also brought at least two other conscientious objectors to speak at the seminary—Herbert Jehle, a scientist, who had been a guest of Bonhoeffer's in London, and Hermann Stöhr, the secretary of the German Fellowship of Reconciliation, who would later be executed for refusing military service.[41]

38. Bonhoeffer, *Life Together*, 91–92.

39. Bethge, *Dietrich Bonhoeffer*, 431.

40. I should explain what I mean by "conscientious objector" here. Bonhoeffer had in several lectures beginning in 1932, as already discussed, argued that Christians should not kill in war and had specifically spoken in favor of conscientious objection. At this point in time Germany was not at war. So in that sense it was a theoretical issue. But as suggested by my comments in this paragraph, his advocacy for conscientious objection was almost unheard of.

41. It should also be mentioned that, in a letter of January 29, 1935, Bonhoeffer suggested that conscientious objection be a central topic for the international, ecumenical youth conference to be held in Switzerland in August of 1935 (see Bonhoeffer, *London*, 289–90). As it happened, in the end Bonhoeffer felt that he couldn't attend the meeting itself.

But Bonhoeffer was, throughout the time at Finkenwalde, also concerned about the ongoing acts of injustice and violence within Nazi Germany. For instance, in a sermon on "Vengeance and Deliverance," given on July 11, 1937, at Finkenwalde, Bonhoeffer said: "It is an evil time when the world lets injustice happen silently, when the oppression of the poor and the wretched cries out to heaven in a loud voice and the judges and rulers of the earth keep silent about it, when the persecuted church calls to God for help in the hour of dire distress and exhorts people to do justice, and yet no mouth on earth is opened to bring justice."[42]

During his time in London, Bonhoeffer had retained his status as a lecturer at Berlin University, though he was not in fact giving lectures.[43] However, when he returned to Germany, he began to lecture at the university again. During his first year at Finkenwalde, he traveled once per week to Berlin to lecture. This was one way Bonhoeffer kept the seminary linked to larger events. As Wilhelm Rott, a seminary student, reported: "[Bonhoeffer] had been in Berlin yesterday; he told us of it. Late in the evening when he came home, he gave those who waited for him one of his exciting reports about the deviations and embroilments of that time of church committees, about spiritual and worldly affairs, politics of the Church and of the State, about those who stood firm, those who wavered and those who fell. But there was more, there were characteristic details which did not escape the sharp observer, and these could not be told to a large audience."[44]

In June and July of 1935 Bonhoeffer wrote an essay titled "The Confessing Church and the Ecumenical Movement."[45] In it he again sounded what were now his expected notes regarding nationalism and peace: "Under the onslaught of new nationalism, the fact that the church of Christ does not stop at national and racial boundaries but reaches beyond them, so powerfully attested in the New Testament and in the confessional writings, has been far too easily forgotten and denied."[46] However, a significant burden of this published essay was to convince Christians outside of Germany that the true

42. Bonhoeffer, "Vengeance and Deliverance," in *A Testament to Freedom: The Essential Writings of Dietrich Bonhoeffer*, rev. ed., ed. Geffrey B. Kelly and F. Burton Nelson (New York: HarperCollins, 1995), 279. He also calls for love of enemies in the same sermon.

43. In August of 1936 Bonhoeffer was forbidden to lecture any longer at Berlin University. In February and March of that year Bonhoeffer had taken his seminary students to Denmark and Sweden. He had failed to notice that a 1935 law had made it illegal for a university lecturer to leave the country without permission.

44. Wilhelm Rott, "Something Always Occurred to Him," in *I Knew Dietrich Bonhoeffer*, 133.

45. Bonhoeffer, "The Confessing Church and the Ecumenical Movement," in *Testament to Freedom*, 139–48.

46. Ibid., 140.

Protestant church in Germany is the Confessing Church. In letters and personal conversations, Bonhoeffer made parallel arguments. However, the fact that many in the ecumenical movement continued to treat the German Christians as a legitimate church caused Bonhoeffer to bow out of active involvement in formal ecumenical gatherings after February of 1937.

Between 1934 and 1937 there were signs of hope for Bonhoeffer within the Confessing Church. The synods at Barmen and Dahlem in 1934 affirmed confessions that helped provide a solid identity for this newly emerging church, an identity that differentiated it from the German Christians. In March of 1935 seven hundred pastors were willing to boldly read a proclamation "Against Idolatry," even though this action not surprisingly led to their arrest. At the end of 1935, when the seminary at Finkenwalde was officially pronounced illegal, the students were given the choice to leave. All elected to stay. In May 1936 officials of the Confessing Church sent a confrontational memo to Hitler—asking for answers to serious questions regarding abusive and unjust behaviors on the part of the Reich government.[47] It boldly stated, for instance, that "Evangelical Christians are convinced on the basis of Holy Scripture that God is the protector of justice and of those to whom justice is denied; hence they regard it as apostasy from Him when arbitrariness finds its way into judicial matters and things happen, 'which are not just in the sight of the Lord.'"[48] Early in the Hitler regime Martin Niemöller naively supported the national socialists. By July 1937 Niemöller, a pastor in suburban Berlin and a significant leader in the Confessing Church, had become so consistently bold in his actions that he was arrested. In March of 1938 he became a personal prisoner of Hitler, and he remained in custody until the end of the war.

In the midst of this, Bonhoeffer attempted to bolster the strength of the Confessing Church. He did so in a provocative lecture at Finkenwalde on April 22, 1936; the text was published two months later. The lecture was an effort to define the boundaries of the church. The central affirmation, hotly disputed by German Christians, was straightforward: "The Confessing Church is the true church of Jesus Christ in Germany."[49] Yet a later section of the essay was even more provocative and often quoted: "The question of church membership is the question of salvation. The boundaries of the church are the boundaries of salvation. Whoever knowingly cut themselves off from the Confessing Church

47. "Protest of the Provisional Leadership to Hitler, 28 May 1936," in *The Third Reich and the Christian Churches: A Documentary Account of Christian Resistance and Complicity During the Nazi Era*, ed. Peter Matheson (Grand Rapids: Eerdmans, 1981), 58–62.

48. Ibid., 61–62.

49. Bonhoeffer, "The Question of the Boundaries of the Church and Church Union," in *Testament to Freedom*, 161.

in Germany cut themselves off from salvation. . . . It must be said again and again that for the church to deny its boundaries is no work of mercy. The true church comes up against boundaries. In recognizing them it does the work of loving others by honoring the truth. *Extra ecclesiam nulla salus*."[50]

In September 1937 the Gestapo forcibly closed the seminary; the doors of the Finkenwalde seminary were locked. The life of this community, in its present form, was over. However, its impact continues to this day. It is fitting that before the year was out [*The Cost of*] *Discipleship* would be published, the book that Eberhard Bethge says was "Finkenwalde's own badge of distinction."[51] A full discussion of this book will wait for chapter 5. But it is worth quoting theologian John Webster, who says that in *Discipleship* "Bonhoeffer is concerned to unleash the critical power of the Scriptural word without the mediation of conceptual sophistication."[52] This commitment is reflected in Bonhoeffer's extraordinary letter to his brother-in-law Rüdiger Schleicher on April 8, 1936:

> To begin with, I will confess quite simply: I believe that the Bible alone is the answer to all our questions and that to receive an answer from it, we only need to ask with persistence and a little courage. One cannot *read* the Bible as we read other books. One must be ready to really ask questions. Only in this way does it open itself up to us. Only when we wait expectantly before it for the ultimate answer does it give it to us. The reason for this is simply that in the Bible it is God who speaks to us. And when it comes to God, one cannot just think things out for oneself; one must ask God. Only when we seek God does he answer. . . . Only when we once dare to read ourselves into the Bible as though it really is God who speaks to us here, the God who loves us and will not finally abandon us to our questions, only then will reading the Bible become a joy. . . . From this point of departure can you then somehow understand that I will not surrender the Bible as this strange word of God; on the contrary, I will ask with all my powers what God is trying to say to us through it. Every other place outside the Bible has become too uncertain for me. I fear that there I will only bump into my own divine look-alike, a reflection of myself. Is it then also conceivable that I am now more prepared for a *sacrificium intellectus* (offering my intellect as a sacrifice [to God])—even in these things and only in these things, that is, in view of the God of truth. And who is there who would not actually offer his or her own *sacrificium intellectus* on some altar or other? This means confessing that one does not yet understand this or that passage of Scripture, in the confidence that it also will be revealed one day as God's own word. I would

50. Ibid., 166.

51. Bethge, *Dietrich Bonhoeffer*, 450.

52. John Webster, "Reading the Bible: The Example of Barth and Bonhoeffer," in *Word and Church: Essays in Church Dogmatics* (Edinburgh: T&T Clark, 2001), 99.

rather do this than to go ahead and say at my own discretion, "This is divine, that is merely human"![53]

As this commitment suggests, Bonhoeffer in *Discipleship* articulates a powerful call from God to live a life defined by divine redemptive grace, a life that provides a powerful witness to the gospel of Jesus Christ because it embodies costly discipleship. And as Ferdinand Schlingensiepen reminds us, Bonhoeffer's title for the book and the seminary lecture course resonate not only with New Testament language but also with political realities in Germany. "At all Nazi public events there were speeches about 'Führer and followers.' During the war these were made into a song with the refrain, 'Führer, command, we'll follow you [*wir folgen dir*].' When Bonhoeffer called his lecture course [and book] *Nachfolge* (following, or discipleship), he was not only using a New Testament concept, but also contrasting it expressly to a term widely used by the Nazis."[54]

The year 1937 was the beginning of a number of especially challenging years for the Confessing Church and for Bonhoeffer. Karl Barth—an important support to both the Confessing Church and Bonhoeffer personally—had already been back in his home country, Switzerland, for more than a year. On November 26, 1935, he had been suspended from his job at the University of Bonn for refusing to give an unconditional oath of allegiance to Hitler.[55] Niemöller, as mentioned earlier, was in prison, where he would remain for the duration of the Reich. Franz Hildebrandt was forced to leave Germany in 1937, and, as Bethge states, "this meant that, after their many years together, Bonhoeffer lost his best-informed and most like-minded friend."[56] In September the doors of the Finkenwalde seminary were locked by the Gestapo. There were numerous arrests within the Confessing Church—for using disciplinary measures against Nazi Party members, for praying in very specific terms for other pastors who were being mistreated by Nazi authorities, and so on. "Because of all this," Bethge says, "church activities came to a virtual standstill. Hardly a day passed without either the administration or the pastors of the Confessing church contravening one of the laws or falling into some form of trap. It became impossible to serve the Confessing church while remaining within the law."[57]

53. Dietrich Bonhoeffer, *Reflections on the Bible: Human Word and Word of God*, ed. Manfred Weber, trans. M. Eugene Boring (Peabody, MA: Hendrickson, 2003), 107–10.

54. Schlingensiepen, *Dietrich Bonhoeffer*, 206.

55. Eberhard Busch, *Karl Barth: His Life from Letters and Autobiographical Texts*, trans. John Bowden (Philadelphia: Fortress, 1975), 255–62.

56. Bethge, *Dietrich Bonhoeffer*, 565.

57. Ibid., 578.

Bonhoeffer had always had differences with the Confessing Church—because of its lack of boldness, its lack of resolve in relation to concerns about the Jews, and its nationalism. But Bethge is right that "in 1938 the greatest weaknesses of the Confessing church became evident."[58] On April 20, 1938, Friedrich Werner, legal director of the German Evangelical Church, in the *Legal Gazette* ordered "that all pastors in active office were to take the oath of allegiance to the Führer."[59] Though Werner himself was not a part of the Confessing Church, in fact for most pastors—including many in the Confessing Church—such an *order* was hardly necessary.[60] Bishop Sasse of Thuringia, for instance, had already asked pastors under his charge to take such an oath. On March 15 he telegraphed Hitler: "My Führer, I report: in a great historic hour all the pastors of the Thuringian Evangelical Church, obeying an inner command, have with joyful hearts taken an oath to Führer and Reich. . . . One God—one obedience in the faith. Hail, my Führer!" Traveling through the Thuringian countryside during his holiday, Bonhoeffer saw an incredible spectacle: "the cross on the Wartburg had been replaced during Holy Week by an immense floodlit swastika."[61] All of this was to celebrate Germany's recent union with Austria. "Bonhoeffer," Bethge says,

> was ashamed of the Confessing church, the way one feels shame for a scandal in one's own family. This Confessing synod had approved the oath to the Führer when it already knew of the impending order that non-Aryans must have a large "J" stamped on their identity cards—an omen of worse things to come, and the thing that finally moved his twin sister's family to flee. And the threat of war against Czechoslovakia was growing. The possibility of a gap between Bonhoeffer and the Confessing church was becoming real.[62]

A few months later Bonhoeffer would again be disturbed by the nationalism that pervaded the German church—including the Confessing Church. On September 27, 1938, Hitler was trumpeting Germany's military strength by parading armored military vehicles through Berlin. Two members of the Confessing Church, Martin Albertz and Hans Böhm, composed a prayer liturgy for use in congregations. It was a confession of guilt for collusion in military aggression and a prayer that the imminent threat of war would be averted. At about the same time, a letter that Barth had written to a colleague in Prague, Josef Hromádka, became public. Barth was encouraging Czech

58. Ibid., 596.
59. Ibid., 599.
60. Ibid., 599–620.
61. Ibid., 599.
62. Ibid., 603.

resistance to German aggression. He said: "Every Czech soldier who fights and suffers will be doing so for us too, and I say this without reservation—he will also be doing it for the church of Jesus, which in the atmosphere of Hitler and Mussolini must become the victim of either ridicule or extermination."[63] Most Confessing Church pastors were furious about both of these challenges to German nationalism; again Bonhoeffer felt shame at such support for Hitler.

November 9, 1938, was the most blatant expression to date of anti-Semitism in Nazi Germany. That night, throughout Germany, many synagogues were set ablaze and many Jewish homes and businesses devastated. Many Jews were tortured; approximately one hundred were murdered and over thirty thousand were sent to concentration camps.[64] Because of all the glass that was broken, the night has come to be called *Kristallnacht*. The ostensible justification for this orgy of violence was the assassination, two days earlier, of a German ambassador in Paris by a Polish Jew. The following Sunday, in a sermon of repentance, Pastor Julius von Jan of Oberlenningen, Württemberg, said:

> Who would have thought that this single crime in Paris could result in so many crimes committed here in Germany? Now we are facing the consequences of our great apostasy, our falling away from God and Christ, of organized anti-Christianity. Passions are being unleashed and the commandments of God ignored. Houses of God which were sacred for others are being burned down, the property of others is being plundered or destroyed. Men who have served our nation loyally and conscientiously fulfilled their duties have been thrown into concentration camps, merely because they belong to another race. Those in authority may not admit to any injustice, but to the healthy good sense of our people it is quite clear, even though no one dares speak of it.[65]

Pastor von Jan was dragged out of his manse by five hundred demonstrators who were from outside his village; he was then beaten severely. He was later interrogated by the authorities and thrown into prison, where he remained until the end of the war.

However, Pastor von Jan's response was unusual. Most of the Confessing Church was silent about this night—and its aftermath. Bonhoeffer himself was in a forest with his ordinands on the night of *Kristallnacht* and only learned about it after the fact. However, later "in the Bible that Bonhoeffer used for prayer and meditation he underlined the verse in Psalm 74, 'they burned all the meeting places of God in the land,' and wrote beside it '9.11.38.' He also

63. As quoted in ibid., 606.
64. Schlingensiepen, *Dietrich Bonhoeffer*, 215.
65. As quoted in ibid., 215.

underlined the next verse, adding an exclamation mark: 'We do not see our signs; there is no longer any prophet, and there is none among us who knows how long.'"[66] Of course, for Bonhoeffer, acting on behalf of Jews was hardly something new. In fact, in September he had helped his sister and Jewish brother-in-law to escape Germany before it was too late.

Bethge is probably correct that "it was during this difficult year [1938] that Bonhoeffer began to distance himself from the rearguard actions of the Confessing church's defeated remnants."[67] Bonhoeffer was certainly disheartened by much within the Confessing Church. However, we must also remember two things about 1938 and Bonhoeffer's relationship with the church. In September he elected to take a month to write the book *Life Together*, as a way to have a record of his own theological reflections on the Finkenwalde experiment in a "new form of monasticism." In June he called together former seminary students for a Bible study on temptation. But more importantly, he continued—through what was called a collective pastorate—to offer theological training to ordinands until that was forcibly halted on March 17, 1940. Thus it would be wrong to think that he had totally given up on the church. He would also continue throughout 1938 and 1939 to give the occasional lecture on topics reflecting the convictions he had been naming over the previous seven years. But severe restrictions had been placed on what he could do. In January 1938 Bonhoeffer was banned from staying in Berlin. (His father intervened with the Gestapo, so that he was only banned from conducting business; he could visit his family.) In September of 1940 Bonhoeffer was forbidden from speaking in public; in March of 1941 he was prohibited from publishing his writings.

It may be true, as some have suggested, that beginning in 1939, or even more in 1940, after the collective pastorate became impossible, Bonhoeffer was more fully connected to his family than the church. For practical reasons this seems likely. Yet as noted before, Bonhoeffer's family was close-knit. Thus I would remind the reader, as I was reminded recently, that to no one was Bonhoeffer more self-revealing than he was in letters to his brother Karl-Friedrich and his brother-in-law Rüdiger Schleicher. Therefore, when he is involved with his family, even if they don't agree with him on some matters, they know who he is.

Ferdinand Schlingensiepen, in a recent biography, claims that by the beginning of the 1940s Bonhoeffer had returned to the ethics he had articulated in Barcelona in 1929. As Bonhoeffer had said then: "There are no acts that are bad in and of themselves; even murder can be sanctified."[68] Schlingensiepen

66. Bethge, *Dietrich Bonhoeffer*, 607.
67. Ibid., 607.
68. Schlingensiepen, *Dietrich Bonhoeffer*, 286.

goes on to say that these words may have been strange coming from a pastoral assistant in 1929 Barcelona. However, "now [in 1940s Nazi Germany] they had become appallingly true and had to be put into action."[69] And this meant that "the central decision of his life, to which everything else had been leading, had finally been taken."[70] Bonhoeffer would join the efforts to kill Hitler. And once he had made this momentous decision "every other consideration had to be subjected to the plans for the assassination."[71] This apparently included, once again, the sanctifying of murder, and—as Bonhoeffer said in Barcelona—war. But is Schlingensiepen correct? That is the question the next chapter will explore, especially as it relates to Bonhoeffer's life between mid-1939 and his execution on April 9, 1945.

69. Ibid., 286, cf. 50.
70. Ibid., 285.
71. Ibid., 281.

3

Dietrich Bonhoeffer, the Assassin?

"As Adolf Hitler and the Nazis seduced a nation, bullied a continent, and attempted to exterminate the Jews of Europe, a small number of dissidents and saboteurs worked to dismantle the Third Reich from the inside. One of these was Dietrich Bonhoeffer—a pastor and author, known as much for such spiritual classics as *The Cost of Discipleship* and *Life Together*, as for his 1945 execution in a concentration camp for his part in the plot to assassinate Adolf Hitler."

This is the opening paragraph of the front inside flyleaf of the book jacket of the *New York Times* bestselling biography of Bonhoeffer by Eric Metaxas, a paragraph intended to lure potential readers.[1] This paragraph reflects the popular opinion that the German theologian and pastor Dietrich Bonhoeffer was arrested, imprisoned, and executed because of his part in the plot to assassinate Hitler. Those who know a bit more of Bonhoeffer's life and thought acknowledge that when he and the Third Reich were young he had a naive attachment to what appear to be pacifist assumptions. But as he matured and the evils of the Nazi regime became more obvious, Bonhoeffer, like his American teacher Reinhold Niebuhr, became more realistic. He abandoned his pacifism, joined the conspiracy, and more specifically joined the military intelligence agency the Abwehr in order to be involved in the attempts to assassinate Hitler.

1. Eric Metaxas, *Bonhoeffer: Pastor, Martyr, Prophet, Spy* (Nashville: Thomas Nelson, 2010).

Larry Rasmussen, in his 1972 book *Dietrich Bonhoeffer: Reality and Resistance*, named the challenge for understanding Bonhoeffer's shift in moral beliefs and practices this way: "All the twisting possible cannot make the author of *The Cost of Discipleship* a volunteer for assassinating even Adolf Hitler."[2] Three claims are implied by this statement. The first is that the author of *Nachfolge*, now translated as *Discipleship*, clearly believed and taught "love of enemies," what Bonhoeffer on occasion referred to as pacifism.[3] The careful theological and exegetical work related to this conviction was in fact displayed most fully in Bonhoeffer's 1937 book, *Discipleship*.[4] However, Bonhoeffer's pacifist rhetoric was most forcefully presented in certain lectures and sermons, beginning in the early 1930s. For instance, in his 1932 lecture "Christ and Peace" he said: "The commandment 'You shall not kill,' the word that says, 'Love your enemies,' is given to us simply to be obeyed. For Christians, any military service, except in the ambulance corps, and any preparation for war, is forbidden."[5]

So this is Rasmussen's first claim: the author of *Discipleship* was a pacifist. The second is that Bonhoeffer, between 1940 and 1943, effectively volunteered to assassinate Hitler and then became actively involved in one or more assassination attempts. And the third is that Bonhoeffer, by the time he became involved in one or more plots to kill Hitler, must have substantially changed his theological ethics, because the author of *Discipleship* would not have been willing to kill anyone, even Adolf Hitler.

The rest of the present book examines the first and third claims (about Bonhoeffer's early pacifism and later theological change), mostly by examining relevant texts. This chapter, however, will examine the second claim—that Bonhoeffer was actively involved in trying to assassinate Hitler. That is to

2. Larry Rasmussen, *Dietrich Bonhoeffer: Reality and Resistance* (Nashville: Abingdon, 1972), 120. This is the most influential book in English to deal at book length with Bonhoeffer's "shift" from pacifism to tyrannicide. This book was rereleased, with no revisions, by Westminster John Knox Press in 2005. For an interesting exchange around the 2005 rerelease of this book, see Clifford Green, "Review of *Dietrich Bonhoeffer: Reality and Resistance*," *Conversations in Religion and Theology* 6 (2008): 155–65; and Larry Rasmussen, "Response to Clifford Green," *Conversations in Religion and Theology* 6 (2008): 165–73.

3. In 1936, in a letter to his girlfriend, Elizabeth Zinn, Bonhoeffer referred to his "grand liberation," in which he became a Christian and, among other things, came to see "pacifism as self-evident." This letter is quoted in Martin Kuske and Ilse Tödt, "Editors' Afterword to the German Edition," in Dietrich Bonhoeffer, *Discipleship*, ed. Geffrey B. Kelly and John D. Godsey, trans. Barbara Green and Reinhard Krauss, vol. 4 of *Dietrich Bonhoeffer Works* (Minneapolis: Fortress, 2000), 291–92.

4. The whole book serves as a call to serious discipleship, of which love of enemies is a component. For direct treatment of "love of enemies," see Bonhoeffer, *Discipleship*, 137–45.

5. Dietrich Bonhoeffer, "Christ and Peace," in *Berlin: 1932–1933*, ed. Larry L. Rasmussen, trans. Douglas W. Stott, Isabel Best, and David Higgins, vol. 12 of *Dietrich Bonhoeffer Works* (Minneapolis: Fortress, 2009), 260.

say, it will examine the factual evidence regarding Bonhoeffer's role in the resistance to Hitler, especially as that resistance is believed to be linked to his involvement in assassination attempts.

It is important at the outset to acknowledge that some of this chapter will be devoted to clarifying what we do *not* know, especially some things that many assume we *do* know with relative certainty. Sabine Dramm, in her recent, careful study *Dietrich Bonhoeffer and the Resistance*, has said, "A closer analysis shows that Bonhoeffer's real part in conspiratorial resistance activities was much slighter than is usually assumed, and this slight share brought hardly any demonstrable results."[6] This is a very helpful and careful statement. However, even here, we need to evaluate what exactly is being referred to by the words "much slighter than is usually assumed." To begin such an evaluation, it is important to distinguish Bonhoeffer's normal work for the Abwehr, the military intelligence agency, from his possible involvements in the attempts to eliminate Hitler as Führer of the Third Reich.

Working for the Abwehr

Bonhoeffer's work for the Abwehr is usually rather vaguely connected to his being in the resistance movement, a part of a conspiracy to overthrow the Hitler government. Apparently, many people assume that the fact that Bonhoeffer was working for a military agency—presumably in a resistance role—signifies that he must have shifted his views from those named most fully in *Discipleship*. In fact, it is sometimes implied that Bonhoeffer sought his position in the Abwehr specifically to be involved with conspirators who were attempting to kill Hitler. Let's examine the relevant issues.

To begin with, it is misleading to focus on Bonhoeffer's employment by a military intelligence agency unless we also look at what his actual work was and

6. Sabine Dramm, *Dietrich Bonhoeffer and the Resistance*, trans. Margaret Kohl (Minneapolis: Fortress, 2009), 240. She goes on to say that "perhaps he was also active in the resistance in ways about which, even today, we still know nothing" (240). For Bethge's assessment of the significance of Bonhoeffer's roles in the conspiracy, see Eberhard Bethge, *Dietrich Bonhoeffer: A Biography*, rev. ed., ed. Victoria J. Barnett (Minneapolis: Fortress, 2000), 795–97. All of us should be grateful that we now have two good sources in English to evaluate Bonhoeffer's work in the resistance movement. Of course for years we have had Bethge's thorough biography (in which pp. 620–797 cover Bonhoeffer and the conspiracy). Now we also have the fresh and thorough account presented by Dramm. Of relevance also is Larry Rasmussen's book *Reality and Resistance*, mentioned earlier. I have worked through Rasmussen's book carefully. But for the purposes of this chapter I will draw primarily from Dramm and Bethge. Of these, I will draw far more heavily from Dramm, simply because she takes Bethge seriously into account in most of her judgments. (I have also perused all the literature listed in Dramm's bibliography that seemed particularly pertinent.)

who his bosses were.[7] We need to be aware, as I mentioned in the introduction, that though the Abwehr has been referred to as a "nest of resisters," Dramm estimates that only about fifty individuals out of a workforce of approximately thirteen thousand were connected to the resistance.[8] That is to say, only a tiny fraction (0.4 percent) of the agency's employees was involved in efforts to undermine the Hitler government.[9] Thus it was not as if working for the Abwehr in itself equaled working for the resistance, broadly or narrowly understood. Going to work did not involve, for instance, regular committee meetings for planning Hitler's assassination. The vast majority of the employees merely did what they saw as the daily work of a military intelligence agency, relevant to their particular job descriptions (though Bonhoeffer in fact used his position to oppose the government in nonviolent ways).

The head of the agency as a whole was Admiral Wilhelm Canaris. Canaris was an opponent of the Hitler regime and repeatedly served as a shield for those within the Abwehr who were actively involved in efforts to overthrow his government, sometimes including plans to kill Hitler. Colonel (and later Major General) Hans Oster was the head of the agency's Department Z, the army's secret service, which began in 1938. Hans von Dohnanyi, a brother-in-law to Bonhoeffer, was a lawyer who took up his position in Department Z on August 25, 1939. Oster and Dohnanyi were actively involved as conspirators, including attempts to assassinate Hitler. All three of these men—Canaris, Oster, and Dohnanyi—worked in the Berlin office. Oster and Dohnanyi were responsible for Bonhoeffer's coming to work for the Abwehr in its Munich office.[10]

Bonhoeffer worked for the agency from the end of October of 1940 until he was arrested on April 5, 1943.[11] On paper, the job of someone like Bonhoeffer was to gather intelligence to assist Germany in its military victory. No one of whom I am aware really imagines that was what Bonhoeffer was doing.

7. On Bonhoeffer's bosses, see Dramm, *Dietrich Bonhoeffer and the Resistance*, 30–38.

8. Ibid., 33.

9. This gives a very different impression from Bethge, who says, "The Military Intelligence was not staffed *solely* by resistance people." Bethge, *Dietrich Bonhoeffer*, 725 (emphasis added).

10. Though I don't want to make too much of it, it is worth noting that Munich is over three hundred miles from Berlin. So the fact that Bonhoeffer worked in the Munich office and that his brother-in-law worked in the Berlin office meant some limitations on their interactions during the time he worked for the Abwehr. Of course it is also true that Bonhoeffer traveled to Berlin regularly, partly because his parents lived there.

11. Dramm devotes a short chapter, pp. 22–29, to discussing when exactly Bonhoeffer began work with the Abwehr. It seems clear to me (as well as Bethge) that he began at the end of October of 1940. It may be that there is a document, or a few, that suggests Bonhoeffer began working for the Abwehr earlier. If so, these documents were probably fabricated to provide Bonhoeffer cover for his claim that he was ineligible for military service already in 1939. For after all, he had already been called to military service in May of 1939, before he left for New York City.

However, to justify his legitimacy as an agent of the Abwehr, he had to appear to be doing exactly that. Bonhoeffer had extensive contacts throughout Europe from his previous ecumenical involvements. Most would have assumed that he was gathering intelligence through these contacts and thus helping the German war effort. As Dramm describes:

> The official reason given for Bonhoeffer's employment was utilization of the excellent relations with prominent members of the ecumenical movement that derived from his earlier work. The ostensible purpose was to acquire information. The real reason was almost identical with this official one, except for the word *acquire*, for the actual purpose was to *pass on* information, of course information of a particular kind. Bonhoeffer, camouflaged as an agent of the Military Intelligence but really a guarantor and contact sent by opponents of Hitler, was supposed to establish links with countries abroad.[12]

Thus he continued and even extended his ecumenical contacts throughout Europe. But he did this to connect the German resistance movements (broadly defined) with significant people in other European countries. On a few occasions this was specifically to discuss the possibility of cooperative efforts between Allied forces and German opponents of Hitler in order to end both the reign of Hitler and the war. As Dramm says:

> His function was to put out feelers about peace conditions, to provide information about the regime opponents, and to win support for them. Countries abroad were to know that there really were "officers against Hitler," and civilian opponents too, people who stood for "another Germany," hoped for an end of the Nazi dictatorship and were developing points of departure for a future Germany in a future Europe.[13]

To give a specific example, in September of 1941 Bonhoeffer met in Switzerland with friends in the ecumenical movement, some of whom were well connected to people in positions of power in their own countries. As Peter Hoffman puts it: "[Bonhoeffer] urged his friends . . . to use their influence to ensure that the Allies would call a halt to military operations during the anticipated coup in Germany."[14] These efforts may have created some goodwill among well-placed people. But unfortunately they did not produce any tangible results. Among other things, it was difficult in the midst of the war

12. Dramm, *Dietrich Bonhoeffer and the Resistance*, 68, emphasis in the original.
13. Ibid., 110.
14. Peter Hoffman, *The History of the German Resistance 1933–1945*, 3rd ed. (Montreal: McGill-Queen's University Press, 1996), 218.

for political officials in other countries to trust a German. For instance, in the British House of Lords, Bishop George Bell could not convince his colleagues of his friend Bonhoeffer's trustworthiness.

There were times when Bonhoeffer collected data for Dohnanyi to add to his chronicle of horrors perpetrated by the Third Reich.[15] Specifically, for instance, after the mass deportations of Jews began in mid-October of 1941, Bonhoeffer and another Confessing Church member and Abwehr employee, Friedrich Justus Perels, compiled an initial report about these deportations. As Dramm says, "What Perels and Bonhoeffer meant to do in October 1941 was to provide objective evidence in objective words for the inhumane measures employed."[16] This report was given to Hans von Dohnanyi and distributed to key people, in order to strengthen the resolve of those who were opposed to Hitler. And there were other times when Bonhoeffer attempted to strengthen the resolve of others—for instance, the Norwegians—in their resistance to the Nazis.[17] Bonhoeffer was also marginally involved, personally, as a mediator in helping Hans von Dohnanyi save the lives of fourteen Jewish men and women by helping them escape from Germany to safe territory (sometimes referred to as "Operation 7").[18] Thus Bonhoeffer was doing some of the same things Helmuth von Moltke was doing, as described in our introduction. However, Bonhoeffer lacked expertise in international and military law and thus had less power than Moltke to bring about changes.

What is striking about both the accounts of Bethge and Dramm is that Bonhoeffer's life as an agent of the Abwehr was truly a cover: a way to avoid military induction while continuing his theological reflection and ministry. Not only did he receive no income from his work for the military intelligence agency, but he continued as much as he was able in his work as a pastor and

15. See, e.g., Dramm, *Dietrich Bonhoeffer and the Resistance*, 120–23. Joachim Fest, in his brief description of Hans von Dohnanyi, specifically mentions: "Forwarded reports from his brother-in-law, Dietrich Bonhoeffer, about the deportation of Jews to senior military leaders in the hope of spurring them to do something." Joachim Fest, *Plotting Hitler's Death: The Story of the German Resistance*, trans. Bruce Little (New York: Metropolitan Books, 1996), 383. "[On November 14, 1942,] Moltke tries in vain to get the Armed Forces High Command to veto the deportation of Jews." "Appendix 2: Chronology of Conspiracy and Imprisonment," in Dietrich Bonhoeffer, *Conspiracy and Imprisonment: 1940–1945*, ed. Mark Brocker, trans. Lisa E. Dahill and Douglas W. Stott, vol. 16 of *Dietrich Bonhoeffer Works* (Minneapolis: Fortress, 2006), 691.

16. Dramm, *Dietrich Bonhoeffer and the Resistance*, 119–23, here 122. A second report was also written by Perels; Bonhoeffer did not help draft it because he was quite ill at the time.

17. Ibid., 146–49.

18. For evidence of his marginal role, see Bonhoeffer, *Conspiracy and Imprisonment*, 352–53. Also see Dramm, *Dietrich Bonhoeffer and the Resistance*, 123–32. I believe Dramm's discussion helps make it clear that Bonhoeffer's role was only marginal in this effort (over against Bethge's interpretation).

theologian.[19] Consider his first few months "on the job." He begins work with the Abwehr in the Munich office on October 30, 1940. The next day he travels to the village of Ettal, where he stays at the local monastery. He lives and works there until the third week of February—mostly to work on manuscripts of what he hopes to be a book on ethics. On February 24, the day after he returns to Munich from Ettal, he leaves on his first "working" trip to Switzerland. He is there for a month—visiting three times with theologian Karl Barth; with W. A. Visser 't Hooft, a key ecumenical leader; with Erwin Sutz, a friend from Union Seminary days; with Friedrich Siegmund-Schultze, a German pacifist; and with many other friends in the ecumenical movement. He also has at least one meeting with Oster, Dohnanyi, and other Abwehr employees.

A number of his ecumenical contacts—Barth, Visser 't Hooft, and Bishop Bell, the Anglican bishop of Chichester—were by 1941 good friends of Bonhoeffer. Speaking with them encouraged and inspired him to keep going in circumstances that were very difficult.[20] Bonhoeffer's friends were also engaging theological dialogue partners. Thus it is the case that, as much as anything, many of his trips for the Abwehr afforded Bonhoeffer the opportunity to engage in serious conversations with keen theological minds—which he was eager to do. But these ongoing ecumenical relationships also reminded him of one of the reasons he sustained such contacts. As he wrote to Swedish theologian and ecumenist Erling Eidem, in a letter on April 11, 1942: "The more hopeless the ruptures in the world become, the more strongly Christians must maintain the bond of peace that unites them in Jesus Christ. Only in this way can the peoples someday find their way back to one another."[21]

As strange as it may seem, these trips, ostensibly undertaken for the Abwehr, gave Bonhoeffer one of the few avenues still open to him to continue doing church work. For instance, he had opportunities to encourage church leaders in their resistance to the Nazis—even if their stance entailed becoming martyrs.[22]

19. Regarding Bonhoeffer's income, see Dramm, *Dietrich Bonhoeffer and the Resistance*, 97–98. (Also see notes regarding a stipend from the Confessing Church in Bonhoeffer, *Conspiracy and Imprisonment*, 93; Bethge, *Dietrich Bonhoeffer*, 701.)

20. For instance, on June 1, 1942, Bonhoeffer wrote to Bishop Bell after a visit with him: "This spirit of fellowship and of Christian brotherliness will carry me through the darkest hours, and even if things go worse than we hope and expect, the light of these few days will never extinguish in my heart. The impressions of these days were so overwhelming that I cannot express them in words. I feel ashamed when I think of all your goodness and at the time I feel full of hope for the future" (Bonhoeffer, *Conspiracy and Imprisonment*, 311–12).

21. Bonhoeffer, *Conspiracy and Imprisonment*, 270.

22. Dramm, *Dietrich Bonhoeffer and the Resistance*, 146–47. Dramm has a brief discussion here about whether or not Bonhoeffer may have encouraged Norwegian church leaders to resist the Nazis "even as far as martyrdom"; she is somewhat skeptical. It seems to me not unlikely

As noted earlier, he also took whatever opportunities he could to continue theological and pastoral writing.[23] He wrote drafts of chapters of *Ethics*, letters to friends, letters (personal and circular) to former seminary students, and a number of theological essays while "working" with the Abwehr.[24] In fact, he had been commissioned to do these very things by the churches.[25]

What was described in the previous few paragraphs is rather typical of what Bonhoeffer did during his time with the military intelligence agency. In what way does Bonhoeffer's work for the Abwehr, in either his official role or his unofficial activities, collide with the convictions he articulated in 1937 in his book *Discipleship*?

This is what is intriguing: there is no evidence that Bonhoeffer joined the Abwehr so that he could be involved actively in assassination attempts. To the contrary, the evidence suggests, as Sabine Dramm's book has shown, that he joined the Abwehr very specifically because he continued to believe what he had said in his 1932 lecture "Christ and Peace," that "for Christians any military service, except in the ambulance corps, and any preparation for war, is forbidden."[26] He had traveled to the United States in June of 1939 to avoid serving in the military.[27] He decided he could not stay there and returned to Germany within a few weeks. However, nowhere does he indicate that he decided to return to Germany because he wanted to be involved in efforts to kill Hitler. Rather, he had come to believe that being in America was cowardly. As he had said in 1932, "There is no peace along the way of safety. For

---

that he may have. After all, he himself returned to Germany in 1939 knowing full well it might cost him his life.

23. Bethge says: "Bonhoeffer lived a remarkable life during the war. For weeks at a time he worked in the peaceful surroundings of the Kieckow fields or the snow-covered slopes of Ettal. In terms of time alone, he had more periods of time for steady work than he had during the Finkenwalde years" (Bethge, *Dietrich Bonhoeffer*, 705).

24. See Bonhoeffer, *Conspiracy and Imprisonment*.

25. After a meeting with a Wolfgang Staemmler, chair of the Old Prussian Union Council of Brethren, Bonhoeffer sent a letter to Bethge on November 16, 1940, in which he said: "The decision, therefore, was that I continue as the director of the Confessing Church pastoral training center and remain available but until then take up my scholarly work, since they are greatly interested in that" (Bonhoeffer, *Conspiracy and Imprisonment*, 83).

26. Bonhoeffer, "Christ and Peace," 260.

27. See, for example, his letter to Bishop George Bell, March 25, 1939, in which he says, "I am thinking of leaving Germany sometime. The main reason is the compulsory military service to which the men of my age (1906) will be called up this year. It seems to me conscientiously impossible to join in a war under the present circumstances." Bonhoeffer, *Theological Education Underground: 1937–1940*, ed. Victoria J. Barnett, trans. Claudia D. Bergmann, Scott A. Moore, and Peter Frick, vol. 15 of *Dietrich Bonhoeffer Works* (Minneapolis: Fortress, 2011), 156. "Under present circumstances" could either be language shaped specifically for Bell or could reflect Bonhoeffer's contextual approach, which, as will be discussed at various points in the book, was a consistent approach to ethics for Bonhoeffer.

peace must be dared. It is the great venture. It can never be safe."[28] Staying in America was "safe." It was not the Jesus way of peace; it was not the way of faithfulness. As he put in a letter at the time, he knew he would "have no right to participate in the reconstruction of Christian life in Germany after the war" if "[I did] not share the trials of this time with my people."[29] Paul Lehman, an American friend of Bonhoeffer, says he remembers a very specific conversation with Bonhoeffer while he was in New York in 1939. They had both recently read *The Revolution of Nihilism*, a book about the situation in Germany. Lehman told Bonhoeffer that this book had turned him from advocating pacifism to advocating revolution. Bonhoeffer replied that the book had actually confirmed his pacifism.[30]

Bonhoeffer returned to Germany in July, after a ten-day stopover in England. In September he applied to be a chaplain in the military. By mid-February of 1940 he knew his application had been denied.[31] Apparently he came to realize, through discussions with his brother-in-law, that if he could be appointed as an agent of the Abwehr, he would be given an exemption from serving on the front lines of the military, where he would have been killing the enemies of Germany in the name of Hitler. Is there not a pattern from Bonhoeffer's leaving for America to his application to work with the Abwehr? Here is the way Dramm puts it in her conclusion, at the head of a list of ten points of focus for thinking about Bonhoeffer and his involvement in resistance movements:

> At the beginning of Bonhoeffer's participation in the political resistance was the question about his call-up for military service. Bonhoeffer was unwilling to perform military service for reasons of faith and conscience, but he of course knew that the penalty for refusal was death. Helped by Hans Oster, Bonhoeffer's brother-in-law Hans Dohnanyi developed a particular construction that made the necessary "uk" status possible [i.e., the official designation that for reasons vital to the war he was not available for military service]. . . . *It was because of his personal, difficult, and risky decision to refuse to perform military service*

28. Bonhoeffer, "The Church and the People of the World," in *London: 1933–1935*, ed. Keith W. Clements, trans. Isabel Best, vol. 13 of *Dietrich Bonhoeffer Works* (Minneapolis: Fortress, 2007), 308–9.

29. This was in a letter to Reinhold Niebuhr, late June 1939 (Bonhoeffer, *Theological Education Underground*, 210).

30. This is reported in Larry Rasmussen, *Dietrich Bonhoeffer*, 58. I want to be consistent with what I say below. This may very well be a faulty memory on the part of Lehman. However, since it does not at all fit with Lehman's expectations and is a specific and unusual conversation, it seems more likely to be accurate.

31. Bethge, *Dietrich Bonhoeffer*, 665–66. If he had returned to Germany specifically to be involved in efforts to kill Hitler, as many suppose, then why did he first try to become a chaplain?

> *that he entered into the political work of the resistance with what was for him (theo)logical consistency.*[32]

To emphasize the importance that avoiding military service had for Bonhoeffer in the years of 1940 to 1943, when he was arrested, Dramm mentions it more than fifteen times, even though this is of no direct relevance to her book's central subject. Bethge says, "The entire three years from 1940 to 1943 were really constantly accompanied by the struggle to renew the UK classifications."[33] What Bonhoeffer would have done if he could not have gotten his position in the Abwehr, and thus an exemption from killing on the front lines, we will never know. Already in August of 1934 we see Bonhoeffer's honesty and humility. He had given his passionate sermon "Church and the People of the World," in which he issued the gospel summons: "There is no peace along the way of safety. For peace must be dared."[34] He spoke in clear terms about obeying the command to pursue peace. During an informal conversation, a Swede asked Bonhoeffer what he would do if war broke out. Bonhoeffer responded: "I pray that God will give me the strength not to take up arms."[35]

One could, of course, argue that his work at the military intelligence agency was not exactly service in the "ambulance corps." And one could argue that it was cowardly to avoid simply saying directly to the governmental authorities that he was a conscientious objector, and thus being subject to immediate execution.[36] However, he did in fact avoid the coward's way out by not staying in the United States, which he could have done. And he did manage to avoid taking an oath of unconditional loyalty to Hitler and killing on the front lines.

32. Dramm, *Dietrich Bonhoeffer and the Resistance*, 235, emphasis added. Dramm's emphasis is on Bonhoeffer's "participation in political resistance." But what she is really referring to is the rationale for Bonhoeffer's work with the Abwehr, which is certainly not just about resistance (and perhaps not "resistance" at all, given Dramm's narrow definition, as will be discussed later).

33. Quoted by Mark S. Brocker, "Editor's Introduction to the English Edition," in *Conspiracy and Imprisonment*, 11.

34. Bonhoeffer, *A Testament to Freedom: The Essential Writings of Dietrich Bonhoeffer*, ed. Geffrey B. Kelly and F. Burton Nelson (New York: HarperCollins, 1995), 228.

35. Bethge, *Dietrich Bonhoeffer*, 389.

36. For some reflections on Bonhoeffer's "conscientious objection" from 1932 forward, see Hans Christoph von Hase, "Turning Away from the Phraseological to the Real," 602; and Clifford J. Green, "Editor's Introduction," 27n130, both found in Bonhoeffer, *Barcelona, Berlin, New York: 1928–1931*, ed. Clifford Green, trans. Douglas W. Stott, vol. 10 of *Dietrich Bonhoeffer Works* (Minneapolis: Fortress, 2008). It seems odd that Green refers to conscientious objection as Bonhoeffer's "personal attitude," as if it were *merely* an internal attitude and not related to specific decisions and behaviors. I hope the several paragraphs of reflections offered here have challenged that notion.

Extraordinarily for a man his age in Germany, he managed quite deliberately to avoid taking up arms.[37]

We need to take stock of important facts here. First, Bonhoeffer's work for the Abwehr did not involve his contributing anything positive to the military efforts of Germany. Second, neither did his normal, everyday work for the agency have anything to do with assassinating Hitler. Instead, his work was quite consistent with what he had articulated in *Discipleship*, but under new conditions, including the reality that he would go to the front lines if he lost his "uk" status. In fact, his apparent reason for entering into work for the Abwehr was to avoid military conscription and thus killing on the front lines in the name of Germany and specifically in the name of Hitler—a position, it should be noted, that was almost unheard of in Germany at the time. This is what we know.

The Conspiracy

Now let us consider the possibility of Bonhoeffer's role in the conspiracy to undermine or eliminate the Hitler government. For even if it is the case that only fifty or so employees of the Abwehr were a part of the resistance, Bonhoeffer was one of them—after all, he had been considered an "enemy of the state" since 1936. Again, Dramm's careful and circumspect statements are worth quoting at length:

> What part did Bonhoeffer play in the resistance, and how should his importance for the resistance be judged? . . . Our answer can only be a tentative one. . . . Or what it was we do not really know. It is true that a closer analysis shows that Bonhoeffer's real part in conspiratorial resistance activities was much slighter than is usually assumed, and this slight share brought hardly any demonstrable results. But perhaps he was also active in the resistance in ways about which, even today, we still know nothing.

She continues:

> What is a matter of certain knowledge in this respect is merely a modest balance sheet of operational steps, specific missions, and factual results. Bonhoeffer's

37. It is true, as Eric Metaxas says, that apart from concerns about being executed Bonhoeffer was hesitant to openly declare himself a conscientious objector because of the repercussions it would have for the Confessing Church. However, it is also the case that Metaxas throughout his biography of Bonhoeffer understates the importance of Bonhoeffer's anti-nationalism and objection to military service (e.g., see Eric Metaxas, *Bonhoeffer*, 321–27). This seems most obvious and willful—and perhaps even deceptive—when he leaves out Bonhoeffer's reference to becoming a pacifist in his 1936 letter to Elizabeth Zinn (ibid., 123–24); compare my quoting of this letter in chapter 1.

> importance does not lie so much in any quantitatively measurable contribution to resistance against the Nazi regime. His importance lies in the ethical foundation for resistance that he offered. He was important for what he said, perhaps less for what he did. The "internal role" that he played in his resistance circle can most readily be described as intellectual pastoral care. Today it might be called "mental support"; and something like the "religious factor" in the German resistance should probably not be undervalued. . . . He was a pastor, a father confessor, a spiritual adviser. . . . Bonhoeffer strengthened other people in what they did at points where the church was silent, and therefore, in spite of some differences, among those involved in the resistance he strengthened believers especially.[38]

However, to get clearer about the import of Dramm's claims in relation to Bonhoeffer's potential, if marginal, roles in assassination attempts, we need first to gain clarity about facts. That is to say, let's be specific: with what assassination attempts might Bonhoeffer have had any connections?

There were numerous times when a coup d'état was contemplated or an assassination attempted between Hitler's assuming power at the end of January in 1933 and July 20, 1944—the final major attempt on Hitler's life. Historians estimate that there were at least forty-two separate plots to kill Hitler but that fewer than half of these are significant enough to merit serious historical study.[39] Only five of these attempts have any perceived connections to Bonhoeffer; thus it is these that will be examined.

There were two attempts to remove Hitler from power in 1938 and 1939.[40] The first and more significant plan unfolded in 1938 under the direction of Hans Oster, the second in command at the Abwehr and the man who came to be known as the "soul" of the resistance movement. Seeds for this attempt were planted especially in the autumn of 1937, when Hitler had a secret meeting with his top generals. It became clear to most of those who met with him that day that Hitler was eager for Germany to go to war. Then, on March 12, 1938, Hitler led a bloodless coup, taking over Austria. In clear violation of one of the most hated tenets of the Treaty of Versailles, Germany annexed Hitler's country of origin. Soon after this, Hitler set his sights on Czechoslovakia.

38. Dramm, *Dietrich Bonhoeffer and the Resistance*, 240.

39. Roger Moorehouse, *Killing Hitler: The Plots, the Assassins, and the Dictator Who Cheated Death* (New York: Bantam Books, 2006), 2. I mention several other key books on the resistance movements in footnote 2 in the introduction.

40. I am speaking here of attempts by groups that could have involved Bonhoeffer. I will mention an individual who by himself also tried to kill Hitler. For a good, brief account of the 1938 plan, see ibid., 79–114. For a detailed account, see Terry Parssinen, *The Oster Conspiracy of 1938* (New York: HarperCollins, 2003). For a brief account of the 1939 plan, see *Oster Conspiracy*, 173–84.

Many military leaders were convinced that Hitler, through an invasion of this country, would lead Germany into war against most of Europe. Thus it was not difficult for Oster and other military leaders to convince a number of officers to join a conspiracy to stop Hitler. They believed that once Hitler ordered a military offensive against Czechoslovakia, they could mount a coup, remove Hitler from his position, and form a new government. Some wanted him arrested and tried for the crimes he had already committed—many of which were documented. Some wanted him killed immediately, believing his power was so great that he was a threat as long as he was alive. What the conspirators were agreed on was the need to remove Hitler from power. They were also agreed on a couple of other matters. First, they needed the German people to see what they had seen. Thus they wanted Britain to stand firm against Hitler, showing Hitler's aggression for what it was. Second, they feared that a civil war might break out in Germany following the coup. Thus they wanted assurances from other nations that they wouldn't take advantage of such a situation. However, British leaders repeatedly refused to listen to the conspirators; instead, they appeased Hitler.[41] In September of 1938, when Britain's Prime Minister Chamberlain met with Hitler in Munich, he colluded in what has been called the "bloodless dismemberment of Czechoslovakia." Hitler for the moment had what he wanted without having provoked a war, namely, the border regions of Czechoslovakia, "leaving the remainder dangerously exposed and denuded of its fortifications."[42] This foiled the plans of the German conspirators, and military support for a coup fell apart.

Nevertheless, some officers, such as Oster, were convinced that Hitler's aggressive desires were far from satisfied. He would still lead Germany into a suicidal war and must be stopped. However, it was now harder to find conspirators who were willing to act. Opportunities were also hard to find.[43] Eventually, Oster found someone willing to kill Hitler. Eric Kordt, deputy to Foreign Minister Joachim von Ribbentrop, had regular access to the Führer, especially in the fall of 1939 as Hitler was moving toward war. Kordt told Oster he was willing to kill Hitler; all he needed was a bomb. Oster said he would provide one. The two men planned a date: November 11, 1939, two days before the planned invasion of Europe. Kordt was to detonate a bomb on his

41. Roger Moorhouse offers some interesting, if brief, reflections on how the appeasement was based on pragmatic concerns, not any "wooly-headed pacifism" (Moorhouse, *Killing Hitler*, 96).

42. Ibid., 103.

43. The following will focus on an attempt on Hitler's life. There were also attempted coups that did not materialize. For instance, also in 1939, General Kurt von Hammerstein-Equord was hoping to lure Hitler to his headquarters in Cologne. Once Hitler was there, he would arrest him. Something similar was contemplated in Paris the following year. In neither case was the plan carried through (ibid., 236).

person while in the presence of Hitler. However, this effort was undermined before it was attempted. On November 8, George Esler, a carpenter acting alone, attempted to kill Hitler.[44] After this attempt was discovered, security was tightened around the Führer and securing explosives became exceedingly difficult. Meanwhile, changing weather conditions forced Hitler to postpone his invasion plans several times. Once again, plans for a coup faded.

No one of whom I am aware provides any evidence that Bonhoeffer had any involvement in either of these plans that unfolded in 1938 and 1939.[45] Bonhoeffer himself did not begin work for the Abwehr until the end of October of 1940. His brother-in-law, Hans von Dohnanyi, did not begin work for the agency until August of 1939. However, it is likely that he was aware of these plans and discussed them with Bonhoeffer. After all, Dohnanyi had connections with many within the conspiracy from early on.[46]

Two assassination attempts that might appear to have more connection to Bonhoeffer were a couple of closely related plots in 1943, during Bonhoeffer's time in the Abwehr.[47] These attempts were made on March 13 and March 21 of that year.[48] The second of these is referred to by Joachim Fest as "the most promising assassination plot of the war years."[49] The central role in organizing and carrying out these plots was played by Colonel Henning von Tresckow, the chief of staff of the Army Group Center, and a small group of conspirators gathered around him.

During 1941 and 1942 many in the German military were being asked to participate in what can only be described as mass murder. Understandably, more than a few officers and infantrymen were having huge problems with what they saw and were sometimes asked to do. Complaints and even formal protests were sometimes made—to no avail. Few officers were willing to do anything extreme, such as participate in a coup or be involved in an attempt to kill the leader of the nation. Someone who was, however, was Colonel Henning von Tresckow. Tresckow was a decorated veteran of the First World

44. On this, see ibid., 49–78.

45. Bethge mentions a "small role" that Bonhoeffer played, but does not name specifics or provide evidence (Bethge, *Dietrich Bonhoeffer*, 671–76).

46. Bethge mentions that Bonhoeffer had removed pages from his diaries at what were likely key points at various times throughout 1938 and 1939. These diary entries likely referred to illegal and treasonous events of which he was aware—and thus would be incriminating of those involved if found (ibid., 626).

47. On these, see Fest, *Plotting Hitler's Death*, 170–201; Nigel Jones, *Countdown to Valkyrie: The July Plot to Assassinate Hitler* (London: Frontline Books, 2008), 112–44; and Hoffman, *History of the German Resistance*, 261–300.

48. Dramm mentions that some recent scholarship even calls into question the "very fact" of these attempts. See Dramm, *Dietrich Bonhoeffer and the Resistance*, 223.

49. Fest, *Plotting Hitler's Death*, 195.

War. Since the 1939 invasion of Poland, Tresckow had been disturbed by the ways in which Hitler conducted Germany's foreign policy. Each new campaign simply solidified his revulsion. By 1941 he was so horrified at the Third Reich's mass murders, particularly of Jews and Eastern Europeans, he decided Hitler must be stopped. Several times between August of 1941 and February of 1943, Tresckow made plans to arrest or kill Hitler himself.[50] However, due to various circumstances, none of these plots came close to being realized. Two later attempts came closer and are much better known.

The first of these later attempts, "Operation Flash," involved placing a bomb on a plane carrying Hitler. On the morning of March 13, 1943, Tresckow was to be involved in a meeting with Hitler. He knew that Hitler would be returning by air to his headquarters in Rastenburg. After the meeting Tresckow approached Colonel Brandt, a member of Hitler's staff who would be returning with the Führer, and asked if he would take a couple of bottles of brandy back to the High Command headquarters as a gift for Tresckow's friend Colonel Stieff. Actually the "brandy" was a British-type explosive, with a thirty minute fuse. Fabian von Schlabrendorff, Tresckow's adjutant in the Army Group Center and his lieutenant in the conspiracy, set the fuse and handed the package to Brandt. It was placed on the plane along with the other luggage. However, the bomb did not detonate, either because of a defective fuse or the extreme cold. Schlabrendorff managed to exchange real brandy for the bombs, thus safely retrieving the explosives before they were discovered.

Just over a week later, on March 21, Tresckow made another attempt. On that date Hitler was to be present for the annual Heroes' Day celebration in Berlin, which included both a speech by Hitler and a tour of an exhibit of weapons captured from the Soviets. Rudolf-Christoph von Gersdorff, a senior intelligence officer of the Army Group Center and a member of the resistance, was assigned to give Hitler the tour of the weaponry. Gersdorff volunteered to carry a bomb with a ten-minute fuse within his jacket pocket. He successfully ignited the fuse at the beginning of what was to be a thirty-minute tour. However, Hitler was distracted and inattentive. He stayed only two minutes, barely looking at anything. Chasing after him would have aroused the suspicions of his bodyguards. Gersdorff hurried into a lavatory and disarmed his bomb. Hitler was still alive.

A few conspirators in the Abwehr were involved in various ways in these attempts. Oster and Dohnanyi transported explosives to be used in these efforts.[51]

50. Moorhouse, *Killing Hitler*, 236–46.

51. For a brief account of these attempts as they relate to Bonhoeffer and those close to him, see Dramm, *Dietrich Bonhoeffer and the Resistance*, 218–30.

Oster was among those who would have seized control of the government after Hitler was killed.[52] However, it is likely there was no substantive involvement or specific planning among most of the fifty or so members of the resistance at the agency. Speaking specifically about these March 1943 attempts, Sabine Dramm says that anyone who includes Bonhoeffer in these efforts "greatly exaggerates Bonhoeffer's role and importance in the resistance."[53] I believe this is Dramm's way of saying that there is not a shred of evidence that Bonhoeffer was linked in any way to these attempts on Hitler's life.

But doesn't Bonhoeffer's arrest on April 5 of 1943, soon after the assassination attempts in March, suggest a closer connection to these efforts? The simple answer is no. To begin with, the assassination attempts were not discovered. Thus *no one* was arrested because of them. The timing of Bonhoeffer's arrest, however strange it may seem, is merely coincidental.[54] Officials in the Reich Central Security Office had long been mistrustful of Canaris, Oster, and the Abwehr. Thus they looked for anything suspicious. In October of 1942 two Abwehr agents working out of the Munich office, Heinrich Ickrath and Wilhelm Schmidhuber, were arrested. The issue that had captured the attention of officials was a matter of financial irregularities.[55] These irregularities were connected to Operation 7, the effort to help originally seven and later fourteen Jews flee Germany by posing as Abwehr agents. Substantial sums of money were used in this effort. Dohnanyi's name emerged in the interrogations of these two men. By early April, Dohnanyi was arrested on the charge of currency violations, related to Operation 7. Bonhoeffer, whose name arose in connection to Dohnanyi, was also arrested. Thus Bonhoeffer was arrested because of his involvement in an effort to save the lives of fourteen Jews.

In September Bonhoeffer was indicted. Dramm says that the only reason given for the indictment was that he had escaped military call-up and thus was "subverting military power."[56] This is not entirely accurate. He was also indicted because he was attempting "to keep others from fulfilling military

52. Parssinen, *Oster Conspiracy*, 178.

53. Dramm, *Dietrich Bonhoeffer and the Resistance*, 223. This therefore implies that Bethge is wrong when he says, in direct reference to these attempts in March, that they "include[d] Bonhoeffer's actual complicity in the plot against Hitler" (Bethge, *Dietrich Bonhoeffer*, 723). He provides no specifics or evidence.

54. On what follows, see Dramm, *Dietrich Bonhoeffer and the Resistance*, 202–5. Also see Anton Gill, *An Honorable Defeat: A History of the German Resistance to Hitler* (New York: Henry Holt, 1994), 213–19.

55. Peter Hoffman, "Introduction to the 1998 Edition," in *Valkyrie: An Insider's Account of the Plot to Kill Hitler*, by Hans Bernd Gisevius (New York: Da Capo Press, 2009), 4–5.

56. Dramm, *Dietrich Bonhoeffer and the Resistance*, 232; Bonhoeffer, *Conspiracy and Imprisonment*, 435–46.

service entirely, partially, or for a time."[57] In fact, these charges also assumed a significant role in the trial of Dohnanyi.[58] Thus Bonhoeffer was imprisoned because the court discovered that his work for the Abwehr was indeed a fabrication. His "job" was a fiction created to keep him from killing on the front lines.

Even though Bonhoeffer was arrested in early April of 1943, his name is often linked to the last serious assassination attempt, the one carried out on July 20, 1944, by Claus von Stauffenberg, which was discussed in the introduction. However, the specific planning for this attempt could not have been done before Bonhoeffer was arrested because Stauffenberg himself did not get involved in the plot until the fall of 1943. And in any event, it did not include the Abwehr conspirators in a substantial way. Dohnanyi was arrested on the same day as Bonhoeffer; Oster was dismissed from his post in the Abwehr the same month. Many assume that Bonhoeffer would not have been executed in April of 1945 if he had not been linked to some assassination attempt, probably the one on July 20, 1944. Yet anyone who imagines that knows little of the atrocities committed by the Nazis. According to Anton Gill, seven thousand people were arrested and forty-five hundred executed following the attempt in July of 1944. Moreover, he goes on to say that "in their last orgy of summary justice and killing, the Nazis brought in many thousands who were innocent of any plot to kill the dictator. . . . The authorities also found themselves with an excuse to execute many more dissidents who had been in prison . . . since before the 20 July attempt."[59] Bonhoeffer was certainly not the only one to undergo execution because of the irrational vengeance of the German authorities. After all, he had been considered an "enemy of the state" by various officials since at least as early as 1936.[60]

So where does this leave us in relation to Bonhoeffer's joining "a conspiracy whose aim was to assassinate Hitler"? Sabine Dramm's statement that "Bonhoeffer's real part in conspiratorial resistance activities was much slighter than is usually assumed" is accurate as far as it goes. However, I would suggest that even this may be an overstatement. If by "activities" we mean actions that contributed directly to attempts to kill Hitler, there is no evidence of any such actions on Bonhoeffer's part. In fact, when one looks at the specific attempts

57. Bonhoeffer, *Conspiracy and Imprisonment*, 435–36.

58. See ibid., 427–46; Gisevius, *Valkyrie*, 99.

59. Gill, *Honorable Defeat*, xiii.

60. To get a feel for how "enemies of the state" were treated by judges and how "justice" was pursued during the last few years of the Third Reich, see footage from trials in the documentary *The Top Secret Trial of the Third Reich*, directed by Jochen Bauer (1979; New York: First Run Features, 2009), DVD.

on Hitler's life, it becomes obvious that it is highly unlikely that Bonhoeffer was "involved" in any of them. However, following a cue from Dramm, I do want to examine one relevant set of acts: acts of speech.

I think Dramm is right that Bonhoeffer "was important for what he said, perhaps less for what he did." She continues by describing what he actually did as "intellectual pastoral care." To expand on this, she says that "he was a pastor, a father confessor, a spiritual adviser. . . . Bonhoeffer strengthened other people in what they did at points where the church was silent, and therefore, in spite of some differences, among those involved in the resistance he strengthened believers especially."[61]

So what does this role mean for our understanding of Bonhoeffer? Let's attempt to summarize what we know, what we don't know, and then what we can hypothesize about. What we know is that Bonhoeffer was involved with the network of conspirators who wanted to defeat the Hitler regime. Moreover, he had relationships with many individuals who were also involved in the conspiracy movement; a few were close friends.[62] Probably all of these individuals had no moral qualms about killing people for what they perceived to be legitimate reasons—although many in the conspiracy had difficulty coming to terms with engaging in treasonous behavior, both apart from and including the possibility of assassinating Hitler. Quite possibly, some of them could agree to engage in treasonous behavior only if they could perceive it as warranted by extreme and evil behaviors on the part of Hitler and those closest to him. The morally serious were willing to try to kill Hitler only if they were convinced that he in fact was a very dangerous and destructive tyrant—and thus to kill him was tyrannicide. This was likely true for Bonhoeffer's brother-in-law Hans von Dohnanyi. Since 1933, when Dohnanyi was working for the ministry of justice, he had been carefully documenting the atrocities committed by the Hitler regime. He appears to have been doing this largely to have hard evidence on record, so the perpetrators of these evils would eventually be held accountable for their actions.[63] However, Dohnanyi's recordkeeping may also have helped him to live more easily with his regular involvement in what were treasonous endeavors and his involvement in efforts to kill Hitler.

61. Dramm, *Dietrich Bonhoeffer and the Resistance*, 240.

62. It is extraordinary simply to see how many people in high places Bonhoeffer knew and, often, was related to. For a list of a number of them, see ibid., 105–8.

63. These records were among those discovered on September 22, 1944, by the Gestapo at the Armed Forces High Command outpost in Zossen. Now called "The Zossen Files," this secret archive of Dohnanyi had varied incriminating evidence regarding conspirators. However, nothing I have seen indicates that there is anything in these files that linked Bonhoeffer to any specific assassination attempts. See Bethge, "Appendix 1: The Zossen Files," in *Dietrich Bonhoeffer*, 935–41; and Dramm, *Bonhoeffer and Resistance*, 232.

So, in short, we know that Bonhoeffer had informal conversations with people involved in seditious activities. Undoubtedly, various efforts to get rid of the Hitler government were discussed. We have decades-old memories from various people about portions of the content of these discussions, especially from Bethge.[64]

But let's be clear. We do not really *know* what Bonhoeffer said in these conversations. To truly know, in any meaningful sense, we would have to have the context for each given conversation—knowing the nature of the subject matter, the occasion for the conversation, Bonhoeffer's tone of voice and facial expressions, the nature of the person with whom he was speaking, and the nature of their relationship. These are the sorts of factors we would need to know in order to discern whether Bonhoeffer's contributions to these conversations indicate he had shifted his ethical views from what he said in the book *Discipleship* or in speeches and sermons from 1932 forward. We simply don't have that information.

Let me give several examples to illustrate why we don't really know what these conversations mean, particularly in relation to Bonhoeffer. It is interesting to read Bonhoeffer's letters, sometimes circular letters, to and about his former seminary students who are serving on the front lines with the German army. These letters are written both in response to correspondence from these students and in response to the deaths of former students.[65] Some students describe prisoners being shot in cold blood, women and children being executed—and such atrocities being justified as saving the lives of German soldiers.[66] No one would guess from reading Bonhoeffer's letters that he continued to believe that killing on the front lines in the German army was wrong.[67] Yet the evidence suggests he did. That was not only why he initially

64. On the subject matter of this whole paragraph, see Dramm, *Dietrich Bonhoeffer and the Resistance*, 39–45; on Bethge's recollection of one specific informal conversation between Bonhoeffer and Dohnanyi, see 42–43. It is clear from Bethge's biography, with the numerous references to Dohnanyi, that Bonhoeffer's relationship with Dohnanyi was close, and they confided in each other about these and other important matters frequently.

65. In a letter to Ernst Wolf, on September 13, 1942, Bonhoeffer mentions that twenty-one of his former seminary students have died as soldiers (Bonhoeffer, *Conspiracy and Imprisonment*, 358–59).

66. See, for instance, this letter in *Conspiracy and Imprisonment*, 251–53. It should be mentioned that what is being described in this letter, by many accounts, violates just war principles. My reading tells me that these sorts of activities had become routine in many quarters of the German army by 1940. To be a German soldier was not simply to not be a pacifist, it was to violate most understandings of the just war tradition. For another firsthand account, see the quotation from Helmut von Moltke in the introduction.

67. See, e.g., Dietrich Bonhoeffer, "Finkenwalde, Circular Letter [May 1940]," in *Conspiracy and Imprisonment*, 44–48. Also see Bethge, *Dietrich Bonhoeffer*, 703–5. One might also look at the records we have in relation to Bonhoeffer's interactions with the Wedemeyer family

joined the Abwehr but also why he guarded his ongoing "uk" status regarding military service as he continued to work for this agency. But he communicated to all of his former students the way he did with Joachim Kanitz, as described in the introduction. As we have seen, Bonhoeffer asked Kanitz in August 1942 how he had received his medal of honor, the Iron Cross. Kanitz says that Bonhoeffer asked with genuine interest and without any sense of judgment. Kanitz further recalls: "It was then that my wish, my desire was strengthened to will only one thing: to survive the war and see to it that such a thing never happened again."[68] Most German soldiers would never have thought this. Kanitz was responding to Bonhoeffer's sensitivity. He was also remembering his teacher's clear teaching about love of enemies and neighbors—teachings that shaped him profoundly.

Bonhoeffer taught clearly and lived with sensitivity. He did, in fact, while training ministers at Finkenwalde, teach pacifism and attempt to get his students seriously to consider being conscientious objectors—a consideration almost unheard of at the time. But later, when war was underway, and many of his former students were on the battlefield, he did not do what Karl Barth did from Switzerland and tell them they should refuse to serve as soldiers.[69] Why? We can only guess. Among other things, Bonhoeffer knew he was privileged. He and his family were well connected. He had managed to avoid directly and formally refusing to serve in the military—and thus facing execution. Of course, it is also the case that he did seek to secure a "uk" status for some of his former students, such as Eberhard Bethge.

The context of Germany in 1940 to 1945 was an extreme situation. In the Abwehr and other resistance circles, Bonhoeffer was friends with individuals who, like him, were challenging the extreme nationalism, militarism, and oppression of the Third Reich. Many of them did not share his Christian faith. Probably none of them had ever shared the convictions he had articulated about not killing in war because of Jesus's teachings about love of enemies. In that context what was he to do? What was he to say, especially when some turned to him for advice, for counsel?

This situation was not totally new to Bonhoeffer. After all, he—a theologian and pastor—was from a tight-knit family but one with mostly loose (and for

regarding the men who were serving in the military. See Bethge, *Dietrich Bonhoeffer*, 788–89, a letter to Maria's mother after her husband died on the front. See also Bonhoeffer, *Conspiracy and Imprisonment*, 350–52, 366–67.

68. Kanitz, excerpt from interview in *Dietrich Bonhoeffer: Memories and Perspectives*, directed by Bain Boehlke (Lansdale, PA: Vision Video, 1983), DVD.

69. Arne Rasmussen, "Church and War in the Theology of Karl Barth," in *Living Theology*, ed. Len Hansen et al. (Wellington, South Africa: Bible Media, 2011), 394.

some, no) ties to the church. He had many conversations throughout most of his life that included topics on which he profoundly disagreed with his family, people he very much loved and respected. And after all, he had clearly had many conversations with his good friend Hans von Dohanyi between 1933 and his involvement in the Abwehr and closer contact with resistance circles; more than likely, at least as early as 1938, assassination had been one of the topics discussed.[70] How did Bonhoeffer's conversations with Dohnanyi proceed, on many topics? Dohnanyi was not only his brother-in-law; he became a trusted friend. Undoubtedly, Bonhoeffer respected him in a variety of ways, knew he had many things to learn from him, valued his resistance to Hitler—and yet never forgot that his brother-in-law did not share some of his own most deeply held convictions. But again, Bonhoeffer had lived with this sort of reality ever since his teens, when he announced to his family that he would be a theologian.

We also need to realize that if, for instance, Bonhoeffer continued to embrace the pacifism he had earlier articulated in various speeches as well as in *Discipleship*, it does not mean he would have had nothing to say to those connected to plots to kill Hitler. Bonhoeffer had known for as long as he had strong convictions about love of enemies that most others in the church did not agree with him. Certainly he did not shy away on occasion from issuing challenging and prophetic words intended to confront his listeners or readers simply with the full force of the gospel call to love enemies concretely in the midst of a world at war. This is what we see, for instance, in his speech at Fanø in August of 1934 and in a sermon to seminarians on January 23, 1938.[71] However, in 1936, at a time when no one doubts that he held to these convictions, Bonhoeffer nonetheless formulates a catechism for instruction in the church that sounds a different note:

> How should the Christian act in war? There is no plain commandment of God on this point. The church can never bless war or weapons. The Christian can never take part in an unjust war. If a Christian takes to the sword, he will daily pray to God for forgiveness of the sin and pray for peace.[72]

70. Dramm says: "There was a constant exchange of ideas and information between [Dohnanyi and Bonhoeffer] from the beginning of the 1930s onward" (Dramm, *Dietrich Bonhoeffer and the Resistance*, 15). Given Dohnanyi's extensive knowledge of the violence and injustices perpetrated by the German government, this challenges the notion that Bonhoeffer was ever naive about the atrocities the German government was committing under Hitler.

71. Bonhoeffer, "The Church and the People of the World," 307–10; and an untitled sermon on love of enemies based on Romans 12:17–21, *Theological Education Underground: 1937–1940*, 465–71.

72. As quoted in Bethge, *Dietrich Bonhoeffer*, 188. Bonhoeffer said something similar in a catechism that he and Franz Hildebrandt wrote together in the late summer of 1931. Bethge

What seems obvious is that Bonhoeffer always sought to discern time, place, and audience. Particularly in relation to this catechism, it is quite possible to see it at least two ways. Perhaps Bonhoeffer is doing this formally on behalf of the Lutheran Church and thus not in his own voice. And perhaps he also knows that getting catechetical students to at least take the just war tradition seriously as basic church teaching will be a major step forward.

Bonhoeffer knew as he interacted with Hans Dohnanyi and others involved in the conspiracy that they did not share some of his convictions. Might it have been the case that Bonhoeffer, in various conversations, was helping those who held different convictions from his own to clarify their own convictions, their own moral parameters for thinking about tyrants, evil, and when killing an evil tyrant might ever be justified—given their own moral framework?

We know that Bonhoeffer was a sensitive, loving, and caring person. We know that he opposed the nationalism, militarism, and cruel oppression and abuses of the Hitler government. We can infer that he would have had empathy with others who also opposed these horrible realities perpetrated by the Third Reich. Do we know that because he had respectful and sensitive conversations with conspirators who were willing to kill Hitler or see him killed, he agreed with them? Or do we imagine that he hoped with Tresckow, the man who was heading up the assassination attempts of March of 1943, that eliminating Hitler would "smooth the way for a military dictatorship"?[73]

I believe we do not really *know* either of these last two things, even though many writings on Bonhoeffer presume that we know the answer to the first and never mention the second.[74]

All of the above few paragraphs are relevant when we reflect on the claims by Eberhard Bethge—drawing on decades-old memories from informal conversations—that Bonhoeffer had said that "if it fell to him to carry out the deed [of assassinating Hitler], he was prepared to do so." Bethge goes on to

comments on how the introduction of the topic of war and peace "was something entirely new" in catechetical training in the Lutheran Church (187).

73. Dramm, *Dietrich Bonhoeffer and the Resistance*, 221. In general we need to be honest about who some of the characters were who were involved in efforts to kill Hitler. For instance, Dramm says that "factually speaking . . . it has to be admitted that a considerable number of those who played a part on July 20, 1944, and who in many cases sacrificed their lives in doing so, were earlier involved in the war of racial extermination, occasionally at least approved it, and in some cases actively pursued it" (239). This is a reminder to be cautious in assuming what it was that Bonhoeffer affirmed of the varied commitments of those involved in "the conspiracy" against Hitler.

74. Some might think the second question absurd. But I believe this is as much as anything because of the biases of most who currently appropriate Bonhoeffer. I would argue that there is no evidence for an affirmative answer to the first question. Dramm argues that in relation to the second sort of question we should be honest about Bonhoeffer's social conservativism.

say that this "was a theoretical statement, of course, since Bonhoeffer knew nothing about guns or explosives."[75] To offer an instance of how memory perhaps is not always accurate, it is worthwhile to look at Bethge's reflections on a conversation Bonhoeffer had with the English bishop George Bell. Bell's memory (recorded in his diary a few years after the fact) was that Bonhoeffer had said, "Hitler is the Anti-Christ. Therefore we must go on with our work and eliminate him whether he be successful or not." Bethge challenges whether or not Bonhoeffer ever referred to Hitler as "the Anti-Christ," saying that this term for Hitler "does not occur anywhere else in Bonhoeffer's writings."[76] That is to say, Bethge reflects on this supposed memory of Bonhoeffer's words the way we in this book are reflecting on the claim that Bonhoeffer made dramatic theological shifts related to involvement in or affirmations of assassination attempts. We examine these claims, based on memories of informal oral comments, in light of texts where Bonhoeffer names his convictions about these and related matters, as well as examining relevant facts.

This leads us, then, to the last statement we want to consider from Sabine Dramm's assertions about Bonhoeffer's contributions through words. She says: "His importance lies in the ethical foundation for resistance that he offered."[77] The best response is probably *yes* and *no*.

For this particular set of statements to have an even fuller meaning, it might be helpful to know Dramm's definition of "resistance." By resistance within Nazi Germany, Dramm means "an active, personally dangerous intervention with the goal of weakening or ending the regime, and putting an end to the National Socialist state."[78] Thus for Dramm some of the activities described in this chapter as Bonhoeffer's work in the Abwehr may count, because they were intended to weaken the Nazi regime. But for her the activities that truly count as "resistance" are those activities directly aimed at eliminating top officials in the government. So these are basically the coups that were contemplated, including assassination attempts. Now, for the *yes* and *no* in relation to Bonhoeffer and resistance.

First, the *no*. I hope this chapter has shown that there is no evidence that Bonhoeffer was "involved in the plots to kill Hitler." Hopefully we have also shown that there is no real evidence that Bonhoeffer himself affirmed the killing of Hitler. Thus, if that's what one means by being involved in the resistance

75. Bethge, *Dietrich Bonhoeffer*, 751–52. For other related claims, see 625, 669–70, 722, 728, 744, 755.

76. Ibid., 722–23. The quote seems to be a memory of a meeting in 1940 that was recounted during a meeting with Bonhoeffer in Sweden in 1942, published in 1945.

77. Dramm, *Dietrich Bonhoeffer and the Resistance*, 240.

78. Ibid., 19.

or offering an ethical foundation for resistance, then the answer in relation to Bonhoeffer is no. Given this, then, it is also dishonest to believe that we can obviously *infer* what Bonhoeffer meant in *Ethics* when he used terms like "responsibility," "guilt," or "living unreservedly in life's duties"—that is, that these were justifications for involvement in the attempts to kill Hitler. (These terms will be discussed later in the two chapters on *Ethics*, especially chapter 7.)

What has been said in this chapter appears contrary to the impression that is given by certain key statements in Bethge's accounts of Bonhoeffer. Bethge suggests that Bonhoeffer entered a new stage of his life, thought, and thus involvements when "in 1939 the theologian and Christian became a man for his times."[79] After he returned from New York in July of 1939, Bonhoeffer entered a new world, says Bethge, where (apparently) upon becoming more deeply engaged and realistic he "entered the difficult world of assessing what was expedient."[80] Dramm, taking cues from Bethge, says, "Bonhoeffer's return from the United States in the summer of 1939 was followed by a long-drawn-out change of course, *as his bystander stance changed* gradually into an independent role in the conspiracy."[81]

Does Bethge truly believe that the Bonhoeffer of 1937 was not "a man for his times"? Or, put the other way around, how do we read any of Bonhoeffer's writings, or his life for that matter, as being driven by expediency? When was it that Bonhoeffer was a "bystander"? Perhaps Bethge desperately wanted his close friend to be perceived as a "political" activist in the midst of the worst years of the Hitler regime. Bonhoeffer, so Bethge wants us to believe, was one of those Germans who *directly* tried to stop the massive slaughter that became the Holocaust of the Jews and World War II; he was a "resister" in the sense in which Dramm defines it.

Though Bonhoeffer was never a bystander, he was also never this kind of activist. This becomes clear as we read the letters of Bonhoeffer and Moltke side by side and note their parallel lives during the same period. Moltke was much more that kind of activist. However, as stated in the introduction, it should again be noted that he too did not—for reasons of principle as well as practical consideration—involve himself in assassination attempts. When he had free time, Moltke met with members of the resistance group known as the Kreisau Circle. When Bonhoeffer had free time, he wrote theology, related to friends, and nurtured relationships through letters; he did not become what some might think of as an "activist."

79. Bethge, *Dietrich Bonhoeffer*, 677.

80. Ibid., 678.

81. Dramm, *Dietrich Bonhoeffer and the Resistance*, 12 (emphasis added).

Now, on the *yes*. If we broaden the definition of "resistance" beyond Sabine Dramm's rather narrow one, then yes, indeed, Bonhoeffer gives us an "ethical foundation for resistance." Almost immediately after Hitler assumed power, Bonhoeffer gave his radio address "The Führer and the Individual in the Younger Generation."[82] A few months later he wrote a prophetic essay, "The Church and the Jewish Question," which was published in June.[83] But even before these more obvious examples, Bonhoeffer was articulating an ethic for resistance. It was manifest in his life, his commitments, and his writings. Thus, if we are to understand his ethical thought on resistance, we don't simply look to writings from 1940 to 1945—not even to writings after Hitler assumed power. We begin with 1932: "A community of peace can exist only when it does not rest on *a lie* or on *injustice*. Wherever a community of peace endangers or suffocates truth and justice, the community of peace must be broken and the battle must be declared."[84] These early words, as much as later ones, are words intended for constructively guiding daily faithful living but also, clearly, for provoking resistance when it is needed—but resistance in line with the commandments of the God known in Jesus Christ.

Many ethicists seem to imagine that Bonhoeffer became more "reasonable" in the 1940s than he had been in his youthful days of flirting with pacifism, proposing a kind of new monasticism, and writing *Discipleship*. However, is it possible that Bonhoeffer continued in the 1940s to believe what he said to his brother in 1935, that if he were to become more "reasonable," he would have to "chuck [his] entire theology"?[85] And since there is no evidence that he did that, might we then see that it is possible that, as Bonhoeffer said in April of 1944, "my life—as strange as it may sound—has gone in a straight line, uninterrupted, at least with regard to how I've led it"?[86]

Therefore, if we are to discern Bonhoeffer's ethics for resistance, we must look at the whole of his writings. This means on the one hand that we do not ignore the rich theological content in *Sanctorum Communio* and *Act and Being*, his lectures on Christology and creation and fall, *Discipleship*, and

82. Bonhoeffer, *Berlin*, 268–82.

83. Ibid., 361–70.

84. Dietrich Bonhoeffer, "On the Theological Foundation of the Work of the World Alliance," in *Ecumenical, Academic, and Pastoral Work: 1931–1932*, ed. Victoria J. Barnett, Mark Brocker, and Michael B. Lukens, trans. Isabel Best, Nicholas S. Humphrey, Marion Pauck, Anne Schmidte-Lange, and Douglas W. Stott, vol. 11 of *Dietrich Bonhoeffer Works* (Minneapolis: Fortress, 2012), 365.

85. Bonhoeffer, *London*, 284.

86. Dietrich Bonhoeffer, *Letters and Papers from Prison*, ed. John W. de Gruchy, trans. Isabel Best, Lisa E. Dahill, Reinhard Krauss, and Nancy Lukens, vol. 8 of *Dietrich Bonhoeffer Works* (Minneapolis: Fortress, 2009), 352.

Life Together, to mention only some of the major early writings relevant for thinking about Bonhoeffer's theological ethics (including an ethic of resistance). We also do not ignore the fact that Bonhoeffer's life and contexts had changed from 1932 to 1941 and from 1941 to 1944. We neither ignore the challenges contained in his provocative writings of his earlier years, such as the 1932 quotations above, nor the rich, evocative, and unfinished writings of *Ethics* and *Letters and Papers from Prison*.

Having just watched again the film *The Pianist*—a powerful, painful film about the Holocaust of the Jews—I am moved by the following excerpt from "Ten Years After," Bonhoeffer's reflections on ten years of the Hitler regime (a memo given to Dohnanyi, Oster, and Bethge):

> We have been silent witnesses of evil deeds. We have become cunning and learned the arts of obfuscation and equivocal speech. Experience has rendered us suspicious of human beings, and often we have failed to speak to them a true and open word. Unbearable conflicts have worn us down or even made us cynical. Are we still of any use? We will not need geniuses, cynics, people who have contempt for others, or cunning tacticians, but simple, uncomplicated, and honest human beings. Will our inner strength to resist what has been forced on us have remained strong enough, and our honesty with ourselves blunt enough, to find our way back to simplicity and honesty?[87]

This memo was written centrally for three friends. It is certainly written by someone who has learned "to see the great events of world history from below, from the perspective of the outcasts, the suspects, the maltreated, the powerless, the oppressed and reviled, in short, from the perspective of the suffering."[88] However, there is every reason to think that Bonhoeffer began this learning process not after 1939 but rather when he worshiped with an African American congregation in New York City in 1930–31. Yet it is this very sensibility interwoven with his convictions about costly discipleship that led him back from New York in the summer of 1939 to endure the hardships of the Third Reich with his fellow Germans.

The thesis of this book is that Bonhoeffer's later writings—important as they are—should be held together with his earlier writings. Taken together, these writings help us to grasp Bonhoeffer's extraordinary and ongoing challenge to our safe and secure existence. Together, these writings help us to see his full-blown theological rationale for daily discipleship, and thus ethics, and for resistance when that is needed. In the midst of all of his writings, we may

87. Ibid., 52.
88. Ibid.

continue to receive with thankfulness the following words, evocative words, moving words, sent from a prison cell:

> God, the Eternal, wants to be loved with our whole heart, not to the detriment of earthly love or to diminish it, but as a sort of cantus firmus to which the other voices of life resound in counterpoint. One of these contrapuntal themes, which keep their *full independence* but are still related to the cantus firmus, is earthly love. . . . Where the cantus firmus is clear and distinct, a counterpoint can develop as mightily as it wants. The two are "undivided and yet distinct," as the Definition of Chalcedon says, like the divine and human natures in Christ. Is that perhaps why we are so at home with polyphony in music, why it is important to us, because it is the musical image of this Christological fact and thus also our *vita christiana*?[89]

That "clear and plain" *cantus firmus* for both Bonhoeffer and the authors of this book is the God revealed in Jesus Christ. It is in service to keeping that centrality clear that this book has been written.

89. Ibid., 394 (emphasis added).

Part 2

The Development of Bonhoeffer's Theological Ethics

In the previous section we considered Bonhoeffer's biography, the people and communities, the tasks and duties that made up his life. The line of inquiry pursued up to this point has sought to trace the contours of Bonhoeffer's existence as a historical agent. We have concerned ourselves with events and facts. In this context, several of Bonhoeffer's key writings have been referenced and placed within the timeline of his life. In this next section we will explore several of these works at greater depth. Our aim is to show that Bonhoeffer's writing, the expressed manifestation of his theological reflection, supports the overall thesis of this book. To do this we will focus on the development of Bonhoeffer's theological ethics. The first chapter in this section covers his early work and focuses on a lecture Bonhoeffer gave in Barcelona, Spain, in 1929. The next three chapters focus on Bonhoeffer's habilitation thesis, *Act and Being*, and the more well-known works *Discipleship* and *Ethics*. We will consider the relationship between these second two at some length and, in the final chapter, examine two key themes in the *Ethics* manuscripts that are often cited as evidence of Bonhoeffer's shift to ethical "realism."

4

Dietrich Bonhoeffer's Amoral Ethics

"An Extremely Awkward Undertaking" Never Again Attempted

Dietrich Bonhoeffer's theological legacy has been read in a variety of ways. Ever since his tragic death in 1945, his interpreters have struggled to articulate his enduring significance. This process of reading the lives of others involves our own lives as well. We comb the lives and thoughts of those who have already lived in order to gain some degree of clarity for our own. Needless to say, then, interpretation of another is inextricably self-involving. And it is understandable that the "portraits" drawn of this particular "Protestant saint" are as numerous as his interpreters, even if it is also true that not all interpretations are necessarily created equal.[1]

The self-involving nature of interpretation, however, is not the only factor that diversifies these portraits of Bonhoeffer. The tumultuous era in which he lived and died fractured his biography and his theological legacy in ways not usually the case under more stable circumstances. An unbroken mirror reflects but one image, but a broken one yields a portrait less uniform. No wonder, then, that Bonhoeffer is understood in such different and often contradictory ways. His was a life lived in a time most trying and in a context rife with

1. For a wide-ranging and accessible account of these "portraits" of Bonhoeffer, see Stephen R. Haynes, *The Bonhoeffer Phenomenon: Portraits of a Protestant Saint* (Minneapolis: Fortress, 2004).

contradictory forces. But despite the turmoil around him, Bonhoeffer the man was still one person. A mirror may be broken, but the ravaged parts are still parts of an intelligible whole.

The fractured wholeness that is Bonhoeffer's life is not unrelated to the written works that are his life's legacy. The book containing his last substantive ethical reflections, his *Ethics*, remains incomplete to this day and was never published during his lifetime.[2] The fragmentation of a book never completed is an apt symbol of the interrupted life of its author. But the incomplete state of Bonhoeffer's last major theological work contrasts with the sense of completion that can be felt in the life that brought it forth. Though Bonhoeffer's life was full of twists and turns, it presents a sense of destiny. His life did not simply end with his death. His life brought him to his death. Whatever disjunctions there may be in Bonhoeffer's legacy must not abrogate the consistency of both his biography and the theological development that was its constant counterpart.

Bonhoeffer's life and theology contain elements of continuity and change, of both consistency and innovation. These changes in thinking were just as much responses to his changing circumstances in Germany as they were results of his own creative insight. Bonhoeffer's thinking over the course of his lifetime demonstrates his ability to integrate new ideas into the existing thought structures, thereby transforming them and being himself transformed. But the overall continuity in Bonhoeffer's thinking despite the changes and innovations is just as apparent, even if often overlooked or underestimated.

The fact that Bonhoeffer's theology has elements of both continuity and discontinuity is obvious to most of his interpreters. Most lives, after all, do contain both of these characteristics. Why would Bonhoeffer's life be any different? What divides interpreters, however, is not the mere fact of both continuity and discontinuity in Bonhoeffer's thinking but the specific locations of these two dynamics throughout the course of his intellectual development. Is Bonhoeffer's life best envisioned as a linear development with the occasional integration of new experiences? Is Bonhoeffer's thought best seen as a systematic extrapolation of foundational theological convictions, albeit in ongoing conversation with new insights? Or, on the contrary, is Bonhoeffer's life best articulated in terms of leaps from one context to another, and his thought best construed as a series of new beginnings? Though these questions may well seem abstract, the various ways in which they are answered affect how any given portrait of Bonhoeffer will be drawn.

2. Dietrich Bonheoffer, *Ethics*, ed. Clifford J. Green, trans. Reinhard Krauss, Charles West, and Douglas W. Stott, vol. 6 of *Dietrich Bonhoeffer Works* (Minneapolis: Fortress, 2005).

There are a number of key events in Bonhoeffer's life that invite questions related to continuity and discontinuity in his thinking. Probably the most well known of these events is his supposed participation in a plot to assassinate Adolf Hitler. Participation in this plot is taken as indicative of and/or a catalyst for an ethical shift from the espousal of pacifism to a position that recognizes the justifiable use of violent measures in certain circumstances. But in addition to a shift away from pacifism, Bonhoeffer's participation also suggests an even deeper shift, a shift in systematic ethical approach. This shift can be documented, it is argued, by comparing the two works that predate and postdate the shift, *Discipleship* and *Ethics*, respectively.[3] This particular construal of Bonhoeffer's ethical thinking is presented in Larry L. Rasmussen's book *Dietrich Bonhoeffer: Reality and Resistance*.[4]

Rasmussen's book is something of a classic in Bonhoeffer interpretation, and the questions Rasmussen raises about Bonhoeffer's pacifism relate to the broader question of ethical development. It is only natural, then, that Rasmussen's arguments will play a role in shaping the arguments of this essay. But there are a number of serious problems with Rasmussen's account of both Bonhoeffer's life and his ethics. The first question is whether Rasmussen has accurately evaluated the degree of Bonhoeffer's involvement in the conspiracy.[5] The second question is whether Rasmussen has accurately understood the development of Bonhoeffer's ethics, particularly when it comes to the relationship between *Discipleship* and *Ethics*. His interpretation suggests a great deal of discontinuity between these two volumes, discontinuities that explain and/or mirror Bonhoeffer's involvement in an assassination conspiracy. But the following interpretation of Bonhoeffer's ethical development argues that there is a greater degree of continuity between *Discipleship* and *Ethics* than is often presupposed by Rasmussen and many others. Furthermore, it goes on to suggest that there is no substantial "break" in Bonhoeffer's thought between these two volumes. Not only is there continuity between the two; there is also fundamental agreement in foundational ethical assumptions. Whatever discontinuities there are between *Discipleship* and *Ethics*, they must be placed within the context of the greater continuity that exists between them.

Assessing the relationship between *Discipleship* and *Ethics* is greatly complicated when they are effectively isolated from the broader theological development that brought them into being. More specifically, the relationship

3. Dietrich Bonhoeffer, *Discipleship*, ed. Geffrey B. Kelly and John D. Godsey, trans. Barbara Green and Reinhard Krauss, vol. 4 of *Dietrich Bonhoeffer Works* (Minneapolis: Fortress, 2000).

4. Larry L. Rasmussen, *Dietrich Bonhoeffer: Reality and Resistance* (1972; repr., Louisville: Westminster John Knox, 2005).

5. See chapter 3 above.

between these two works cannot be determined with any degree of accuracy unless it is compared to the relationship between Bonhoeffer's first reflections on Christian ethics in Barcelona in 1929 and the work of *Discipleship* that it preceded. There is a very clear contrast between Bonhoeffer's Barcelona ethics and his ethics in *Discipleship*. No one denies that this is the case and that the contrast between these two ethical works is a sharp one. But this generally recognized fact has not been as fruitful as it could be when applied to other questions of Bonhoeffer interpretation.

One of the truisms of interpretation is that the obscure or the questionable should be interpreted by the clearer and less arguable. The method of the following chapters is to apply what is learned about the relationship between the Barcelona lecture and *Discipleship* to the relationship between *Discipleship* and *Ethics*. The first relationship, which evidences a strong shift in thinking, will provide a basis for adjudication and evaluation of the second relationship, the less evident and contested one between *Discipleship* and *Ethics*.

The suggestion that there are continuities between *Discipleship* and *Ethics* is not a new one. In the editors' introduction to the critical edition of *Discipleship*, for instance, Geffrey B. Kelly and John D. Godsey take issue with those who have pitted *Discipleship* against *Ethics* or have seen the former work as representing an aberration in Bonhoeffer's more credible thought and practice.[6] So it is not as if the current argument is completely without precedent. But in addition to confirming these general affirmations of continuity, this chapter and those that follow it hope to make it even more obvious that the relationship between *Discipleship* and *Ethics* is best seen in terms of development rather than disruption.

The Theological Structure of Bonhoeffer's Barcelona Ethics

Bonhoeffer completed his first dissertation, *Sanctorum Communio*, in July 1927.[7] Less than one year later, in February of 1928, Bonhoeffer began a temporary assignment as an assistant pastor to a German-speaking congregation in Barcelona. In addition to his regular pastoral duties, Bonhoeffer delivered three theological lectures; the third was titled "Basic Questions of a Christian Ethic." Unlike *Sanctorum Communio*, which evidences a superlative degree of systematic integration and theological insight, this lecture is fraught with

6. Geffrey B. Kelly and John D. Godsey, "Editors' Introduction to the English Edition," in *Discipleship*, 19–23.

7. Dietrich Bonhoeffer, *Sanctorum Communio: A Theological Study of the Sociology of the Church*, ed. Clifford J. Green, trans. Reinhard Krauss and Nancy Lukens, vol. 1 of *Dietrich Bonhoeffer Works* (Minneapolis: Fortress, 1998), 9.

difficulties. It is, after all, something of a first attempt at discussing ethical foundations and their concrete application.[8] Nevertheless, there is reason to suppose that if things had gone differently, this particular lecture would have contained the germ of Bonhoeffer's ethical thought, a germ he could have developed further. In point of fact, this is a road Bonhoeffer did not follow. But examining what proves to be a false start will demonstrate all the more the significance of the shift that happened to make *Discipleship* possible. One of the most striking things about the ethics lecture in Barcelona is its emphasis upon moral relativity. Not only is this something of a surprise given the circumstances of the lecture—Bonhoeffer was, after all, lecturing to congregants for whom he was a pastor—it also seems uncannily "postmodern." But more to the point, the fact that Bonhoeffer begins his lecture by presuming and indeed arguing for the relativity of moral norms is significant because this recognition shapes his entire discussion of Christian ethics in the Barcelona lecture.

Bonhoeffer's recognition of moral relativity, which is essentially in line with the approach of the Danish philosopher Søren Kierkegaard, is also significant because it will shape his ethical thinking throughout his lifetime. This is especially apparent when it comes to his critique of moral absolutes and principled forms of morality. If there is one motif that is recognizably present in all three of Bonhoeffer's major works on ethics, it is this one. However, as shall become readily apparent, when discussion turns to *Discipleship* and *Ethics* in chapters 5 through 7, we will see that Bonhoeffer employs this aversion to principled ethics and moral absolutes to very different ends depending upon the piece of writing in question. Bonhoeffer is always critical of moral absolutes and moral principles, but the rationale for this critique changes over time. Following this motif and its various uses and rationales will thus aid in our overall goal of tracing the contours of Bonhoeffer's ethical development.

From the very beginning of Bonhoeffer's lecture, and indeed throughout its entirety, he insists that all morality is context specific, time sensitive, and culturally shaped.[9] It arises from and is thus bound to sociocultural enterprises

8. This is not to suggest, however, that Bonhoeffer was not interested in ethics at all until he gave his lecture in Barcelona. Bonhoeffer's critique of German idealism (and, to a lesser degree, Kantian epistemology) in *Sanctorum Communio*, for example, pinpoints the failure of these systems to accurately describe the ethical nature of human interaction. See Dietrich Bonhoeffer, *Sanctorum Communio*, 34–57, esp. 49–50. With this said, however, it is primarily in the Barcelona lecture that Christian ethics becomes a focused topic of attention.

9. This and the following subsection have been informed by Nathan Kerr, *Christ, History, and Apocalyptic: The Politics of Christian Mission* (Eugene, OR: Cascade Books, 2009), 23–92. Kerr's description and critique of both Troeltsch and Barth were helpful in informing my analysis of Bonhoeffer's early ethics. This should not be surprising considering the fact that Bonhoeffer was indebted both to Barth and Berlin.

and the thought constructions and ideologies upon which culture and society are founded and which they embody. As Bonhoeffer states, "Ethics is a matter of blood and a matter of history. It did not simply descend to earth from heaven. Rather, it is a child of earth, and for that reason its face changes with history as well as with the renewal of blood, with the transition between generations. There is a German ethic as well as a French ethic and an American ethic."[10] Because ethics is firmly rooted in earth, because it is a product of specific cultures and the specific needs of a given moment in time, it would be an act of extreme naïveté, or of simple ignorance, for the Christian theologian to undertake the ethical task simply by defining and applying one or several moral absolutes. Thus Bonhoeffer's critique of moral absolutes is meant to be total. His insistence upon the relativity of moral sentiment applies just as much to one culture as to another culture, to any epoch, and, more important theologically, to the Scriptures as well. Morality as such is relative. Despite its frequent enshrinement in a canon backed by divine authority, all morality is a product of social and cultural forces.

But this is not the end of Bonhoeffer's discussion. Though he recognizes the relativity of morals, he does not treat this as warrant for complete relativism. The fact is that Bonhoeffer's central concern in this lecture is to define Christian ethics such that it can avoid completely succumbing to relativity. Thus Bonhoeffer actually has two motives for writing and delivering this lecture: to acknowledge the obvious implications of historical consciousness upon moral axioms and also to free Christian ethics from morality and thereby guarantee its universality and absolutely binding nature. Bonhoeffer's twin motivations can be seen when he asks,

> What about the idea of a so-called Christian ethic? Are these two words not perhaps intrinsically utterly incompatible, "Christian" and "ethic"? Does such a combination not secularize the idea of what is Christian? Does the so-called Christian ethic not thereby become merely one alongside others, one of many, perhaps a bit better or even a bit worse, but in any case not drawn wholly into historical relativity? . . . Hence talking about a Christian ethic while at the same time maintaining the exclusive claim of such an ethic will apparently be an extremely awkward undertaking.[11]

10. Dietrich Bonhoeffer, "Basic Questions of a Christian Ethic," in *Barcelona, Berlin, New York: 1928–1931*, ed. Clifford Green, trans. Douglas W. Stott, vol. 10 of *Dietrich Bonhoeffer Works* (Minneapolis: Fortress, 2008), 360.

11. Bonhoeffer, "Basic Questions," 362. Bonhoeffer's way of posing this question bears strong resemblance to Ernst Troeltsch's own way of posing the question. See Kerr, *Christ, History, and Apocalyptic*, 23–28. Their solutions to the problems of historicism may differ, but their starting points are remarkably similar.

Because Bonhoeffer recognizes the relative nature of ethics, the "Christian" and the "ethical" are fundamentally "incompatible." But it is also clear that by making such a distinction, Bonhoeffer wants to maintain the "exclusive claim" of Christian ethics. Rather than being a total relativist, then, Bonhoeffer wants to articulate a solid foundation for Christian ethics. He cannot base Christian ethics upon the universal or absolute nature of moral imperatives, however, because moral imperatives are relative by their very nature. Something else must provide a bulwark against the force of relativity.

Bonhoeffer articulates the basis of Christian ethics not in terms of universal moral standards but in terms of God's action. The Christian message cannot be treated as merely a moment in the many moments of time and place, history, and culture, but as the event to which all moments and all times, all histories, and all peoples are related. But morals cannot possibly provide the necessary comprehension of all things relative. Thus Bonhoeffer cannot follow the lead of many down through the Christian centuries who have articulated the faith primarily in moralistic terms. On the contrary, Bonhoeffer looks to a more recognizably Protestant approach. He frames the issues involved in reference to the classic theme of God's justification of the ungodly. God and God's action can do what morality could not do. As Bonhoeffer states,

> Christianity and ethics represent two entities that at first are not entirely compatible and in fact are quite disparate. And why? Because Christianity speaks of the exclusive path from God to human beings from within God's own compassionate love toward the unholy, the sinful, while ethics speaks of the path from human beings to God, about the encounter between the holy God and the holy human being, in other words, because the Christian message speaks of grace, while ethics speaks of righteousness. Because there are innumerable paths to God, there are also innumerable ethics. But there is but one path from God to human beings, and that is the path of love in Christ, the path of the cross.[12]

Here Bonhoeffer is requisitioning the doctrine of justification and using it to solve the problem posed by moral relativity. He is doing so by applying the traditional Lutheran distinction between law and gospel to the distinction between the relative and the absolute. The law could not justify humanity before God; it could only accuse humanity before God and thus demonstrate our own limitations. But the gospel as God's free forgiveness and acceptance of the sinner does what the law could not do: reconcile us to God. Just so, the relativity of morals cannot provide the necessary basis for Christian ethics; it

12. Bonhoeffer, "Basic Questions," 362–63.

can only demonstrate the futility of such an endeavor. But while the relativity of morality fails to become truly absolute, the absolute and unlimited nature of God's grace succeeds. Thus God's action in Christ is the only basis for Christian ethics.[13]

One of the most important yet misunderstood aspects of Bonhoeffer's ethics is its aversion to abstract ideas and values. Bonhoeffer's recognition of moral relativity is one reason for this aversion. The other reason for Bonhoeffer's rejection is rooted in his understanding of the ethical encounter. For Bonhoeffer, human relationships and the relationship between God and humanity are dynamic, historical, and unique. God encounters the human being and summons him or her to responsible action. So also, human beings encounter one another, impinge upon each other's freedom, and elicit responses of responsibility and reciprocity. These encounters—between divine and human, human and human—are ongoing. This is the "historical" aspect of ethical encounter to which Bonhoeffer sometimes alludes.[14] Because one encounters human beings in a variety of circumstances, and because any given human being is always changing, an ethical encounter between two persons is always unique. And because the interaction between two persons is an interaction between different wills, two different centers of subjectivity, the ongoing history of encounter is dynamic rather than static. It can only be described in existential rather than essentialist terminology.[15]

By defining the ethical encounter in terms of unique moments between persons, Bonhoeffer must necessarily reject moral absolutes or universal principles of moral action. The unique can never be predicted or replicated. But a morality that is based upon absolutes and universals can only comprehend the recurrent and the predictable. It cannot, therefore, accurately describe or prepare one for the actual moments of ethical encounter that will happen throughout one's lifetime and in interaction with others. Thus, moral absolutes

13. Bonhoeffer is clearly thinking in terms of the relationship between gospel and law as defined by the Formula of Concord. And yet it is important to point out that his understanding of the law is not in keeping with the Lutheran tradition's emphasis upon the "third use of the law," which highlights the positive role of the law in shaping Christian action. Furthermore, Bonhoeffer's presumption of moral relativity stands in contrast to the Reformers and thus complicates the second use of the law (to make people aware of sin and dependent upon God's grace). For the classic Lutheran position on the relationship between law and gospel, and on the threefold use of the law, see *The Book of Concord: The Confessions of the Evangelical Lutheran Church*, trans. and ed. Robert Kolb et al. (Minneapolis: Fortress, 2000), 581–91.

14. By "historical" Bonhoeffer does not mean historiography but the time- and place-boundedness of human being. See Bonhoeffer, *Sanctorum Communio*, 48–49.

15. Bonhoeffer's understanding of the ethical encounter is based upon his definition of the "social ontic-ethical basic-relations of persons" as defined in *Sanctorum Communio*. See Bonhoeffer, *Sanctorum Communio*, 40–50, esp. 48–50.

are problematic not only because morality is relative but also because human interaction is both contextual and fundamentally unique.

The primary reason Bonhoeffer invokes the doctrine of justification within the context of his deconstruction of moral absolutes is to highlight God's action. The primary point is not, therefore, to speak of God's forgiveness, even though Bonhoeffer obviously does not wish to question humanity's guilt and need for divine pardon. Rather, Bonhoeffer wishes to draw attention to God's active word, God's self-communicative activity to humanity. At the heart of Bonhoeffer's theology is his insistence upon God's free, spontaneous action. This model of God contrasts, for instance, with a divinity that is defined primarily in terms of abstract being or as inert substance. God is here understood as living being, as a center of subjectivity engaging other subjectivities, that is, human beings. While humanity, with all of its moral action, strives in vain toward God, like Icarus toward the sun, God engages humanity on God's own terms and in God's own freedom to save and deliver. Another problem with morality, then, is its insufficiency vis-à-vis God's action. But it is the problematic relationship between morality and God that suggests a solution to the problem of relativism.[16]

Bonhoeffer defines the foundations of Christian ethics not in terms of universal moral absolutes but in terms of God's unique action. What morality could not do, God's command can accomplish. A morality of law, imperative, and value belies the uniqueness of human activity as well as the relative nature of morals. But by emphasizing the unique and unrepeatable command of God, and the equally unique response of the human actor obedient to that command, Bonhoeffer preserves the uniqueness of human action and therefore dispenses with moral absolutes. Bonhoeffer replaces the usual grounding of Christian ethics in moral absolutes and universal norms with the spontaneous freedom of God's actions through commanding.

Bonhoeffer's use of the divine command in the Barcelona lecture is related to his emphasis upon ethical encounter. Just as human beings encounter other

16. This emphasis upon God's action, subjectivity, and freedom is hardly unique to Bonhoeffer. Bonhoeffer is clearly dependent upon the work of Karl Barth and the broader intellectual milieu Barth represented. Bonhoeffer's manner of emphasizing the divine command shares much in common with Barth's ethics. But it is also similar to other, less prominent figures, such as Emil Brunner. For a readable overview of Barth's significance in German theological circles, see Gary Dorrien, *The Barthian Revolt in Modern Theology: Theology Without Weapons* (Louisville: Westminster John Knox, 2000). Though written much later than 1929 when Bonhoeffer gave the Barcelona lecture, for an example of Barth's distinctive approach to Christian ethics, see Barth, *The Doctrine of God*, ed. G. W. Bromiley and T. F. Torrance, trans. G. W. Bromiley et al., vol. 2 of *Church Dogmatics* (1957; repr., Peabody, MA: Hendrickson, 2010), 509–781. For an approach to ethics similar to Bonhoeffer's but published only a few years after Bonhoeffer's lecture, in 1932, see Emil Brunner, *The Divine Imperative*, trans. Olive Wyon (Philadelphia: Westminster, 1947), esp. 122–31.

human beings, so also God encounters human beings. This emphasis upon God's action and God's encounter with the human subject is what prevents Bonhoeffer's ethics in the Barcelona lecture from becoming totally relativistic.

God, by definition, is not subject to the historical process of which morality is a product. For this reason God is the only real and foundational basis for Christian ethics. Furthermore, the God of whom Christian theology speaks is a God who, though not a product of history, acts in and upon history. For this reason God's action can be ethically significant while at the same time transcending fixed moral categorization.

By basing Christian ethics in God and God's action, Bonhoeffer has made good on his intention, evident at the very beginning of his lecture, to acknowledge the relative nature of morals. On the other hand, despite his aversion to moral absolutes and his description of Christian ethics as "beyond good and evil," Bonhoeffer is obviously very concerned about grounding and securing real human action within history. This is partly the reason why he searches for a proper foundation for Christian ethics to begin with.

Bonhoeffer's practical concerns, as well as his use of the divine command to secure human action, can be seen when he says, "The ethical can be found only within the bonds of history, in concrete situations, in the moment of the divine call, of being addressed, of the demands made by concrete crisis and the concrete circumstances of decision, of a demand I must answer, to which I am accountable."[17] Here Bonhoeffer talks about an accountability to a concrete demand that is contextually apropos. It is important to stress, furthermore, that this accountability is directed toward the "divine call" that reaches the human person through concrete interactions with others. The divine command encountering the human person is the guarantee of the ongoing validity of Christian ethics no matter the culture, time, or social situation of its recipients.

Before moving on to discuss Bonhoeffer's emphasis upon Christian freedom, it is necessary to further specify the nature of God's command. Bonhoeffer's notion of God's command employs a model of a God who is absolutely free. God's command must be based on nothing other than God's own freedom. God commands when God chooses. God commands what God chooses. What this means is that what God may have commanded in the past is no longer necessarily what God will command in the present or in the future. God is free to command what God will. Thus God is not bound to any morality or any moral dictate, not even to the past record of God's commanding in the Old and New Testaments, that is, the "laws" or "commandments" found in the canon.

17. Bonhoeffer, "Basic Questions," 377.

Bonhoeffer's particular way of using God's command further undermines the use of moral principles. As Bonhoeffer suggests, "There is absolutely no possibility for establishing universally valid principles, since each individual moment lived before God can confront us with completely unexpected decisions."[18] Because God's command is always free from conditioning, it always appears to its recipients as completely new. Nothing in prior experience could prepare a human being for God's command, even if nothing will be the same subsequent to its occurrence. It is this stress upon the unique actuality of God's command that both grounds Christian ethics and preserves it from the normal relativity of morals. Because the divine command cannot be anticipated, it is not subject to the dynamic that makes moral principles possible or useful. After all, the reason moral principles are used, or come into being in the first place, is that human conduct is in some ways regular and predictable. One given phenomenon in place and time is not genuinely new but analogically related to phenomena that came before it and will come afterward. If this were not the case, then moral principles or any rules of conduct, in addition to being irrational, would never be useful enough to be remembered. If every situation were *sui generis*, there would be no need for rules or guidelines of human behavior. In fact, the possibility of their arising in consciousness would never occur. But because God's command is *sui generis*, it can provide the only adequate foundation vis-à-vis moral similitude.

The fact that God is absolutely free to command anything at any time has direct bearing upon Bonhoeffer's model of human freedom in the Barcelona lecture. Bonhoeffer suggests that for the Christian person to be genuinely free, he or she must be free from moral principles. This is a consequence of both the constraints of morality as well as the absolute nature of God's freedom to command.

Morality binds and shapes human action. But freedom is not bondage but liberation from that which binds. For this reason authentic Christian freedom, on the one hand, and obedience to a moral dictate, on the other hand, are fundamentally at odds for Bonhoeffer, at least at this early stage of reflection. As Bonhoeffer says,

> Those who surrender their freedom also surrender their status as Christians. Christians stand in freedom, without any backing, before both God and the world; they alone bear the entire responsibility for how they will deal with this gift of freedom. Through precisely this freedom, however, Christians become creative in their ethical actions. Acting according to principles is unproductive

18. Ibid., 368.

> and merely reflects or copies the law. [But] Christians draw the forms of their ethical activity out of eternity itself, as it were, put these forms with sovereignty in the world, as deed, as their own creations born of the freedom of God's children. Christians create their own standards for good and evil.[19]

The juxtaposition between morality and Christian freedom could not be more strongly stated. Bonhoeffer goes so far as to say that obedience to a concrete commandment is an abrogation of Christian freedom. Clearly, then, true freedom and directing oneself by a moral dictate are utterly incompatible.

Bonhoeffer's understanding of Christian freedom is obviously a mirror image of his model of God's freedom. God is absolutely free from morality, and so Christian freedom must be free from morality as well. Nevertheless, the Christian's free action is not absolute. Though Christian action is not conditioned by the constraints of any divine or human law, it is not a self-willed freedom. In fact, though Bonhoeffer does not spell this out in any great detail, the freedom of the Christian is dependent upon God's freedom. It is the moment of encounter between God and a human being that enables the freedom of the human respondent.

All that has been said so far about divine and human freedom invites the question of whether morality, as normally understood, has any positive role to play for Bonhoeffer in shaping Christian action. On one hand, it seems that morality of any kind cannot be a positive thing for Bonhoeffer because both Christian freedom and divine freedom transcend morality altogether. On the other hand, Bonhoeffer's definitions of Christian and divine freedom depend logically upon some underlying degree of regularity in human conduct. God's command as absolutely new obviously does not impinge upon something that is already always absolutely new—otherwise the notion of "impinge" loses all meaning. The regular exists, in other words; and its existence is predicated upon the disruptive actuality of God's command, which disruption in moral regularity creates Christian moral transcendence. If God's command is disruptive, then there must be something to interrupt prior to God's doing so. Morality must exist for there to be bondage to it. The alternative would be both a complete relativity in human action in the created order paralleled by a divine power that has no reason to encounter human beings at all. Bonhoeffer's notions of divine and human freedom, then, seem to imply the presence of moral norms of some sort shaping human behavior.

Yet this particular problem, the necessary presence and thus relative value of normal morals in the face of God's command, does not seem to have become

19. Ibid., 366.

obvious to Bonhoeffer at this point in his theological development. Be this as it may, Bonhoeffer does presuppose some degree of validity for morality without explicitly acknowledging the fact. This must be the case, because he speaks quite plainly in his lecture about different ethics shaping their respective national cultures.[20] He acknowledges the fact of human righteousness even though denying its Promethean pretensions.[21] And though he defines Christian action as essentially "beyond good and evil," this does not mean that there is no good and evil.[22] It just means that Christian action is not Christian on the basis of its being good or evil. Thus Bonhoeffer simply presumes that there are forms of ethical discourse that bind and shape human affairs, just as he must also presume that morality has some degree of positive value in human society.

However, the fact that Bonhoeffer seems to evade implicit evaluation of morality as it is commonly understood and frequently employed does call for explanation. And although there may be several different reasons explaining this lacuna, sufficient reason for it can be found in consideration of Bonhoeffer's primary goal in the Barcelona lecture. Bonhoeffer's central focus throughout the lecture is to define the essence of particularly Christian ethics. That essence is the unique ethical encounter between God's free command and the human actor's obedient response. The fact that Bonhoeffer defines this as the essence of Christian ethics makes sense of his dismissive attitude toward moral norms. The abstract norm cannot capture the eventuality of unique ethical encounter. But the fact that Bonhoeffer defines this encounter as the essence of Christian ethics does not mean that all moral norms are thereby abolished or that there are no meaningful distinctions to be made between what is moral and what is immoral. The essence of Christian ethics is not the moral as such but the freedom of God's command and the Christian freedom to act that it engenders. But that does not mean that Bonhoeffer denies the reality of what is not essentially Christian about morality. Nor is it his fundamental contention to deny how morals shape human behavior, even Christian behavior. Bonhoeffer means that the essence of Christianity, of the Christian God, of particularly Christian action, cannot be the morality of the action but the freedom of the act. It is not what God commands that is essential; it is the freedom with which God commands. It is not what Christians do but the freedom with which they do it that constitutes the action as Christian.

Bonhoeffer's discussion of New Testament ethics in the Barcelona lecture is really only understandable given his emphasis upon the uniqueness of God's

20. Ibid., 359.
21. Ibid., 362–63.
22. Ibid., 363.

command and the relative nature of normal morals. This is because Bonhoeffer's treatment of New Testament ethics is simply a consequence of his prior understanding of morality. What he has said about morality in general also applies to the New Testament; and so, the relationship between God's command and New Testament ethics is the same as that between God's command and any ethic whatsoever.

Bonhoeffer defines the essence of Christian ethics in terms of the unique moment of divine and human freedom. Morality as such is not unique but general, governing as it does the regular in human affairs. This definition of morality guides Bonhoeffer's discussion of New Testament ethics. So one of his tasks in the lecture is to argue against the supposed uniqueness of New Testament morality. Jesus's love command, for instance, was shared by both the Jewish rabbi Hillel as well as the Roman philosopher Seneca. The primary point in making this comparison is to demonstrate the nonuniqueness of New Testament morality. Once this is recognized, it becomes apparent that New Testament morality cannot provide the type of foundational basis for Christian ethics that Bonhoeffer desires.[23]

The obvious question that arises in response to Bonhoeffer's understanding of New Testament law is prompted by its conspicuous presence in the New Testament. If the essence of distinctively Christian action is an existential freedom that transcends morality, then what role, if any, does New Testament morality play in shaping Christian action? Bonhoeffer's answer to this question mirrors the question, posed to him above, concerning the relative value of morality.

First, Bonhoeffer insists that it is not the substance of New Testament law that is distinctively Christian. The essentially Christian in New Testament commandments is, rather, the formal claim of the divine command expressed through them and the humble submission before God such a command requires from its human recipients. It is the divine "thou shalt" in the commands and the human reply of "I will" that constitutes the essence of New Testament morality. The essence of New Testament morality is the recognition of the continual need of Christians to submit to God because God alone is the only valid basis for faithful human action. Obviously, this formal definition of New Testament ethics is nothing other than a transposition of what constitutes the ethical encounter between persons.

This formal definition of New Testament law implies that the actual content of New Testament morality is not morally binding. Indeed, the more one interprets New Testament law in terms of its content and seeks to be obedient

23. Ibid., 364–65.

to a specific commandment, the less likely one's action is specifically Christian. The specifically Christian is, as has already been seen, moral transcendence, and so obedience to the content of New Testament law is not freedom but the grossest form of bondage. As Bonhoeffer says, "The familiar radical edge that Jesus' demands have acquired derives from the radical renunciation of one's own person and one's own will that is required of Christians in ethical decisions before God. But not every one of Jesus' behavioral rules is valid for us; merely imitating them would be slavish and unfree."[24]

Now, however, there is another question related to Bonhoeffer's understanding of New Testament ethics. Just because the definitively Christian act is freedom from morality does not necessarily mean that New Testament morality has no role to play in shaping Christian behavior. This follows from the fact that Bonhoeffer seems to recognize a relative value for morality in general, even though he sees morality as accidental to what is essential to Christian action. New Testament morality, like all morality as such, does have some effect upon human affairs. However, this is a purely formal sort of recognition on Bonhoeffer's part, and it plays no role in prescribing what God commands. Because Bonhoeffer has already defined the essence of Christian action as freedom from morality, there is no way for him to adjudicate between the conflicting claims that different moral values pose to the moral agent. New Testament morality and any morality whatsoever stand in the same relationship to God's command and to Christian freedom.

The Application of Bonhoeffer's Barcelona Ethics to Concrete Cases

Bonhoeffer's Barcelona lecture on Christian ethics is composed of two roughly equal portions. The first portion of the lecture specifies the foundations of Christian ethics, foundations that are meant to guide concrete action. Naturally, then, in the second part of the lecture Bonhoeffer turns his attention to concrete cases of ethical decision. It is here, in the second half of the lecture, that Bonhoeffer applies ethical theory to actual practice. More specifically, in this part of the lecture Bonhoeffer deals with moral quandaries. It deals with situations in which a moral agent must choose between two or more courses of action. The fact that a decision is involved points to the various possibilities of action that could be taken. If there were only one possible course of action, there would be no need to make a decision. The reason such a decision presents a moral quandary, furthermore, is because all the options contemplated seem to involve moral ambiguity. If one option is clearly morally superior to the

24. Ibid., 368.

others, there would be no real quandary of a moral nature; the option closest to the norm of action is obviously the right decision.

One reason an ethicist might engage in analysis of hypothetical moral quandaries is that it allows him or her to show how a particular moral norm resolves difficult decisions. The underlying assumption is that the moral norm with the power to resolve the most quandaries is both more useful and perhaps more valid than any alternative. Or, in more complicated cases, situations involve a multiplicity of competing value judgments; discussion of a quandary allows the ethicist to articulate a hierarchy of values by which to adjudicate the course of action that is right in relation to those alternative actions that involve moral determinates of lesser value. This is precisely what Bonhoeffer is doing in the second half of his lecture, and yet this procedure seems to fly in the face of Bonhoeffer's previously stated ethical foundations.

Bonhoeffer's ethical foundations specify that it is only God's command in the concrete situation that decides the course of action to be taken by the human agent concerned. Because God's command is absolutely free, it cannot be specified in relation to any moral norm prior to its eventuality. Only after God's command has been given can the moral agent know what the justified course of action is. When this particular model of God's free command is applied to the present context, it becomes clear that only God can resolve moral quandary. God does this by commanding what God chooses to command. This command, in turn, liberates the agent from the constraints of morality to issue in genuinely free action. But if it is the case that only God can resolve moral quandaries, then what is the point of discussing them at all? If the decision is not one's own to make ahead of time, then why discuss the options that might be available before they actually present themselves?

Bonhoeffer seems aware of the contradiction involved here between the practice of moral analysis and his insistence upon the undetermined moment of free action. This is why he prefaces the second part of his lecture with a qualification. He says, "All we can do [in the following discussion] is examine the concrete situation of decision and point out one of the possibilities for decision that emerges there. The decision demanded in reality, however, must be made in freedom in the concrete situation by the individual involved."[25] In other words, he means only to discuss the various options available in any given moral decision and leave it up to the actual moment of decision to justify the action that will be taken. Nevertheless, though this is what Bonhoeffer intends to do, it is not what he actually ends up doing. He goes well beyond a

25. Ibid., 369.

discussion of various possibilities to clearly specify one option among several to be morally appropriate. This becomes particularly apparent when Bonhoeffer discusses war and pacifism.

A number of concrete moral questions constitute the last section of Bonhoeffer's lecture—for example, war, economics, truth telling, and sexuality. The present discussion will focus only upon the first of these questions, for two basic reasons. Although Bonhoeffer discusses several different moral quandaries, he resolves all of them in very similar ways. There is enough similarity in his analysis of them all to make four separate discussions unnecessary. The second reason is related to the question of Bonhoeffer's ethical development. Bonhoeffer will address the issue of war in all three periods of his ethical writing—in the Barcelona lecture, in *Discipleship*, and finally in *Ethics*—in very different ways. Focusing specifically on his treatment of war in the Barcelona lecture will provide a basis for comparison with how this issue is treated in Bonhoeffer's subsequent ethical works. In other words, focusing on the specific question of war contributes the most to advancing our overall argument.

Bonhoeffer frames his discussion of moral quandary in terms of broader conflict between various facts or metaphysical factors within history. The discussion of war, for instance, involves the conflict between historical development, on the one hand, and love of others, on the other hand. Love of all people, which Christ clearly commands, inevitably conflicts with the duty of personal and national self-actualization. The quandaries that Bonhoeffer examines, then, are ongoing precisely because reality is in conflict with itself.

The conflictual nature of reality apparent in Bonhoeffer's dualistic thinking at this early stage of his ethical thought clearly depends upon the traditional Lutheran distinction between the two realms, or orders, of church and world. One of the hallmarks of this model is its ability to comprehend two very different and often conflicting moralities applicable to two spheres of life. It is true that this is just one of the possible ways in which two-kingdoms thinking can function. But it is the most pertinent use when it comes to Bonhoeffer's thinking in the Barcelona lecture. He is clearly working with two very different sets of moral imperatives with distinct realms of applicability.[26] On the one hand, Christ's commands in the Sermon on the Mount, about loving one's enemies, turning the other cheek, forgiveness, and so on, are the basis for rejecting war and violence.[27] This set of morals corresponds roughly to the

26. See Clifford Green's editorial comments in ibid., 368–69n25.
27. Bonhoeffer, "Basic Questions," 370.

realm of the church or, alternatively, of the spiritual. The other set of morals stems from God's providential call for people groups to conquer and expand.[28] When Bonhoeffer talks about the conflict between "historical development" and "love," then, he is talking about the conflict between a duty to one's own people and the alternative duty to love one's enemies during a time of war.[29] This conflict is shaped, in turn, by a presupposed conflict between the two realms of church and world.

During a time of war, whether defensive or offensive, one's own nation enters into violent conflict with another. It is precisely at this time that the moral quandary begins for the Christian person. One is torn between the call of Christ to love the enemy and the call to defend and/or advance the prerogatives of one's nation or people. This moral conflict can be resolved only by choosing to prioritize one moral value over the other. The Christian is forced to choose in such a situation precisely because his or her responsibilities are divided by conflicting allegiances to both church and world. The only question is how the Christian should resolve the conflict and on what basis.

The irony is that Bonhoeffer is very clear on how this particular quandary should be resolved. When faced with such a decision, one should decide to defend one's own people rather than abandon them in their hour of need. In other words, Bonhoeffer makes a definite choice between moral options. He justifies prioritizing allegiance to the world over the church's call to peace. As he says,

> The situation seems clear to me. In such cases, I no longer have the choice between good and evil; regardless of which decision I make, that decision will soil me with the world and its laws. I will take up arms with the terrible knowledge of doing something horrible, and yet knowing I can do no other. I will defend my brother, my mother, my people, and yet I know that I can do so only by spilling blood; but love for my people will sanctify murder, will sanctify war. As a Christian, I will suffer from the entire dreadfulness of war. My soul will bear the entire burden of responsibility in its full gravity. I will try to love my enemies against whom I am sworn to the death, as only Christians can love their brothers. And yet I have to do to those enemies what my love and gratitude toward my own people commands me to do, the people into whom God bore me. And finally I will recognize that Christian decisions are made only within the ongoing relationship with God, within a constantly renewed surrender of oneself to the divine will. I can rest assured that even if the world does violence to my conscience, I can make only one decision, namely, the one to which God

28. Ibid., 373.
29. Ibid., 369.

> leads me in the sacred hour of encounter between my will and God's will, in the hour in which God conquers my will.[30]

Now, from this quotation Bonhoeffer's own position regarding participation in war and conscientious objection is quite clear. He decides against conscientious objection to war, against pacifism, and for participation in a war effort on behalf of one's people. What is far from clear, however, is how anything he says about this decision for war can be reconciled with his explicitly stated ethical foundations.

The first half of the Barcelona lecture articulates a moral theory that is incompatible with the resolution of moral quandary prior to the moment of decision. But the second half of the lecture proceeds to resolve a number of moral quandaries by prioritizing the Christian's worldly responsibilities over the moral claims of the churchly realm. Thus Bonhoeffer's discussion of moral quandary seems incompatible with his fundamental moral convictions. How should this incompatability be explained or understood?

A number of inconsistencies are readily apparent. The first problem is that Bonhoeffer is working with two incompatible definitions of New Testament law in the Barcelona lecture. When he talks about New Testament law in the first half of the lecture, he argues that New Testament commandments are but past instances of God's commanding. They do not specify what God will always command, and so they cannot be used to specify the course one's actions should take in the future. This seems to imply that it is not possible to become guilty by disobeying a specific New Testament commandment. But when Bonhoeffer suggests in the second half of the lecture that the commandment to love one's enemies creates a moral quandary with respect to one's commitments to one's own people, he is clearly treating the New Testament as a source of morally binding value. Now, of course, they are not binding enough to actually dictate one's action. But they obviously have some sort of morally binding status. Otherwise Bonhoeffer would not have treated the moral quandary as morally ambiguous at all. The value of one's people would simply have outweighed the value of one's allegiance to enemy love in the hierarchy of values; and one would have been justified in going to war without the least bit of guilt. But the fact that guilt is involved when one has chosen to participate in war demonstrates the binding character of New Testament law despite Bonhoeffer's theoretical words to the contrary. Thus Bonhoeffer's formal and nonbinding interpretation of New Testament law is inconsistent with its use to create moral quandary.

30. Ibid., 372.

Moral quandary can only occur when two binding moral values conflict. But if New Testament law does not bind, then it cannot conflict with any other moral value.

The second problem, closely related to the first one, is that Bonhoeffer ends up utilizing a value that transcends the moment to determine the way in which the moral quandary should be resolved. In the first part of the lecture Bonhoeffer said that only God's command within the moment of decision itself could dictate the course of action that must be taken. But this insistence upon the moment seems incongruous with the resolution of moral quandary in the second part of the lecture. If the moral quandary is resolved prior to the moment of decision, then it appears to be specifying the course God's command will take despite not knowing what will actually happen. Or even more problematic, resolving moral quandaries appears to be dictating the course God's command must take and thus usurping God's absolute freedom to command. As Clifford Green points out,

> Allegedly only the moment itself, the concrete situation, can determine which decision a person should make. Nonetheless Bonhoeffer relates the decision [whether or not to participate in war] to a criterion that transcends the situation, namely ties to one's own people (*Volk*), as a divine order. In time of war, when one's own blood relatives are threatened, these ties cause the Christian notion of love of one's neighbor . . . to recede.[31]

In other words, despite Bonhoeffer's critique of moral principles, his contextualism, and his emphasis upon God's freedom to command, he ends up using a principle that transcends the moment and limits God's freedom so that he can highlight the super-value of the *Volk* and justify one's duty to commit violence in their name.

The fact that there are some serious problems with Bonhoeffer's Barcelona lecture on Christian ethics is both difficult to understand and all too understandable. Bonhoeffer composed and delivered this particular lecture shortly after completing a dissertation that demonstrates the highest degree of intellectual skill and logical rigor. Thus it is somewhat perplexing, given the caliber of Bonhoeffer's gifts, that his ethics lecture should contain such obvious internal discrepancies. On the other hand, the lecture is a first attempt by a young mind delivered to the members of the church he was serving, and not in a lecture hall in Berlin. Given these circumstances, it is not surprising that Bonhoeffer's thinking would show signs of haste and contain some logical inconsistencies.

31. See editorial footnote 32 in ibid., 371.

Despite the ambiguity that the Barcelona lecture on ethics contains, however, many of its themes will continue to play a role in Bonhoeffer's later work in both *Discipleship* and *Ethics*. This does not mean, though, that the transition from the lecture to subsequent ethical reflection is a smooth one. Indeed, the transition is not smooth at all. There is a shift in thinking after the Barcelona lecture that influences the nature and consequences of Bonhoeffer's ethics; and this shift must be taken seriously if the true development of Bonhoeffer's ethics is to be understood.

The nature and significance of this shift in thinking will be the subject of the next chapter, and so there is no reason to develop it further at this point. The only task that now remains is to explore in what ways Bonhoeffer's Barcelona lecture could have been made internally consistent. The reason for engaging in such hypothetical reconstruction is twofold. First, exploring how the Barcelona lecture could have been "fixed" gives some sense of how Bonhoeffer's ethics may have developed if he had not experienced a significant spiritual and theological transformation several years after the lecture was given. Exploring the path not taken will make apparent the contrast with Bonhoeffer's postconversion thinking. Second, exploring the ways in which these internal contradictions could have been resolved may shed light upon some of what Bonhoeffer will later say in *Ethics*. There are significant themes in the Barcelona lecture that seem to reappear in Bonhoeffer's final thoughts on Christian morality; and this reappearance invites the question of how *Ethics* is related to the Barcelona lecture. Does *Ethics* represent a reversal of the shift in thinking that made *Discipleship* possible, as the dominant account of Bonhoeffer's ethical development would suggest? Or is it possible to detect the impact of *Discipleship* upon the very themes *Ethics* seems to share with the Barcelona lecture? Answering these questions can only be simplified if the inherent possibilities of the Barcelona lecture are more fully explored.

At the heart of Bonhoeffer's positive theological agenda in this early lecture is his concern to stress the freedom of God from moral constraints, divine freedom that results in the moral freedom of distinctively Christian action. His aversion to principles, his insistence that Christianity lies beyond both good and evil, his peculiar understanding of New Testament ethics—all these elements serve his insistence on Christian freedom. But the fact that Bonhoeffer seems to know ahead of time what God will command in a given context tends to subvert the very possibility of the moral freedom Bonhoeffer intends to uphold. Though he suggests that participation in war is a free option, the fact that he discusses only that one option leads the critical reader to assume that he implicitly suggests it is the only option. But if this is the case, then Bonhoeffer's freedom is just another form of bondage. He has liberated his listeners from bondage to New Testament law only to bind them all the more to the nation-state and the cultural milieu such a nation embodies.

In order for Bonhoeffer to be more consistent with his own definition of Christian freedom, he has two options. The first option is that he could discuss both conscientious objection and participation in war as potentially valid avenues of Christian action in response to the quandary brought upon by a war. If a Christian could be free to go to war, there is no reason why a Christian could be free to abstain from going to war. It is just as possible for God to lead one into freedom to make war as it is for God to free one from war. If distinctively Christian acts are marked by freedom rather than any particular behavior, then these two behavioral responses could be equally legitimate, equally "sanctified." If being a Christian means transcending good and evil, and thus being open to subjection to guilt no matter the action undertaken, then there is no way anyone can prescribe what a Christian should do in the event of war. The second option open to Bonhoeffer, in a bid for greater consistency, would simply be a refusal to discuss any concrete action at all as a possibility of resolution to moral quandary. There is, after all, an infinite number of possibilities God may prescribe in response to any given moral quandary. Just to leave particular action in God's hands seems the safest form of moral casuistry given the inexplicable nature of God's freedom.

In summary, Bonhoeffer's understanding of God's action in Christ should have led him to affirm the freedom of the moral agent to bear the guilt incurred by both moral options he provides in the cases he discusses. The fact that Bonhoeffer does not discuss the possibility of conscientious objection and actually validates the possibility of participation in war demonstrates his failure to pursue his insights to their logical conclusions. The second major inconsistency in Bonhoeffer's lecture concerns his contradictory uses of New Testament law. As has already been mentioned, the lecture seems to undermine the capacity of New Testament commandments to form human behavior while at the same time suggesting that disobedience to them makes one guilty. In order to be more coherent, Bonhoeffer must either admit that the New Testament laws are morally binding or exclude the possibility that New Testament laws could create a moral quandary. He cannot have it both ways.

One possible resolution to this particular impasse is to recognize that the binding nature of New Testament law is relative to God's command. Bonhoeffer's primary concern in the Barcelona lecture is defining the essence of divine and human action in terms of freedom. God's freedom is absolute, and so God can command anything. Morality, including New Testament morality, cannot determine God's command. So also, human freedom is determined only by God's command and not by obedience to moral imperatives. But this understanding of divine and human freedom does not absolutely exclude the possibility that any given New Testament law could become morally binding. It just defines under what conditions New Testament law or any form of morality may become morally binding: by being commanded by God in the moment of decision.

God's freedom to command entails the possibility of God's use of past law, past instances of his commanding, to express God's will for the present circumstances. There is no reason, then, to exclude the possibility that God may command one to love one's enemies. But the absolute nature of God's freedom also means that there is no reason to exclude the possibility that God may command one to do the exact opposite or something else entirely.

The recognition that God may command one to do exactly what God commanded others to do in the New Testament is completely consistent with the above suggestion regarding moral quandary. Just as Bonhoeffer should include the possibility of conscientious objection in addition to his recommendation of military participation in his discussion of the moral quandary posed by war, so also Bonhoeffer should admit that God's command may be entirely consistent with what God has commanded in the Scriptures, even if it is still the case that God can also use any moral sentiment whatsoever, canonical or extracanonical, to accomplish God's will on earth. God may wish one to kill in the name of one's *Volk*, or God may command one to resist killing in their name. Only God knows what God will command. In the meantime, it is only appropriate to be prepared for anything, or to be prepared to be caught quite unprepared for the new thing God's freedom for us shall entail.

Looking Ahead: The Transition to *Discipleship*

The primary goal of this chapter and the next two is to demonstrate the continuities between *Discipleship* and *Ethics* over against alternative readings that contrast the two. However, because these continuities can best be ascertained by being placed within the broader lineage of Bonhoeffer's ethical development, it has been essential to begin at the beginning. Because *Discipleship* represents a significant departure from the Barcelona lecture, it is only natural to examine the lecture first so that the true differences and similarities can be most easily seen.

That Bonhoeffer's basic starting point in the Barcelona lecture will undergo radical reinterpretation is indisputable. Even interpreters who stress the discontinuities between *Discipleship* and *Ethics* agree that the Barcelona lecture contains some ideas Bonhoeffer will never again espouse.[32] First and foremost among these is his dependence upon German nationalist sentiment. And it is also indisputable that while Bonhoeffer endorses war and participation in war in the Barcelona lecture, he will later reverse this judgment and become a self-described pacifist. This reversal in practical ethics is no more evident than when comparing the lecture with *Discipleship*, because the latter clearly upholds nonresistance and enemy love as natural consequences of obedience to Jesus.

But what is often overlooked by interpreters, despite their acknowledgment of Bonhoeffer's change on the issue of violence and recrimination, is the depth of the change involved. Not only does Bonhoeffer become a pacifist—not only does his mind change regarding practical applications in morals, in other words—but his work in *Discipleship* also demonstrates a fundamental reworking of the very foundations of Christian ethics. Bonhoeffer's entire system of thinking is drastically altered just a few short years after having lectured in Barcelona, and the depth and significance of these changes makes it unlikely that they are anything other than irreversible.

If the Barcelona lecture represents Bonhoeffer's first attempt at Christian ethics, then his work in *Discipleship* is not merely his second attempt; it is also a milestone in his ethical thinking that will continue to influence all subsequent attempts on his part to think through the basics of Christian ethics. Thus analysis of the relationship between the Barcelona lecture and *Discipleship* will provide a helpful key for interpreting the ambiguous relationship between *Discipleship* and *Ethics*, a relationship that is contested and which these chapters attempt to clarify.

32. Rasmussen, *Dietrich Bonhoeffer*, 96–100.

5

Obedience to Jesus Christ

Narrating God's Command in Bonhoeffer's Discipleship

Shortly after he gave his lecture on Christian ethics to the congregation in Barcelona, Bonhoeffer returned to his native Germany. But even before this, Bonhoeffer had begun work on his second dissertation, a work that would significantly influence his understanding of Christian ethics, altering the ethical judgments and conclusions he had just presented to his congregation. While back in Berlin, working as a teaching assistant for a new professor of systematic theology, Bonhoeffer labored on the manuscript, submitting it to the faculty in the spring of 1930,[1] later revising it for publication in September 1931 as *Act and Being*.[2] After finishing his dissertation and giving an inaugural lecture before the Berlin theological faculty, Bonhoeffer again left Germany, this time to study in New York City. Bonhoeffer spent a year in postdoctoral study at Union Theological Seminary, giving the occasional lecture and touring the continent. It was in the United States that Bonhoeffer encountered

1. Clifford J. Green, "Editor's Introduction to the English Edition," in *Barcelona, Berlin, New York: 1928–1931*, ed. Clifford Green, trans. Douglas W. Stott, vol. 10 of *Dietrich Bonhoeffer Works* (Minneapolis: Fortress, 2008), 12–17.

2. Wayne Whitson Floyd Jr., "Editor's Introduction to the English Edition," in *Act and Being: Transcendental Philosophy and Ontology in Systematic Theology*, ed. Wayne Whitson Floyd and Hans-Richard Reuter, trans. Martin Rumscheidt, vol. 2 of *Dietrich Bonhoeffer Works* (Minneapolis: Fortress, 1996), 5.

the compelling Christian pacifism of Jean Lasserre, the deeply convicting faith and witness of the African American church he was a part of, and the emphasis on social justice some of his American professors and colleagues both espoused and embodied. Bonhoeffer's time spent in the United States was a rich experience that influenced him both personally and theologically.[3]

Bonhoeffer returned to Germany in June of 1931. Between 1930 and 1932 he experienced a profound personal reorientation that affected his life and changed his ethical convictions irrevocably.[4] In fact, as has been described in the first chapter of this book, this particular set of experiences is so significant that Bonhoeffer talks about it in terms of a personal conversion to authentic Christian faith. In a recollection of these experiences, Bonhoeffer emphasizes how the "Bible, especially the Sermon on the Mount," freed him and turned his life "sharply around," and entailed "the renewal of the church and the pastorate" as well as a new commitment to the Christian pacifism he had previously "combated passionately."[5] The book *Discipleship*, published in 1937, is just one of the fruits of Bonhoeffer's newfound commitments.[6] His life spent living and working together with other members of the Confessing Church in Nazi Germany is another.

Discipleship is one of the most significant textual milestones in the development of Bonhoeffer's theological ethics. *Discipleship* is significant partly because it expresses most fully Bonhoeffer's own peace convictions, convictions that show to what degree his ethical thinking changed since giving his first lecture on the topic. As the previous chapter detailed, Bonhoeffer's 1929 Barcelona lecture on Christian ethics constitutes both a repudiation of pacifism and an endorsement of participation in war. But in less than ten years after expressing these convictions, Bonhoeffer publishes a book in which he completely contradicts them. The clear calls for nonresistance and enemy love he voices in *Discipleship* stand in the strongest possible tension with his previous thoughts on war and violence.

Because of the obvious contradictions between the Barcelona lecture and *Discipleship* pertaining to war and peace, it is only natural that those seeking to explain how Bonhoeffer got from one position to the other would focus primarily on his pacifism. But such a focus, as self-evident as it seems, can

3. Green, "Editor's Introduction," 19–35. Also see chapter 1 above.

4. Ibid., 34–43. Also see chapter 1 above.

5. Clifford J. Green, *Bonhoeffer: A Theology of Sociality*, rev. ed. (Grand Rapids: Eerdmans, 1999), 141, emphasis omitted.

6. Geffrey B. Kelly and John D. Godsey, "Editors' Introduction to the English Edition," in *Discipleship*, ed. Geffrey B. Kelly and John D. Godsey, trans. Barbara Green and Reinhard Krauss, vol. 4 of *Dietrich Bonhoeffer Works* (Minneapolis: Fortress, 2000), 2.

also prove misleading if Bonhoeffer's "pacifism" is isolated from the broader stream of theological and ethical development that makes this commitment intelligible. Narrowly focusing on the development of Bonhoeffer's pacifism can, of course, yield insight into the possible biographical sources of his pacifism or locate the point in time when Bonhoeffer's pacifism becomes subsequently ingrained in his life and thought. But such an endeavor cannot explain why certain biographical sources affected Bonhoeffer's thinking and others did not, nor can it explain to what degree Bonhoeffer's conversion was, in fact, preceded by the very theological vocabulary that made it possible to describe the shifts. Furthermore, when Bonhoeffer's pacifism is isolated from the broader theological developments of which it is a part, it is easily treated as an extraneous idea as easily espoused as it is transcended and overcome. In other words, treating "pacifism" as its own cause rather than the effect of a much larger shift in Bonhoeffer's thought structure is an interpretive act that already presupposes that Bonhoeffer's commitment to peace is short-lived because it was never truly his own. Such a reading does not attend carefully enough to the actual nature of the theological shifts that occur to make *Discipleship* possible. Another reading is necessary.[7]

In order to make sense of Bonhoeffer's ethical development, including the emergence of his pacifism, it is vital to see the relationship between the Barcelona lecture on Christian ethics and *Discipleship* in terms of a transition from one theological whole to another. The endorsement of violence in the first thought structure is merely a part of the overall ethical and theological foundations that legitimate such an endorsement. So also, the peace ethic in *Discipleship* makes sense only within the framework of its own foundational theological commitments. The question, then, is not how to relate violence to peace, the endorsement of war to committed pacifism, but how to relate one systematic theological whole that justifies violence to another systematic whole that condemns it. Only once the transition between these two mutually inconsistent works is made comprehensible can one understand both the fact of Bonhoeffer's pacifism and the reasons behind its emergence (as well as its endurance).

The first section of this chapter will highlight the theological factors that explain the transition from the Barcelona lecture to *Discipleship* by drawing

7. Larry Rasmussen's discussion of Bonhoeffer's "pacifism" in *Dietrich Bonhoeffer: Reality and Resistance*, though helpful in many ways, is also misleading because it does not carefully and patiently attend to the larger developmental, conceptual whole of which Bonhoeffer's pacifism is a part. Rasmussen's discussion thus misunderstands Bonhoeffer's pacifism as well as the nature of Bonhoeffer's ethical development. See Larry Rasmussen, *Dietrich Bonhoeffer: Reality and Resistance* (1972; repr., Louisville: Westminster John Knox, 2005), 94–126.

upon Bonhoeffer's work in *Act and Being*. The rest of the chapter will then proceed to examine *Discipleship* in its own right to ascertain how the previously assessed theological factors—the factors that caused the transitional development—are employed in this second attempt at Christian ethics. The successful examination of both theological wholes in their own right—as expressed in the Barcelona lecture in the previous chapter and *Discipleship* in the latter part of this chapter—as well as the causal factors that explain the transition between them, will yield an accurate narrative of Bonhoeffer's ethical development. In the process, it will also shed light upon the character of Bonhoeffer's pacifism.

Act and Being: Incarnating Divine and Human Freedom

Bonhoeffer's primary concern in *Act and Being* is to substantiate the social nature of the church and the historical nature of human being, both of which are described in *Sanctorum Communio*.[8] He intends to do this while preserving the fundamental insistence, which he learned from Karl Barth, that human knowledge of God is only possible as a result of God's self-disclosure. Bonhoeffer is convinced that in order to do full justice to human life as it is actually lived and experienced, it is necessary to effect a relative rehabilitation of certain categories of theological and philosophical thought implicitly neglected by Barth's early theology.[9] Bonhoeffer suggests that by consistently neglecting the categories of being (continuity, duration, history, development, etc.), Barth's theology demonstrates an untenable preference for categories of act (sheer eventuality, contingency, eternity, immediacy, etc.), which frustrates the continuity of human life and thus the divine/human integrity of the incarnation. Bonhoeffer's solution, in light of Barth's overdependence upon categories of actuality, is to see both act and being in the person of Jesus Christ.[10]

8. Dietrich Bonhoeffer, *Sanctorum Communio: A Theological Study of the Sociology of the Church*, ed. Clifford J. Green, trans. Reinhard Krauss and Nancy Lukens, vol. 1 of *Dietrich Bonhoeffer Works* (Minneapolis: Fortress, 1998).

9. Reference to Barth's "early theology" is meant to name a phase in Barth's theological development that Barth later eschewed as inadequate before beginning again on his mature *Church Dogmatics*. I leave unanswered the question of whether Barth's theology ever demonstrates the corrections that Bonhoeffer, in *Act and Being*, found necessary.

10. This particular reading of *Act and Being* is convincingly presented by Michael DeJonge. See Michael P. DeJonge, "The Fact of the Person of Jesus Christ: Dietrich Bonhoeffer's *Act and Being*" (PhD diss., Emory University, 2009). A revised version is published as *Bonhoeffer's Theological Formation: Berlin, Barth, and Protestant Theology* (Oxford: Oxford University Press, 2012). Much of the basic framing of the discussion in this section is drawn from DeJonge's work.

This integration of act and being in the person of Jesus Christ may seem, at first, to be only tangentially related to the question of Bonhoeffer's ethical development post-Barcelona. But this is far from correct. On the contrary, this christological integration is the primary theological catalyst for the ethical transition from Barcelona to *Discipleship*, and is also the foundational theological basis for his renewed *Discipleship* ethic. Because this is the case, an examination of Bonhoeffer's christological integration of act and being in the person of Jesus Christ will shed considerable light upon the nature of Bonhoeffer's theological development, the meaning of *Discipleship*, and the nature of his pacifist commitments.

Through the lenses provided by his focus on Christology in *Act and Being*, Bonhoeffer gains the theological tools necessary both to deconstruct the ethics of the 1929 Barcelona lecture and subsequently to articulate his new ethics in *Discipleship*. Bonhoeffer's conversion supplies the necessary personal or spiritual impetus for such an ethical revision, but the conceptual tools for this revision are already available to him in *Act and Being* by 1930. Bonhoeffer's thinking subsequent to his conversion draws upon his work in *Act and Being*, putting such work into critical dialogue with the tenets of the Barcelona lecture on Christian ethics, critical dialogue that eventually yields a theological ethic of peace in *Discipleship* that stands in stark contrast to his earlier ethic of justified violence.[11]

Bonhoeffer's mature christological integrationism is articulated in dialogue with many theologians, ethicists, and philosophers within the pages of *Act and Being*. But there is one particular interlocutor, the theologian Karl Barth, whose own early theology is of special interest. This is because Bonhoeffer's critical interactions with Barth's early theology expose a weakness in Barth's thought that Bonhoeffer seeks to resolve through his own christological integrationism. More specifically, in *Act and Being* Bonhoeffer finds Barth's model of divine and human freedom to be especially troublesome insofar as it frustrates any coherent theological account of either divine consistency or faithful human continuity.

Bonhoeffer's critique in *Act and Being* of Barth's models of divine and human freedom is particularly germane to the question of Bonhoeffer's ethical development, because the same critique can also be applied with equal force to Bonhoeffer's own model of divine and human freedom in the Barcelona lecture on Christian ethics. Bonhoeffer's critical distance from Barth's theological model of freedom is thus simultaneously a distancing from his own previous

11. *Discipleship* is of course about much more than peace—in fact, it is fundamentally about Jesus Christ. The emphasis on peace is both because of the emphasis of the present book and for purposes of clarity regarding the shift in Bonhoeffer's theological ethic from Barcelona to *Discipleship*.

theological convictions as well. Thus exploring Bonhoeffer's critical interactions with Barth will shed light upon the transition away from the ethics of the Barcelona lecture. Yet it is just as important to recognize that Bonhoeffer's christological solution to what he finds problematic in Barth's early theology is also relevant in explaining the nature of Bonhoeffer's ethical development. Just as Bonhoeffer's critique of Barth is also an act of theological self-criticism, so also Bonhoeffer's christological integrationism is a resolution of problems found in Barth and Bonhoeffer's own previous system of theological ethics. As such, this christological solution grounds *Discipleship*, Bonhoeffer's second major work of theological ethics.

What is it about Barth's early theology that Bonhoeffer finds so problematic? To determine this we must consider Barth's solution to the problem of theological knowledge. The theology of Karl Barth, from its genesis to its culmination, is a theology of revelation. Despite his various shifts, Barth is always focused on the possibility, nature, and effects of God's revelation. Although it is true that Christian theology has always presupposed a doctrine of divine revelation, it is Barth more than anyone else before him who most thoroughly explores the logic of divine revelation to engage contemporary questions about the veracity of theological language. Barth's focus on God's revelation, then, is not merely a repetition of a traditional theological commonplace. Rather, it is best understood against the backdrop of the critical questions posed to the Christian faith by Barth's own intellectual milieu, most especially those questions prompted by Immanuel Kant's (1724–1804) critique of metaphysics.[12]

Though Kant's critical philosophy has affected theology in more ways than one, it is his account of human knowledge and the critical impact of that account upon metaphysics that is of most significance in relation to Barth's theological agenda. Human knowledge, according to Kant, is the product of an interaction between the object experienced and the subject that experiences. Sense impressions must enter consciousness in order for there to be experience of an object, and to do so these impressions must be organized by certain innate properties or presuppositions. These innate categories are not the result of experience but are what the mind must presuppose in order to experience anything at all.[13] The fact that all knowledge is a product of

12. Situating Barth vis-à-vis Kant is obviously not the only way to explain Barth's significance, but it is one that is especially helpful when it comes to relating Barth's early theology to Bonhoeffer's critical appropriation of the same, evident in *Act and Being*. The following discussion draws from the insights of Charles Marsh. See Charles Marsh, *Reclaiming Dietrich Bonhoeffer: The Promise of His Theology* (New York: Oxford University Press, 1996), 7–15.

13. Frederick Copleston, *Modern Philosophy: From the French Enlightenment to Kant*, vol. 6 of *A History of Philosophy* (1964; repr., New York: Doubleday, 1994), 235–72. W. T. Jones,

the interaction between the knowing subject and the objects known makes human knowledge of divine reality problematic. The exercise of pure reason is only valid when there is some object to be known. But because divine reality must necessarily transcend objects of awareness to remain divine, the divine cannot be known through pure reason. This categorical limitation frustrates any attempt to know whether a divine reality corresponds to the human mind's notions of divinity. Because human cognition is conditioned by the finite, any ideas it may conceive about the divine are purely speculative and thus not subject to empirical verification.[14]

Kant's critical reflections upon human knowledge prompt him to question the epistemic value of metaphysics. Kant is convinced that the primary reason that metaphysical questions are answered in such a variety of mutually contradictory ways is because the questions themselves lead human reason beyond its arena of competence.[15] The problem with metaphysics down through the ages, then, is that it presumes to extend pure reason beyond the realm of human knowledge.

Kant's epistemology challenges traditional metaphysical speculation. It also poses serious problems to theology, and this is especially true when it comes to the doctrine of divine revelation. If all of the mind's acts of perception are constituted and made possible by finite categories that exist within the mind's own subjective composition, and if God exists outside of and independent from the world's finite categories, then knowledge of God is impossible.[16] This may not have been what Kant himself intended when writing his *Critique of Pure Reason*, but it is difficult to see how Kant could have prevented these consequences without ignoring the implications of his own thinking. At any rate, it is very clear that Kant's epistemology problematizes religious knowledge in ways not previously entertained. The biblical narratives, for instance, clearly presume that the God of the universe has spoken to humanity. God has communicated God's will to God's chosen people Israel and then through the life, death, and resurrection of Jesus Christ. Not only so, but traditional theology has always assumed that the Scriptures themselves are also divine communications to humanity. Kant's epistemology is problematic to the degree that God and religious objects cannot be brought together or related in

---

Kant to Wittgenstein and Sartre, vol. 2 of *A History of Western Philosophy*, 2nd ed. (New York: Harcourt, Brace & Jovanovich, 1969), 37–43.

14. Copleston, *Modern Philosophy*, 283–306; Jones, *Kant to Wittgenstein and Sartre*, 55–62.

15. Immanuel Kant, *Critique of Pure Reason*, trans. J. M. D. Meiklejohn (1787; repr., New York: Barnes & Noble, 2004), xvii.

16. This description of the effect of Kant's epistemology upon metaphysical questions is sufficient for the purposes of this chapter but is also a generalization. For a more expanded and nuanced discussion, see Copleston, *Modern Philosophy*, 277–307.

a positive way. God's reality transcends both the words of Scripture and the human mind that perceives them. Thus Kant's epistemology calls into question both the veracity of metaphysical speculation and the Scriptures as God's communication to humanity.[17]

One way to respond to Kant's epistemology is to question the gulf he posits between God and worldly categories, reasserting the traditional analogical relationship between the two.[18] Another, completely opposite strategy is to work within the limits imposed upon theology by Kant's epistemology. This approach would accept Kant's critique of metaphysics and relegate the referents of theological language to the mundane realms of moral practice or religious feeling.[19] And yet neither of these two theological responses to Kant describes Barth's distinctive approach to the question of divine knowledge. Barth's theological approach cuts across the horns of the Kantian epistemological dilemma to insist upon the possibility of divine knowledge. Barth's insistence upon the possibility of divine reality respects rather than questions the epistemological gulf between human perception and divine reality to which Kant rightly draws attention. Thus Barth's response to Kant presents a novel approach to theology to Barth's contemporaries—including the young Dietrich Bonhoeffer.

Barth's solution to Kant's transcendentalism is both simple and elegant in the way it uses Kantian epistemology to call into question Kant's own agnosticism. Barth agrees with Kant that God is not simply an object of human awareness. God's existence and nature are not merely "given" to human awareness in the sense that an object is given and perceptible. Barth surmounts the Kantian impasse between God's transcendence and the object-boundedness of the human mind by insisting upon God's revelation through God's Word. Barth does not take issue with the epistemological gulf that Kant sees between the transcendent God and the limited cognition of the human mind. But while Barth agrees with Kant that the human mind cannot itself bridge this gulf, he does not believe God is constrained by the same limitations. God does what human capacity cannot do by bridging the gulf between divinity and humanity from the divine side rather than from the human side.

17. Helmut Thielicke, *Modern Faith and Thought*, trans. Geoffrey W. Bromiley (Grand Rapids: Eerdmans, 1990), 285–88.

18. For the early Barth's rejection of analogy, see Karl Barth, "Fate and Idea in Theology," in *The Way of Theology in Karl Barth: Essays and Comments*, ed. H. Martin Rumscheidt, trans. George Hunsinger (Allison Park, PA: Pickwick, 1986), 32–42. For commentary and context, see Gary Dorrien, *The Barthian Revolt in Modern Theology: Theology without Weapons* (Louisville: Westminster John Knox, 2000), 92–96.

19. Examples of this approach include Albrecht Ritschl and his student Wilhelm Herrmann, the second of whom was one of Barth's teachers. For a helpful discussion of both Ritschl's and Herrmann's Kantianism, see Thielicke, *Modern Faith and Thought*, 324–44.

Barth's theology appropriates the Kantian model of the subject in order to both respect and transcend Kantian transcendentalism. The subject is that which knows the object known, and as such can only know what is proper to its own capacities. This is the basic insight of Kantian epistemology. But Barth suggests that, while it may be true that God is not an object nor deducible on the basis of our knowledge of objects, if God is understood as the divine subject, then human knowledge of God is made possible on the basis of God's subjectivity, which acts to reveal God's self to humankind. Thus, according to Barth, and in agreement with Kant, God is not a thing. But over and beyond Kant, Barth suggests that God is a center of agency. God is a self or a subject, and because this is the case, God can be known when God speaks God's Word.

God's freely given, revelatory Word speaks to human beings from the realm of divine transcendence by coming into contact with the object world of sensory experience. Because this Word is always *God's* own, it is transcendent; but because it is God's *Word*, it makes itself known. Because God makes God's self known in God's Word, human beings can hear that Word and know God through that Word. The Word is revelation of God inasmuch as it is God's Word; and inasmuch as God's Word is God's, it is revelation of God to humanity. The possibility of knowledge of the divine is grounded in God's capacity alone rather than in human capacity. The priority of God's grace in the economy of salvation applies with equal force to the economy of revelation. It is only God's way to us that makes possible our way to God. God's revelation grants to humanity the possibility of true knowledge of God, and in so doing exposes the inherent limitations of the human mind to arrive at divine knowledge through its own reflection.[20]

Humanity is always creating its own concepts of the divine, as Feuerbach famously posited. But according to Barth, this does not mean that there can be no true knowledge of God. What it does mean is that the theologian who wishes to ground human knowledge of the divine cannot do so with reference to human capacity. Therefore Barth's account of God as the subject that encounters human reality is one that portrays God engaging the human mind and will as an alternative reality to be reckoned with, acknowledged, and obeyed; and it is in this way that Barth intends to overcome the constraints of human knowledge and guarantee the possibility of God's communication to humanity. God judges the objectifying capacity of the human mind by revealing not another human construct but God's very self. This act of divine self-disclosure abolishes and reconfigures human objectifications of the divine.

20. The idea that Barth appropriates the notion of subjectivity to beat Kant at his own game is not my own. See Marsh, *Reclaiming Dietrich Bonhoeffer*, 11.

The epistemological acts of the human mind in creating divine objects can only be subverted by the act of another active mind, the divine mind. And though God as subject encounters human subjects through objects of perception, God can never be exhausted by the objects through which this encounter occurs.

Bonhoeffer's interest in Karl Barth's theology began while he was still a student at the University of Berlin, and it continued until his death.[21] Part of Bonhoeffer's attraction to Barth had to do with the intellectual alternative that Barth provided for theology at the time. By grounding theology in divine revelation rather than in human reason or religious affections, Barth was countering an already venerable German theological tradition, a tradition in which both Barth and Bonhoeffer were educated and from which both later distanced themselves.[22] But though Bonhoeffer was strongly influenced by Barth and would take occasion to explain or defend Barth and the theological movement Barth represented, Bonhoeffer's appreciation did not come without reservation.[23]

There is much in Barth's theological approach with which Bonhoeffer agrees and so integrates into his own theology. Most important, Bonhoeffer shares Barth's insistence upon locating the possibility of divine knowledge with God alone rather than in human reason. But while Bonhoeffer agrees in general with Barth's insistence upon the necessity of divine revelation for human knowledge of God, he finds fault with some of the consequences Barth draws from this necessity. More precisely, the manner in which Barth describes God's revelation to humanity is problematic from Bonhoeffer's point of view, because it trades upon distinctions that frustrate any account of God's revelation persisting through space and time. A positive theological account of such persistence is necessary given both the historical continuity of human existence and so also of God's incarnation in Jesus Christ.

Bonhoeffer notices that because Barth's theology eschews any categories of "being," opting instead for categories of "acting," Barth cannot really make good on his insistence that knowledge of God is made known in Jesus Christ or that such knowledge shapes human identity. In general terms, Barth's solution to the Kantian dilemma causes as many problems as it solves. It problematizes objects of revelation vis-à-vis God, and it subjectivizes God's action and human

21. Eberhard Bethge, *Dietrich Bonhoeffer: A Biography*, rev. ed., ed. Victoria J. Barnett (Minneapolis: Fortress, 2000) 67, 73–77, 843.

22. The fact that Bonhoeffer was interested in Barth even while studying at the University of Berlin is evidence enough of his critical (but appreciative) distance from theological liberalism. For an eminently readable description of Barth's turn against liberal theology, see Dorrien, *Barthian Revolt in Modern Theology*, 14–46.

23. Dietrich Bonhoeffer, "The Theology of Crisis and Its Attitude toward Philosophy and Science," in *Barcelona, Berlin, New York*, 462–76.

knowledge of that action. These problems contribute to Barth's so-called actualism, which is precisely the presenting problem that Bonhoeffer finds so disagreeable with Barth's theology. Why? Because it disrupts human continuity.

Bonhoeffer's refinements of Barth's emphasis upon God's subjectivity in *Act and Being* are meant to correct flaws in an approach to theology that Bonhoeffer otherwise affirms. Bonhoeffer is just as convinced as Barth that God's special revelation through God's subjectively given Word is the necessary and only condition for human knowledge of God. He does not, then, attempt to appropriate realist philosophy for theology or rehabilitate a doctrine of general revelation. He is equally convinced with Barth that unaided human reason cannot obtain true knowledge of God. Furthermore, despite the fact that Bonhoeffer finds Barth's employment of divine subjectivity to be unbalanced, he does not dispense with Barth's emphasis upon God's subjectivity altogether. What he does do is show that Barth's emphasis upon God's subjectivity results in a formal model of divine freedom, which frustrates the way God's acts of revelation are related to duration—time, space, and historical life.

Bonhoeffer's solution is not to eliminate the emphasis on God as subject or the contingency of God's revelation through acts. However, rather than concentrate on God as subject, Bonhoeffer focuses on the person of God—act and being united in the God-man, Jesus Christ. Thus God's acting is not occasional but has decisively entered history in the person of Jesus. The freedom of God is no longer formally defined but made flesh and given substantive definition in Christ. The redemptive power and persuasive, commanding Word of God are expressed through this God-man. Shape is given to divine continuity through the incarnation. God has entered history. In Christ God has created a people—a body of Christ—who have historical continuity, who occupy space and time. Bonhoeffer will rhetorically, in subsequent writings, attempt to name the ways in which God has acted to reconcile the world to himself, has spoken with clarity through commands, has created a people—and yet is still the living God, a transcendent Subject whose act and being are revealed in the God-man, Jesus Christ.

Whether Bonhoeffer realized that he was engaging in self-critique by critiquing Barth is not entirely clear. In all likelihood he was not fully aware of the potential impact upon his own prior theological ethics that his new definitions of freedom possessed until sometime after his experiences in New York City, perhaps even during the process of working on *Discipleship*. But this is to be expected. After all, it is often the case that ideas new to a mental web of knowledge fail to reach their full critical and reconfiguring potential until well after the time when they were initially absorbed. The latent potential in new ideas is, no doubt, exacerbated if—as is the case with Bonhoeffer—the initial target of one's criticism is another person's system of ideas rather than one's own. Be this as it may, the question of when or whether Bonhoeffer ever gained critical distance from the development of his ethical thought to realize the actual sources of its shift cannot be the burden of the present discussion. As interesting as this particular biographical question may be, it is not as important to answer for present purposes as it will be to note both the fact of these new definitions of freedom and the significant impact they have upon the course of Bonhoeffer's ethical development.

Discipleship: Narrating God's Command

Now that the transition between the Barcelona lecture on ethics and *Discipleship* has been described, it is appropriate to examine *Discipleship* in more detail and on its own terms. The discussion of the transition to *Discipleship* has been conducted on a formal conceptual level in order to understand the nature of Bonhoeffer's theological development. Specifically, Bonhoeffer's redefinition of divine freedom as freedom in and for duration has the capacity to drastically reorient his theological ethics. The following examination of *Discipleship* will demonstrate to what degree and in what ways Bonhoeffer draws upon this theological reorientation to read the Jesus story and articulate its moral significance for Christian discipleship.

With the argument of *Act and Being* in mind, our analysis here concentrates on the model of christological authority Bonhoeffer employs in *Discipleship*. What we will find is that the distinctive approach to morality in *Discipleship* depends on the christologically specified definition of divine freedom in *Act and Being*. This focus will further describe the nature of the transition from the Barcelona lecture to *Discipleship* and will pave the way for a subsequent discussion of concrete ethics.

The opening chapter of *Discipleship* is well known. There the usually irenic Bonhoeffer unleashes a polemic against what he calls "cheap grace."[24] The obvious moral passion of this chapter, stressing as it does the importance of distinctive Christian patterns of living, should be evidence enough that Bonhoeffer has done some significant rethinking of his 1929 ethical positions. But what is most important to realize about his polemic against "cheap grace" for the current discussion is its deconstructive character. It prepares the way for Bonhoeffer's own positive theological agenda.

One of Bonhoeffer's most important insights in *Discipleship* is his definition of the nature and effects of Christ's authority. His understanding of

24. Bonhoeffer, *Discipleship*, 43–56.

Christ's authority will allow him to depict God's subjectivity in the Christ narratives. It will allow him to appropriate Jesus's commandments and obedience to them as theologically suitable. But Bonhoeffer's particular model of Jesus's authority will also enable him to bring together grace and obedience without succumbing to either legalism or antinomianism. Thus his model of Christ's authority is the positive insight that his deconstruction of "cheap grace" anticipates.

At times, however, Bonhoeffer's emphasis upon Christ's authority has not been adequately understood or fully appreciated. Clifford Green, for example, thinks that Bonhoeffer's emphasis upon the authority of Christ can sometimes verge on divine coercion. Green argues that the "power Christ" in *Discipleship* can all too often oppress the disciple and preclude a healthy sense of selfhood.[25] As helpful as Green's work is in emphasizing the relationship between Bonhoeffer's earliest theology and *Discipleship*, his work falls short when it comes to articulating the nature and function of Christ's authority. This is unfortunate, because once one grasps the full significance of Bonhoeffer's portrayal of Christ's authority, it becomes clear that Bonhoeffer's intention is to show how Christ's authority properly construed is the source of existential liberation rather than domination. Bonhoeffer's emphasis upon the true nature of Christ's authority is meant to bring together the call to obedience and the grace of the one calling.

In *Discipleship* Bonhoeffer describes Christ's authority by contrasting two models of Christ's identity, one focusing on his moral teaching and the other focusing on his personhood. The first is insufficient, as it misconstrues Jesus's identity by reducing Jesus's commandments to abstract moral principles. This procedure tends to articulate the significance of Jesus's moral teachings without reference to its foundation in Jesus's identity as God's freely contingent self-revelation. In other words, what is important in this false reading are the universally valid moral dictates Jesus expresses rather than his personhood. The second model of Jesus's authority, the one Bonhoeffer leverages in *Discipleship*, grounds Jesus's commandments in the person of Jesus and his distinct history. Because Jesus Christ is God's selfhood in the flesh, it is possible to do justice both to the validity of Jesus's concrete commandments *and* to the dependence of those commandments upon his person for their authorization and legitimacy.

Bonhoeffer begins his description of Christ's call to discipleship by quoting Mark 2:14, where the obedient response of the disciple Levi is so immediate it

25. Green, *Bonhoeffer*, 170–79. This is, no doubt, due to Green's preoccupation with the psychological backdrop of *Discipleship*. But as helpful and accurate as his account may be, a strictly theological account of the genesis of *Discipleship* is also necessary.

seems inexplicable. Contrary to interpretations of this passage that make the immediate act of obedience more humanly reasonable, Bonhoeffer grounds the nature of the obedient act in Jesus Christ himself. As Bonhoeffer notes,

> The text is not interested in psychological explanations for the faithful decision of a person. Why not? Because there is only one good reason for the proximity of the call and the deed: Jesus Christ himself. It is he who calls. That is why the tax collector follows. This encounter gives witness to Jesus's unconditional, immediate, and inexplicable authority. Nothing precedes it, and nothing follows except the obedience of the called. . . . Jesus calls to discipleship, not as a teacher and a role model, but as the Christ, the Son of God.[26]

In this passage Bonhoeffer is determined to maintain the inexplicable nature of Levi's obedience to Christ by rooting it in the "unconditional, immediate, and inexplicable authority" of Jesus. The distinction between two very different models of Jesus's authority—between Jesus "as a teacher and a role model" and "Jesus as the Christ, the Son of God"—is meant to maintain the inexplicable nature of Jesus's call as well as the inexplicable nature of Levi's obedience. But this raises the question: why is it so important that both Jesus's authority and the disciple's obedience be inexplicable in the first place?

There are two answers to this question, the first one more obvious than the other. The easy answer is that Bonhoeffer is attempting to do justice to the close proximity between Jesus's "call" and the resulting "obedience" that is present in the text. The text itself offers no explanation other than Jesus's authority as the Son of God. After all, the New Testament contrasts Jesus's own power with the authority of the "scribes" and other religious teachers.[27] But to reference the New Testament alone gives only a partial explanation for Bonhoeffer's emphasis.

Bonhoeffer's emphasis upon the inexplicable nature of Christ's command and the disciple's response, though serving what is portrayed in the New Testament, is best understood against the backdrop of his critical appropriation of Barth's theology of revelation. Bonhoeffer critiqued Barth's concept of divine freedom because it was too formal and not sufficiently defined by the incarnation. But this critique does not mean Bonhoeffer finds fault with Barth's emphasis upon God's divine subjectivity and God's freedom in revelation. The fact is that Bonhoeffer, in *Act and Being*, wanted to do justice both to God's subjective freedom and to God's subjective freedom making itself known in Jesus Christ. This intention is also at work in *Discipleship*.

26. Bonhoeffer, *Discipleship*, 57.
27. See Matthew 7:29, Mark 1:22, and Luke 4:32 for examples of this contrast.

In focusing on the Jesus narrative for ethics, Bonhoeffer does justice to God's *subjectivity* in Christ while also doing justice to God's subjectivity making itself *available* in Christ. The former emphasis is evident when Bonhoeffer roots Christ's commands in Christ's person. The latter emphasis is evident when he stresses that it is precisely in Christ's commands that his person is made known. Thus it is of vital importance for Bonhoeffer that Jesus's commandments not be abstracted from Jesus's person as God's self-disclosure. Emphasis upon the second of the two christological models is meant to preclude objectification of Jesus's commandments into reified moral principles. Such objectification is inevitable, however, if Christ's commandments are interpreted independent of his selfhood. The implication, then, is that understanding Jesus merely as a role model or teacher cannot do justice to the necessary bond between Christ's person and Christ's commandments.

Just as there are two models of Christ's authority, one problematic and one sound, there are also two corresponding models of moral anthropology. If understanding Jesus simply as a teacher runs the risk of abstracting his teachings from his person, the corresponding moral anthropology is a form of moral idealism. If, on the other hand, one sees that Jesus's commandments are inextricably bound to his person, then the corresponding moral anthropology is personal obedience. As Bonhoeffer says,

> Discipleship is commitment to Christ. Because Christ exists, he must be followed. An idea about Christ, a doctrinal system, a general religious recognition of grace or forgiveness of sins does not require discipleship. . . . One enters into a relationship with an idea by way of knowledge, enthusiasm, perhaps even by carrying it out, but never by personal obedient discipleship. . . . Discipleship is bound to the mediator, and wherever discipleship is rightly spoken of, there the mediator, Jesus Christ, the Son of God, is intended. Only the mediator, the God-human, can call to discipleship. Discipleship without Jesus Christ is choosing one's own path. It could be an ideal path or a martyr's path, but it is without promise. Jesus will reject it.[28]

Here Christ as person is being contrasted with Christ as notion or idea. Bonhoeffer's preference is obviously for the former. Because Christ is a person, he calls others to himself in an obedience that is bound to his person, to his own subjective reality as God in the flesh. Such personal obedience is *obedience* because it is Christ who calls the person to follow; it is *personal* because it entails being bound to Christ's person, and it affects the obedient one at the very core of his or her identity. Interestingly enough, however, Bonhoeffer is

28. Bonhoeffer, *Discipleship*, 59.

not denying that moral idealism can actually look like personal obedience to Christ insofar as it can "carry out" the concrete implication contained in a moral idea. But the crucial distinction is that such an action is not a response to Christ's call but a choice to affirm an idea or principle. Closely related to this distinction is the fact that action in response to an idea is a self-chosen agenda. Moral idealism grows out of one's own self-affirmation, while obedient discipleship is, by definition, self-sacrificial.

It is important to note Bonhoeffer's distinction between true and false models of christological authority as well as the respective distinctions between true and false moral anthropologies, because these distinctions are what make it possible to bring together God's grace and human obedience to Christ's commandments while doing justice to both God's initiative and human response. The correct model of Christ's authority does justice to God as the divine subject, to Christ as God's freedom incarnate, and thus to God as the source of grace and empowerment. The model of Christ as moral teacher cannot do justice to the disciple's dependence upon God's gracious and active call in Jesus because it has employed an objectified and objectifying model of God and of Christ. This model has reduced Christ to an object of reflection and his teachings to lifeless moral values, principles, or absolutes. Thus this model, in not doing justice to Christ as the divine subject incarnate, reduces obedience to legalism and Christian freedom to self-grounded moral striving.

Here it is clear, in the distinction between the two models of Christ's authority, that Bonhoeffer has borrowed from Barth's emphasis on divine subjectivity. From Barth, Bonhoeffer realized that God is the divine subject and not an inert object of human investigation. God, by God's very nature, cannot become a mere object of human reflection. God is always ever the subject of God's own disclosure, the source of his being known by those who receive revelation. By taking over this model of divine subjectivity and applying it to Christ, Bonhoeffer has found a way to ground discipleship not in human action but in God's own prior action to and for the disciple. He has used Barth's model of divine subjectivity and applied it to axiology. What this implies, however, is that Christ's call to discipleship is itself an act of grace. Christ's call is costly, but it is full of grace nonetheless. But, by implication, the alternative model of Christ as teacher or role model, and the resulting moral idealism in response to such a model, precludes God's active call through Christ and thus fails to be an act of salvation for the human subject.

In addition to bringing God's grace and human action together by grounding axiology in God's subjectivity, Bonhoeffer also brings together God's subjectivity and soteriology. Because God is active in Jesus Christ, Christ's call is both an act of grace and an act of salvation without failing to be a call to obedience at the same time. But in order to better appreciate how discipleship can be God's act of salvation for the believer, it is important to understand Bonhoeffer's model of the sinful self and God's subjectivity as the solution to the self's dilemma. Only then can Bonhoeffer's insistence in *Discipleship* upon the subjectivity of Christ and personal obedience be fully appreciated.

At the center of Bonhoeffer's soteriology is his insistence that the unredeemed human subject is trapped inside itself. Such entrapment are isolating. If humanity is left to its own devices, then atomization and solipsism is the result. No true human community can be derived simply from a conglomerate of isolated and isolating egos. Furthermore, this dilemma cannot, by definition, be overcome by human effort alone. The acts of the self-enclosed subject, whether reflective or outwardly embodied, can only ever be acts of further egoism; and so such acts can only ever result in further isolation from others and further alienation between others.[29]

The only solution to the dilemma of human sin, given this particular model, is personal encounter with God's own Word. Only as the sinful human subject is encountered by God's own self can the human person be liberated from his or her own self-imposed entrapment, isolation, and the resulting alienation from others. Neither human action nor human reflection is capable of delivering humanity from its self-enclosed isolationism. Only by being actively confronted by the living God can the human self be freed from its distorted selfhood to be free for God and for others in community. Self-reflection is not the solution to the problem; it only compounds the problem. As Bonhoeffer says in his lecture before the Berlin theological faculty, "It is not in self-reflection that the human being understands himself but in the act-of-relating to God, that is, only where the person genuinely stands before God."[30] Indeed, "the human being understands himself only in his act-of-relating to God, which only God can establish."[31] Only in being encountered from outside one's own epistemological world can one be liberated. Thus only in encounter with the living God, and God's divine subjectivity, can the human being's own self be fractured and transformed.

It is important to notice how Bonhoeffer brings together epistemology, soteriology, and axiology not only in the above quotations but also throughout the whole of *Discipleship* by trading upon the distinction between God as subject and God as object. Bonhoeffer focuses so much on distinguishing

29. For a fuller treatment of Bonhoeffer's model of guilty humanity, see Green, *Bonhoeffer*, 48–52, 71, 76–83.

30. Dietrich Bonhoeffer, "The Anthropological Question in Contemporary Philosophy and Theology," in *Barcelona, Berlin, New York*, 405.

31. Ibid.

one model of Christ from another, for instance, because it is our perceptions of Christ that shape our relating to him. God's subjectivity in Christ means that God is not under our epistemological control. But it also means that God in Christ is not under our moral control either. God in Christ must ever be perceived as the subject impinging upon us. Furthermore, it is precisely through maintaining an emphasis upon God's free subjectivity in Christ that axiology and soteriology are brought together in the closest possible harmony. God's call in Christ is a call to obedience, but the call itself comes freely and gratuitously to the disciple. God's call in Christ is a call that saves because only by being encountered by God's self can the sinful human self be liberated.

It may indeed be difficult at times for readers to hear the grace in Bonhoeffer's insistence upon "costly grace," because he so consistently and repeatedly emphasizes obedience as self-denial in contrast to self-affirmation. Perhaps it is true that this emphasis could be complemented by theological recognition of healthy self-affirmation, as Green suggests.[32] But from all that can be gathered about Bonhoeffer's soteriology, it is clear that the self that needs to be broken—and broken into—is the guilty self, the self fallen way from God and others, hopelessly entangled in its own falsely construed world. Only because this bondage is so pernicious—it is, after all, a bondage where one is enslaved by oneself—does Bonhoeffer feel it necessary to emphasize the intrusive and disrupting influence of God's call in Christ in words that are often quite forceful. Thus it should never be forgotten that the purpose of defeat of the selfish self is its liberation, its salvation, and its being made free for God and for others in community rather than its destruction or corruption.

Bonhoeffer's critique of Barth in *Act and Being* centered not upon the notion that God is the divine subject but upon the abstract notion of freedom that defined that subject's activity. But once he has subjected that abstraction to theological scrutiny, Bonhoeffer can himself employ it in a way that does justice to both God's subjectivity in Christ and the narrative form in which that subjectivity moves and is revealed.

Thus in *Discipleship* Bonhoeffer utilizes the model of God as subject appropriated from Barth to ground Christ's commandments in the activity of Christ's own person. The alternative is to see God or Christ as an object of moral concern. When Bonhoeffer distinguishes between two models of christological authority, he is clearly opting for the subjective model of God in Christ over the alternative.

This contrast between two models of christological authority informs, in turn, two models of human action vis-à-vis Jesus Christ. The moral

32. Green, *Bonhoeffer*, 177.

anthropology Bonhoeffer emphasizes as correct follows from the christological model that depends upon God's subjectivity. The moral anthropology Bonhoeffer downplays as inadequate is the one that relates to God in Christ as an abstract moral principle, that is, as an object of perception. The choice of the former model over the latter, in turn, enables Bonhoeffer to bring together God's grace and human obedience, soteriology and axiology, by mediating God's action to the human subject through the incarnate subject, Jesus Christ.

Furthermore, by contrasting two models of christological authority, opting for the one that emphasizes God's subjectivity, and thereby bringing together soteriology and axiology, Bonhoeffer has established a genuine alternative to "cheap grace" without lapsing into legalism. The problem with cheap grace is that it precludes obedience to Jesus Christ through selfish inactivity. The problem with moral idealism is that it also precludes obedience to Jesus Christ through an activity all too selfish. At the heart of both is a refusal to see Jesus as the divine subject breaking into the self and claiming it for the divine purpose. But if God's subjectivity in Christ is taken seriously, then the human subject encountered thereby will become free for Christ, just as God in Christ is free for others. Because God's subjectivity is enacted in and through Jesus's history, obedient attention to Jesus conforms one's own history to God's.

Simple and Paradoxical Obedience to Commandments

The first five chapters of *Discipleship* articulate the true nature of Jesus Christ as well as the true nature of Christian obedience to him. Only after making clear to his readers that his treatment of Christian ethics is not meant to deny grace or succumb to legalism does Bonhoeffer turn to interpret and apply the Sermon on the Mount. This chapter has itself followed Bonhoeffer's lead. Only now that the proper model of Christ's authority is understood in all its dimensions can the discussion turn toward the more practical implications such authority has for Christian behavior in *Discipleship*.

In the following discussion it will become clear that just as the foundational themes of divine and human freedom, grace and obedience, ethics and salvation have undergone drastic modification subsequent to the Barcelona lecture on ethics, so also has the concrete ethical substance. Bonhoeffer will emphasize simple obedience to Jesus Christ in *Discipleship* in a way not possible in the Barcelona lecture. He will also emphasize the importance of Christ's mediation between the self and other people in a way that qualifies the Barcelona lecture's appeal to immediate relationships with one's *Volk* and family. He will stress literal obedience to Christ's command not to resist the evil person and to love the enemy with a sincerity and straightforwardness that stands in stark contrast to the Barcelona lecture's previous denunciation of literal obedience to these commandments. Finally, he will use the distinction between church and world to come to conclusions completely opposed to his previous endorsements of justified violence.

It has already been shown that the confrontation between persons (i.e., the person of Christ and the disciple) that effects graced obedience is rooted in and depends upon the proper model of christological authority as well as the proper model of moral anthropology. This has the effect of bringing together God's grace in Christ and human obedience. What remains to be seen, however, is how in *Discipleship* Bonhoeffer makes good on his critique of Barth's model of the fragmented self. Bonhoeffer suggested that Barth's understanding of both faith and obedience were impossible to describe in real history. Thus it is now important to examine to what degree Bonhoeffer himself sees obedience as historical, that is, as embodied duration.

One of the ways Bonhoeffer presses home both the disruptive nature of Christ's commands and the importance of the embodied response such a disruption makes possible is to insist upon "simple obedience." Simple obedience is literal obedience to Jesus's commands. Thus, for example, when Jesus tells the rich young ruler to sell all his possessions, he means for the ruler to do exactly that.[33] Now, one way to avoid the implications of such literal obedience is to stress the obedience of the heart over the obedience of a concrete embodied life. In other words, one way in which simple obedience to Christ's commands is circumvented is precisely by playing the interior over against a person's exterior acts. As Bonhoeffer explains,

> If Jesus said: leave everything else behind and follow me, leave your profession, your family, your people, and your father's house, then the biblical hearer knew that the only answer to this call is simple obedience, because the promise of community with Jesus is given to this obedience. But we would say: Jesus's call is to be taken "absolutely seriously," but true obedience to it consists of my staying in my profession and in my family and serving him there, in true inner freedom. Thus Jesus would call: come out!—but we would understand that he actually meant: stay in!—of course as one who has inwardly come out.[34]

As is clear, Bonhoeffer contrasts the simplicity of the biblical hearer with the evasive sophistry of the modern interpreter. The implication of this contrast is that the modern interpreter does not do justice to the true nature of

33. Bonhoeffer, *Discipleship*, 78.
34. Ibid., 79.

Jesus's call or to the obedience of the one who is to follow. The false interpretation confines obedience to the interior realm of disposition alone because it precludes a real and embodied break with social ties and responsibilities. Bonhoeffer's stress upon simple obedience, in contrast, is meant to preserve the disruptive claim of Jesus's call by attending to the break in immediate relationships such a claim entails.

This break in the immediacy of social ties, especially those that bind the person to his or her family and people, was unimaginable for the Bonhoeffer of the Barcelona ethics lecture. There one's allegiance is split between two competing loyalties because true Christian action can only transcend moral decisions. God's command, as it is understood in the Barcelona lecture, can only relativize moral norms, it cannot specify which norms should guide behavior. But here, in *Discipleship*, God's command unifies moral allegiances by breaking the ties of immediacy with those social realities that demand action contradictory to God's commands in Christ. There is no longer any need to discuss the inevitable conflict between competing loyalties because those loyalties have already been rearranged by God's command itself. Thus while the Barcelona lecture employed God's command to transcend morality, *Discipleship* employs God's command to change morality. God's command in Christ can now specify distinct behavior because God's freedom exists in being bound to the distinct behavioral pattern of Jesus Christ.

Whatever Bonhoeffer may have been thinking prior to writing *Discipleship*, clearly his definition of the self's transformation has broadened to include not only the interior ego but also the exterior social world in which it is nested. Christ's call disrupts the self not only in a personal sense; it does so precisely by breaking the ties of immediacy and responsibility that obtain between any given self and its social worlds including, for example, the worlds of family, broader community, and people. Indeed, it is precisely through deconstructing one's "given" relationships to others that one is transformed and formed to exist in relation with others in a distinct manner, in a manner that befits having heard Christ's call to obedience. Thus simple obedience to Christ has both personal and social ramifications, not only because Christ's commandments demand embodiment by their very nature, but also because a self transformed through encounter with Christ cannot but become embodied in concrete life, thus affecting social relations.

Bonhoeffer wishes, therefore, to do justice to two aspects of obedience to Christ, both interior dispositions *and* exterior behavior. Though these two aspects of human obedience can be distinguished, there is no reason to juxtapose them. Though it is important that the egotistical self be redeemed in confrontation with the living God, for instance, because it is no longer necessary to pit God's freedom against God's duration in Christ, it is now possible to see that God's confrontation through Christ's call to obedience affects both the person's identity as well as that person's actions over time. Obedience to Jesus is both existential and an embodied response.

This holistic account, an account that holds together interiority and behavior, stands in stark contrast to what was once articulated in the Barcelona lecture on ethics. There Bonhoeffer could not envision human freedom in any other way than transcendence over moral constraint. But what is "morality" other than a way to specify or commend for emulation a distinctive form of behavior? Because this is the case, regardless of Bonhoeffer's intentions, his initial model of Christian freedom implies the impossibility of embodied freedom to the extent that it denies the possibility of freedom formed by distinctive behaviors and behavioral expectations. Not only so, but this abstract notion of Christian freedom also implies not merely a distinction between freedom and embodiment but an antagonistic dualism. But then this is to be expected. After all, the model of divine freedom employed in the Barcelona lecture on ethics was abstracted from all duration and from embodiment as well. Why would Bonhoeffer's definition of Christian freedom have been any different?

It is only after subjecting evasions of simple obedience to critical scrutiny that Bonhoeffer, in turn, concedes the element of truth in these evasions. Though it is true that both the interior life and exterior obedience should be held together, this does not mean that one element does not have a certain priority over the other. The element of truth contained in the evasive answers Bonhoeffer combats with simple obedience is the emphasis upon interiority over behavior. It is clear, then, that just as Bonhoeffer does not want to separate faith from obedience, neither does he want to suggest that an act of obedience can be considered faithful if it does not follow from faith in Jesus Christ. As Bonhoeffer says,

> Jesus' command to the rich young man [to sell all of his possessions and follow] or his call into a situation that enables faith really has only the one goal of calling a person to faith in him, calling into his community. Nothing finally depends on any human deed at all; instead, everything depends on faith in Jesus as the Son of God. . . . Nothing finally depends on poverty or riches, marriage or the single state, having or leaving a profession. Rather, everything depends on faith. To this extent, we really are right that it is possible to believe in Christ while we have wealth and possess the goods of this world, so that we have them as if we did not have them. But this is a last possible form of Christian existence, a possibility of living in the world, only in light of the serious expectation that Christ would return in the immediate future.[35]

35. Ibid., 80.

These comments may seem to be in tension with much of what Bonhoeffer has already said about the importance of obedience, not to mention his polemic against “cheap grace.” But this is not the case. In fact, there is a profound connection between the prioritization of faith found in this passage and the grounding of Christ’s commandments in his person, which is also the basis for Bonhoeffer’s insistence upon obedience. But as this passage insists, obedience exists for the sake of faith in Jesus Christ and not the other way around. Christ’s call to do something specific, then, should not mean that the only thing required is behavior modification. Rather, true obedience has commitment to the person of Jesus Christ as its ground and goal. Obedience without commitment to Jesus Christ is not obedience at all but self-chosen moral idealism. Without Jesus Christ, then, “obedience” is disobedience no matter what concrete behavioral form it may take.

Now, because faith in Christ has priority over any given concrete action, it is also the case that authentic faith in Christ is possible in a variety of concrete activities and roles. This is the case even if one’s activities and responsibilities—say, as a father, as a spouse, or in an occupation—entail commitments and embody actions that seem to contradict Christ’s commandments. Take, for example, Christ’s commandment not to lay up treasures on earth (Matt. 6:19–21). A commitment only to simple obedience would imply that being a disciple of Christ and having a savings account, for example, are somehow fundamentally incompatible. Bonhoeffer’s suggestion that there is a “paradoxical obedience,” however, envisions the possibility of authentic obedient faith in Jesus Christ while having a bank account. But—and Bonhoeffer goes to significant pains to make this clear—paradoxical obedience can in no way be used as an excuse to evade the transformative force of that same commandment taken literally and obeyed simply. In fact, Bonhoeffer goes so far as to say that only those who have already obeyed this command in simplicity can have any legitimate claims to paradoxical obedience at all.

The dialectic relationship between simple and paradoxical obedience cannot be resolved into a higher theoretical synthesis. Bonhoeffer is not offering here a comprehensive theory of obedience that sees the prophetic role of simple obedience only from within the higher perspective provided by the necessity of paradoxical obedience. This type of easy resolution could all too easily be used to exclude the possibility of simple obedience altogether.

The fact that Bonhoeffer does not seek systematic resolution in this particular matter is itself bound up with his insistence upon the transformative power of Christ’s call to obedience, as well as the nature of the human self. The purpose of simple obedience is transformation in Christ for a life formed and shaped by Jesus’s own identity. Because human beings are not simply minds or hearts, but bodies of action in space and time, it would be fundamentally misleading to imply that Jesus commands an obedience only of the "heart" and not also of the entirety of one's embodied existence. Though Jesus Christ's commandments aim at the center of one's self, they do not bypass the activities of the body. Indeed, Bonhoeffer suggests that it is precisely by calling for specific changes in behavior that the self can be transformed by Jesus Christ through faith in him. Thus to preclude simple obedience would be tantamount to eliminating the possibility of salvation, because it is precisely the extremity of Christ's commandments that affect the fallen egotistical self for its own liberation and reconciliation with God and others. In other words, fundamentally eliminating simple obedience would be to lapse into "cheap grace." But, on the other hand, it would also be problematic to eliminate paradoxical obedience from the equation. When paradoxical obedience is rigorously denied as an authentic possibility for faith, the results are a lapse into legalism.[36]

The other reason Bonhoeffer insists upon both simple and paradoxical obedience is to do justice to the concrete examples of obedience to God given in Scripture. More specifically, it is to do justice to those particular examples where God confronts his people with extraordinarily difficult choices, choices that force them to make a decision for or contrary to faith in God.

Obviously, given Bonhoeffer's particular focus in *Discipleship*, his primary illustrations of obedience draw from the New Testament. But Bonhoeffer finds a similar pattern of obedience at work in the Old Testament as well. Take, for instance, the example of obedience portrayed by Abraham. On the one hand, Abraham's response to God's Word to sacrifice Isaac was one of simple obedience (see Gen. 22:1–10). This act of simple obedience entailed a harsh break in Abraham's given relationships as the father of his son and as the head of the household in relation to those within his care. Abraham's willingness to sacrifice Isaac is taken as evidence of simple obedience, as is Abram's prior willingness to leave his father's household and country to journey toward Canaan. On the other hand, the fact that Abraham receives Isaac back after having been prevented from killing him signals the presence of paradoxical obedience in Abraham's life. He remains a father to his son just as before. But from that point onward his relationship with Isaac is no longer only that of

36. It should be pointed out, however, that Bonhoeffer's primary concern in *Discipleship* is to insist upon the importance of simple obedience. Given the state of Christian ethics in his time, especially in relationship to Christ's commandments in the Sermon on the Mount, there was no need to conduct an *apologia* for paradoxical obedience. The very opposite was the case. See Clarence Baumann, *The Sermon on the Mount: The Modern Quest for Its Meaning* (Macon, GA: Mercer University Press, 1985).

a father to a son. Rather, the fact of Abraham's past willingness to let go of Isaac continues to form Abraham's relationship to Isaac for the rest of their lives together. As Bonhoeffer says,

> Abraham received Isaac back, but he has him in a different way than before. He has him through the mediator and for the sake of the mediator. As the one who was prepared to hear and obey God's command literally, he is permitted to have Isaac as though he did not have him; he is permitted to have him through Jesus Christ.[37]

What was previously an immediate relating of father to son becomes a relationship mediated through God's command.

Bonhoeffer's use of the Abraham story clarifies why he affirms both simple and paradoxical obedience. The reason that simple obedience must always be the first response to God's command in Christ is that through this action we are empowered to "let go" of our relationships with and responsibilities to others, the world, and our very selves, in favor of allegiance to Jesus Christ and his body, the church. Jesus's command forces the hearer to decision, to a stark "yes" or "no" response to his call. But if we refuse to be led through this break with given worldly ties, then we have already refused our allegiance. We have failed both to believe and obey. Christ's call has not formed us as it could have, and thus we fail to see reality as it is in truth. We will have no claim to paradoxical obedience. But if we allow ourselves to let go of all our relationships for Jesus's sake, then and only then can we be restored to ourselves and to our relationships—although we now exist in these relationships in a manner different from before we gave them up in response to Christ's call.

Thus the reason simple obedience is the first response to Christ's commandments is that otherwise one could not be transformed (e.g., if one appeals to paradoxical obedience as a way out of the rigors of simple obedience). But the reason paradoxical obedience is also admitted is that it is possible to be in places of concrete responsibility (e.g., as a husband, wife, child, parent, or worker) as a person for whom those responsibilities have already been severed in response to Christ's radical call. In other words, simple obedience is maintained because otherwise Christ could not become one's ultimate Lord, while paradoxical obedience is maintained because one can have Jesus as Lord even when one "returns" to one's concrete daily responsibilities.

In focusing upon simple obedience Bonhoeffer demonstrates his clear concern for a break with given worldly realities. But Bonhoeffer is not content

37. Bonhoeffer, *Discipleship*, 97.

simply to insist upon the need for simple obedience and its paradoxical complement. He presses on to give the redeemed self a new vision of itself and its relationships to God and others. The break of one's self away from one's false self and one's social ties results in a new vision of the nature of the world and one's place within it. The self is broken away from one vision of reality in order to be given a new vision, which is itself true perception of the world. Thus, according to Bonhoeffer's account, discipleship to Jesus is *metanoia* in a twofold sense: the sense of existential breakage, repentance, and liberation from selfishness, and of a transformation in knowing and seeing. There can be no other way that true discipleship can take place, because the "self" is partly constituted by what it sees.[38] If the false self is to be truly changed, it must see a fundamentally new view of the world.

This new vision, according to Bonhoeffer, is the perception of Christ's mediating role in human relationships. The old vision was, on the contrary, a view of the world where human relationships are understood immediately. The call of Jesus Christ, the call that intrudes upon the selfish self and liberates it from its egoism, the call that breaks the self from its worlds and given natural responsibilities, is the same call that delivers the obedient person from immediacy to christological mediation. As Bonhoeffer says,

> Jesus' call itself already breaks the ties with the naturally given surroundings in which a person lives. It is not the disciple who breaks them; Christ himself broke them as soon as he called. Christ has untied the person's immediate connections with the world and bound the person immediately to himself. . . . Not the caprice of a self-willed life, but Christ himself leads the disciple to such a break.[39]

Here it is clear that the break that takes place is possible only through Jesus's call. Thus it is not as if one creates a break with family, friends, social ties, and responsibilities as an arbitrary act. Neither does one will these breaks into being through self-will. Rather, it is Christ's call impinging upon the acting subject that disrupts that subject's given relationships and responsibilities to those who compose its social world.

38. On the relation between vision and selfhood, see Stanley Hauerwas, "The Significance of Vision: Toward an Aesthetic Ethic," in *Vision and Virtue: Essays in Christian Ethical Reflection* (Notre Dame, IN: Fides, 1974), 30–47. Charles Taylor has similar statements regarding the relationship between identity and one's commitments. See Charles Taylor, *Sources of the Self: The Making of Modern Identity* (Cambridge, MA: Harvard University Press, 1989), 25–52. Both Taylor and Hauerwas show that the objects of our moral attention both show us the world and shape our identities.

39. Bonhoeffer, *Discipleship*, 93.

But Bonhoeffer does not leave the discussion here, for to do so would be simply to transfer the arbitrary nature of a break in social immediacy from the will of the human subject to the will of the divine subject in Jesus Christ. The break in social immediacy would still seem arbitrary and forced. So what Bonhoeffer does is to suggest that in addition to creating a "break" in social immediacy, Christ's call also places the acting subject into the truth—the truth of christologically mediated social relationships. As Bonhoeffer says:

> In becoming human, [Christ] put himself between me and the given circumstances of the world. I cannot go back. He is in the middle. He has deprived those whom he has called of every immediate connection to those given realities. He wants to be the medium; everything should happen only through him. He stands not only between me and God, he also stands between me and the world, between me and other people and things. He is the mediator; not only between God and human persons, but also between person and person, and between person and reality. Because the whole world was created by him and for him (John 1:3; 1 Cor. 8:6; Heb. 1:2), he is the sole mediator in the world.[40]

Here Bonhoeffer presses his insight on the necessity of the break in immediate relationships to new levels of meaning. He is concerned to demonstrate that the priority of grace leads to truth. Grace from God leads to a perception of what is already the case about the world, even if perception of the world's truth remains hidden from those who have not encountered the intrusive call of Christ to obedience and costly discipleship.

Prior to being called by Christ and responding in simple obedience, the hearer of the word not only possessed immediate relationships with family, in a profession, and in the world; he or she also had a vision of reality in which the only possible relationship with these phenomena was an immediate one. But this is precisely the illusion that Christ's call serves to destroy and transform. As Bonhoeffer insists,

> [Discipleship] is about accomplished facts and recognizing them, and therefore about the person of the mediator himself, who has come to stand between us and the world. That is why there must be a break with the immediacies of life; that is why a person called must become an individual before the mediator.
>
> So people called by Jesus learn that they had lived an illusion in their relationship to the world. The illusion is immediacy. It has blocked faith and obedience. [But] now they know that there can be no unmediated relationships, even in the most intimate ties of their lives, in the blood ties to father and mother, to children, brothers, sisters, in marital love, in historical

40. Ibid., 93–94.

> responsibilities. Ever since Jesus called, there are no longer natural, historical, or experiential unmediated relationships for his disciples. Christ the mediator stands between son and father, between husband and wife, between individual and nations, whether they can recognize him or not. There is no way from us to others than the path through Christ, his word, and our following him. Immediacy is a delusion.[41]

In saying these things Bonhoeffer is trying to combat a common misunderstanding or misreading of Jesus, the Gospels, and the New Testament. Broadly speaking, alternate readings of Jesus's commands and the Sermon on the Mount in particular have juxtaposed a concept of unmediated "reality" with the commands of Jesus. "Certainly Christ calls us to forsake father and mother and our own lives, but in reality we have responsibilities to our parents and must take care of ourselves for the sake of our posterity and indeed the faith itself," one may suggest. In light of what was quoted above, Bonhoeffer would argue that such a mind-set employs unredeemed categories. What does it mean to say "in reality" when it is actually only through obedience to Christ that reality is seen in truth? What does it mean to have responsibilities that would vie for our attention when it is only through breaking with such responsibilities, in response to Christ's call to do so, that we can establish our proper (mediated) relationship to them in a way that is faithful to the truth of Christ? Thus it is not so much that following Christ, reality, and responsibility must somehow be related. Rather, Bonhoeffer suggests that the decision for Christ in obedience is the decision to embrace a different vision of reality altogether and thus to redefine our responsibilities in light of what is now seen to be real.

The importance of a christological vision of mediation between persons clearly distinguishes *Discipleship* from the Barcelona lecture. The Bonhoeffer of 1929 thought primarily in terms of competing spheres of responsibility—for example, love of enemy versus love of neighbor. Christ's call to faithfulness and obedience in faith could not resolve this dichotomy. In fact, it was precisely Christ's commandment to love the enemy that catalyzed the ethical dilemma posed between these two competing responsibilities. On the one hand, in *Discipleship* Bonhoeffer does not dismiss the possibility of paradoxical obedience, and thus does not dismiss vocational allegiances that are in tension with the literal implications of Jesus's commands. Nevertheless, clearly his emphasis is upon a holistic vision of the world mediated through Christ rather than the tragedy of moral dilemmas as in the Barcelona lecture.

41. Ibid., 94–95.

Toward the Sermon on the Mount

The final consequence of Bonhoeffer's shift in theological perspective is a positive construal of New Testament law. As has already been seen in the previous chapter, the primary reason Bonhoeffer hesitated to stress "simple obedience" in the Barcelona lecture was because of his concern to preserve God's freedom, and in turn preserve the freedom of the Christian. One practical result of this hesitancy was that the Sermon on the Mount was not morally binding. But after his work in *Act and Being* and his subsequent conversion, Bonhoeffer has redefined his understanding of God's freedom. As a result, his hesitancy to stress simple obedience is no longer necessary. In fact, it is precisely by simple obedience to Christ's commandments that one is made free.

What was once necessary to transcend in order to be free has now become freedom's source. In effect, then, Bonhoeffer has demonstrated the crucial role that New Testament commandments play in the order of salvation. The commandments of Christ are the vocative force of Christ's person. They convey grace just as they effect personal and social transformation. They change persons and reorient them in the light of the truth of the world in Christ. Thus to bypass them or ignore them in the name of "grace" is a contradiction in terms. Indeed, because of the particular nature of Bonhoeffer's overall theological account in *Discipleship*, it is all the more important to stress the rigor and force of Christ's commandments. To soften them or explain them away would be to misunderstand them and to deny to others the possibility of their own transformation.

Christ's commandments not to resist the evildoer and to love the enemy (Matt. 5:38–42 and 5:43–48, respectively) are particularly relevant to the current discussion of Bonhoeffer's theological development. In the Barcelona lecture Bonhoeffer appealed to God's command to justify participation in war, that is, in an action that contradicts the command to love the enemy. But in *Discipleship* he reverses this judgment entirely. Appealing to God's command in this manner is no longer theologically tenable. God's commanding should not be understood without reference to God's commandments as articulated and specified in Jesus Christ. Thus there is now no cogent theological rationale for not taking seriously the Sermon on the Mount in all its literal rigor, nor is there any reason to hesitate in insisting upon "simple obedience" to its dictates.

It is crucial to realize that in his interpretation of the Sermon on the Mount in general, and the commandments of enemy love and nonresistance in particular, Bonhoeffer is employing many of his insights into the nature of Christ's authority and the dynamics of obedience as his hermeneutic. Thus it is not surprising to see him recapitulate many of the themes already discussed in his interpretation of these commandments' meanings and implications.

One theme Bonhoeffer employs is his polemic against principles and against principled interpretations of New Testament law. This theme is obviously not a new one for Bonhoeffer. Indeed, it has been present in his ethical thinking since the Barcelona lecture. Nevertheless, the implications that Bonhoeffer draws in *Discipleship* from the nonprincipled nature of the commandments of nonresistance and enemy love are very different from the implications he drew in the Barcelona lecture.

In the Barcelona lecture, Bonhoeffer's primary purpose was to problematize love of enemy by suggesting that it meant hatred of one's own people. His primary goal in arguing against simple obedience to this commandment was to demonstrate that such obedience does not free one from becoming guilty of the deaths of one's neighbors, family, and friends during a time of war. In thus arguing, Bonhoeffer also shored up his point that moral absolutes are problematic to begin with. They do not deliver one from the bondage of morality and the contradiction to freedom implied by moral dilemma. This became, in turn, Bonhoeffer's grounds for dismissing the possibility of simple obedience to Jesus's commandments.

Now, in *Discipleship*, Bonhoeffer is no more intent than he was in the Barcelona lecture to interpret Jesus's commandments in an absolute or principled manner. Thus he is also no more insistent than he was in the Barcelona lecture that Jesus's commandments imply moral purity if obeyed. The difference, however, is that in the Barcelona lecture he thought the inability of the commandments to make one guiltless was an argument against simple obedience; but in *Discipleship* this is no longer a damning argument, because the rationale for obedience is not in the commandments' capacity to make one guiltless but in their capacity to make one like Christ.

Thus Bonhoeffer states his case for obedience to Jesus on grounds different from those at the basis of a system of moral principles. He grounds obedience on the basis of Jesus Christ alone. For instance, Bonhoeffer's rhetorical interlocutors ask him about the practicality of Jesus's commandments, saying, "How can Jesus's statement [not to resist the evil person] be justified in the light of our experience that evil seeks out the weak and rampages most wildly among the most defenseless? Isn't Jesus's statement just an ideology which does not take into account the realities of the world, let us say the sin of the world? . . . Because we live in the world and the world is evil, therefore this statement [of Christ's] cannot be valid." But Bonhoeffer's answer is to suggest that the rationale for obedience to Jesus's commandments is not based upon ignorance of the world's evil, nor upon denying or minimizing that evil, but upon the way Jesus lived in and dealt with the world's evil. Thus Bonhoeffer answers in rejoinder, saying, "Jesus says: because you live in the world and because the world is evil, that is why the statement is valid: do not resist evil. [Indeed] it would be difficult to accuse Jesus of not knowing the power of evil, Jesus, who battled with the devil from the first day of his life onward."[42] That Jesus's commandments should be obeyed is not based upon the fact that they deliver one from all guilt but upon the fact that Jesus Christ was in the world in a way that did not resist the evil person.

Another component of Bonhoeffer's interpretation of the commands in the Sermon on the Mount is his insistence that they require God's grace to obey. The above discussion has already made it plain that Jesus's command is grace in the form of enabling power. Though this grace is first experienced by the would-be disciple as existential disruption, it is also experienced as super-added ability and freedom to obey. In Bonhoeffer's interpretation of the love commandment, it becomes clear precisely why this model of moral engagement between Jesus and his disciples is so necessary: by nature the would-be follower of Jesus is unable to love his or her enemy. Only after being encountered with God's free commanding power in Christ can one be enabled to so love. As Bonhoeffer says,

> Loving one's enemies is not only an unbearable offense to the natural person. It demands more than the strength a natural person can muster, and it offends the natural concepts of good and evil. But even more important, loving one's enemies appears to people living according to the law [i.e., Old Testament Torah] to be a sin against God's law itself. Separation from enemies and condemning them is what the law demands.[43]

To love one's enemy is not something that can possibly emerge naturally from a person; it comes as a super added gift of grace. But because Bonhoeffer has already grounded the capacity for obedience in Jesus Christ rather than in the disciple's human capacities, obedience is made possible despite its impossibility for human nature. Obedience requires Christ precisely because Christ's commands transcend human ability. With this account of human inability, it is no wonder Bonhoeffer is so adamant to distinguish his account of Christ and discipleship from moral idealism. Moral idealism presumes the very human capacity that Bonhoeffer denies humans possess in relation to Christ.

It has already been seen that Bonhoeffer's account of obedience embraces personal salvation as well as social transformation. Because the person is

42. Ibid., 135.
43. Ibid., 138–39.

fundamentally altered by means of Christ's call, his or her relations with others are altered as well. Thus it would be a distortion of both the nature of Christ's commandments and the social nature of personhood to confine Jesus's commandments to a purely interior or purely personal arena.

With this holistic account of obedience in mind, it comes as no surprise that Bonhoeffer takes issue with the traditional Lutheran distinction between "person" and "office," especially as that has been used to limit the application of Jesus's commandments to the realm of "personal ethics." Against this false limitation, in his discussion of both nonretaliation and enemy love, Bonhoeffer insists that the follower of Jesus is to love the enemy not only in the personal realm but in one's social role as well. As Bonhoeffer says,

> The Reformation interpretation [of nonresistance and enemy love] introduced a decisively new concept, namely, that we should differentiate between harm done to me personally, and harm done to me as bearer of my office, that is, in the responsibility given me by God. In the former case I am to act as Jesus commands, but in the latter case I am released from doing so. Indeed, for the sake of true love, I am even obligated to behave in the opposite way, to answer violence with violence in order to resist the inroads of evil. This is what justifies the Reformation position on war, and on any use of public legal means to repel evil. But this distinction between private person and bearer of an office as normative for my behavior is foreign to Jesus. . . . [In fact, both] "private" and "official" spheres are all completely subject to Jesus's command. The word of Jesus claimed them undividedly. He demands undivided obedience.[44]

Jesus calls us as whole persons because there is no other type of person but the whole person. Obedience to Jesus, then, cannot divide reality into two contradictory zones, one operating in obedience to Jesus and the other operating independent of Jesus's influence. All of reality is the legitimate place for holistic obedience to Jesus Christ.

But there are further implications to this holistic understanding of obedience. Because disciples of Jesus must obey him in all circumstances in life, there may well be certain roles in a society that are inappropriate to perform given their very nature. It is at this point, when the disciple can no longer be in a particular social role and also with good conscience be a follower of Jesus, that the hidden break with the world becomes evident for all to see. Although it is true that "the body of Christ is . . . deeply involved in all areas of life in this world," Bonhoeffer also insists that "there are certain points where the complete separation remains visible, and must become even more

44. Ibid., 134–35.

visible."[45] Church history demonstrates, in fact, that "even as early as the first few centuries of the church, certain professions were considered incompatible with being a member of the Christian community."[46]

Given the fact that Bonhoeffer envisions the possibility of conscientious refusal to act in certain social roles, it is no surprise that when insisting upon "nonresistance" he realizes that the church exists in a form fundamentally distinct from the larger society of which it is a part. Bonhoeffer argues that Jesus's commandment not to resist the evil person "releases his community from the political and legal order, from the national form of the people of Israel, and makes it into what it truly is, namely, the community of the faithful that is not bound by political or national ties."[47] The distinction between person and role is not definitive for the Christian, and so the distinction between the church and the world can now become determinative. But this distinction between church and world is but the corollary of Bonhoeffer's insistence that obedience to Christ is rooted not in human nature but in grace. Thus the church/world distinction is part and parcel of Bonhoeffer's entire theological ethics in *Discipleship*; it is deeply rooted in his understanding of God's command in Jesus Christ.

What is said in *Discipleship* about love of enemy and the possibility of an open break with given social roles stands in stark contrast to Bonhoeffer's arguments in the Barcelona lecture. There Bonhoeffer trades upon the very distinctions that he subjects to critique in *Discipleship*. He suggests that one's role as a member of a particular *Volk* entails the moral necessity of transgressing Jesus's commandments as understood literally or obeyed simply. Bonhoeffer based the legitimacy of participating in war upon the independent value of the *Volk*. Thus one's duty as a part of the *Volk* was to defend it by becoming a soldier. What does this form of argumentation suggest except the very distinction between person and social role Bonhoeffer denies in *Discipleship*? Furthermore, given the split between person and social role that Bonhoeffer maintains in the Barcelona lecture on ethics, it comes as no surprise that he does not comment on the distinctive nature of the church community. In stark contrast, then, in *Discipleship* Bonhoeffer speaks clearly about the distinctive nature of the Christian community precisely because it takes Jesus's commandments seriously. Here he expects Jesus's commandments to be obeyed in all spheres of life so that a church community of authentic faith and obedience can take up space in the world.[48]

45. Ibid., 247.

46. Ibid., 246. Most important, for current purposes, Bonhoeffer lists the professions of police officers and soldiers as incompatible with Christian discipleship.

47. Ibid., 132.

48. Ibid., 110–14, 225–52.

In wrapping up this analysis of *Discipleship* it will be helpful to remember that this chapter has, broadly speaking, pursued two distinct tasks. In relation to the preceding chapter, it has demonstrated the nature, cause, and extent of Bonhoeffer's ethical development from the 1929 account of Christian ethics to the 1937 account in *Discipleship*. In relation to the two chapters that will follow, the current chapter has established a basis of comparison by which to adjudicate the nature and extent of Bonhoeffer's ethical development subsequent to *Discipleship* and leading up to the end of the writing of the *Ethics* manuscript in 1943.

Understanding the nature of the transitions from the Barcelona lecture to *Discipleship* makes clear the extent of those transitions as well. The argument of both this chapter and the next is that the extent of the transitions in ethical thought from Barcelona to *Discipleship* will not be repeated. Neither will these transitions be reversed. On the contrary, because of the definitive nature of both Bonhoeffer's conversion and the transmogrification of theological and ethical substance prior to and clearly present in *Discipleship*, *Discipleship* itself will not be surpassed by *Ethics*. In fact, *Ethics* can be properly understood only as a continuation of the ethical tradition begun in *Discipleship*. *Ethics* presupposes *Discipleship* even as it revisits some of the loose ends, so to speak, of *Discipleship*. Thus rather than being a repudiation of *Discipleship* either in its parts or as a whole, *Ethics* is its confirmation, as it is its continuation, amendment, clarification, and culmination.

Because the nature of the transition from the Barcelona lecture to *Discipleship* is definitive for all subsequent ethical reflection, understanding Bonhoeffer's conceptual development in this phase of his intellectual biography yields specific benchmarks by which the constitutive central theological themes of *Ethics* can be compared and contrasted. This will allow perception of both the continuity and possible discontinuity between *Discipleship* and *Ethics* by examining how a specific theme is understood and employed in both works.

The results of this examination cannot be spelled out in detail here, but by way of anticipation it can be said that none of the foundational theological tenets of *Discipleship*—tenets that resulted from the transition subsequent to the Barcelona lecture—are either denied or repudiated in *Ethics*. That God is subject-in-duration, divine freedom in the incarnate Christ, will not change. Thus neither will Bonhoeffer's insistence that faith is both an eventuality and a faith-in-duration. God's command as commanding within a history will not be modified, and so neither will the insistence that God's command is inseparable from the concrete commandments of the canon. God's freedom will persist through history in Christ, and so disciplined freedom will also exist in history. The insistence upon the priority of God's action, and the resulting emphasis upon God's command as grace and as power to obey, will not be downplayed. Thus grace and obedience will remain closely harmonized. Because God's command is in God's commandments, there will be no reason nervously to avoid all ethical specification. Finally, both the duration of obedience and the disruptive elements of God's command to obey will be done justice by being presumed to be united.

Furthermore, in *Ethics* Bonhoeffer will continue to trade on the distinction between God as object and God as subject, opting for the latter model. Thus, as in *Discipleship*, he will repudiate absolute principles in favor of concrete commandments. He will emphasize the importance of Jesus's person as God incarnate and not employ a model of Jesus as teacher or moral exemplar. Moreover, commandments—God's speaking—will be tied to the scriptural witness to who God, who Christ, is. Bonhoeffer will continue his polemic against principles also, in the same way he always has, that is, to deconstruct those ethical alternatives he sees as theologically problematic because abstract. As a result of these particular christological distinctions, Bonhoeffer will also continue to use the moral-anthropological distinctions that follow. He will insist upon personal obedience over moral idealism. He will envision Christ not as part of one's ideational world but as the disruptive subjectivity of God entering into and transforming one's conceptions again and again. Thus he will continue to see personal obedience as empowered by grace and as imposed from beyond the confines of the self rather than as self-willed or self-chosen. Therefore his model of obedient faith and faith in obedience will continue to be both axiological and soteriological.

Despite these continuities and preservations of foundational theology, however, *Ethics* does shed light upon some of the less developed ideas in *Discipleship*. But rather than being a repudiation of *Discipleship*, this development of themes presupposes the framework first articulated in *Discipleship*. In *Discipleship* Bonhoeffer clearly and sharply distinguishes between two understandings of God (as object verses subject), two models of Christ's authority (Christ as teacher versus Christ as God in the flesh), and two models of moral anthropology (moral idealism versus personal obedience). But in addition to distinguishing these two forms of moral discourse, he also tends to downplay the significance of one over the other. In *Ethics*, without denying the validity of the distinctions between these two forms of moral discourse, Bonhoeffer is wishing to more positively evaluate the one he found so theologically problematic in *Discipleship*.

While the first form of discourse corresponds broadly to natural morality or the natural good, the second form of discourse corresponds to the order of grace. Without wishing to imply that Bonhoeffer will become a Roman

Catholic theologian or a Thomistic moral philosopher, it is the case that in *Ethics* Bonhoeffer will focus more closely upon the relationship between the order of nature and the order of grace than he does in *Discipleship*. This he does by asking about the relation between the penultimate and the ultimate. By focusing upon this distinction and its relationship to the other themes of *Ethics*, it will be possible to see how Bonhoeffer could stand by *Discipleship* even as he took his own final stand.

6

The Penultimate and the Ultimate

Negotiating the Discipleship *Tradition in* Ethics

On July 21 of 1944 Dietrich Bonhoeffer wrote to Eberhard Bethge. In his letter Bonhoeffer discussed topics as diverse as music and Scripture, but more pointedly he told Bethge that he had come to a greater understanding of the "profound this-worldliness" of Christianity. He wrote, "I do not mean the shallow and banal this-worldliness of the enlightened, the bustling, the comfortable, or the lascivious, but the profound this-worldliness that shows discipline and includes the ever-present knowledge of death and resurrection."[1] He went on to recount a conversation he once had with a young French pastor named Jean Lasserre. The two had talked about what they wanted to do with their lives. Lasserre wanted to become a saint; Bonhoeffer wanted to learn to have faith, something he thought he could do by living a saintlike life. Reflecting on the conversation years later in his letter to Bethge, Bonhoeffer concludes that he penned *Discipleship* at the end of that path. He told his friend, "Today I clearly see the dangers of that book, though I still stand by it."[2] By the time he wrote Bethge, the

1. Dietrich Bonhoeffer, *Letters and Papers from Prison*, ed. John W. de Gruchy, trans. Isabel Best, Lisa E. Dahill, Reinhard Krauss, and Nancy Lukens, vol. 8 of *Dietrich Bonhoeffer Works* (Minneapolis: Fortress, 2009), 485.
2. Ibid., 486.

imprisoned Bonhoeffer had been forced to end his work on *Ethics*. All of his working manuscripts, which were published later as *Ethics*, had been written before that point.[3] What should we make of Bonhoeffer's comments? We have alluded to this question in this volume already, but it is really only now, after the work of the preceding chapters, that we can begin to properly assess the relationship of *Discipleship* and the manuscripts Bonhoeffer intended to be something of a magnum opus, his *Ethics*. After following the trajectory of Bonhoeffer's ethical thinking over a significant period of his life, we are in a better position to determine what themes are the most enduring and what may simply be the coincidental assertions of one discreet context.

That there are such coincidental themes in Bonhoeffer's ethics should already be apparent. It has already been seen, for instance, how Bonhoeffer's early nationalist ideology expressed in the Barcelona ethics lecture was displaced by the peace ethic of *Discipleship*. But if such fundamental transition occurred once, might it not be possible that Bonhoeffer's later experience led him to fundamentally reconstrue his ethics once again? That is to say, if Bonhoeffer once substituted pacifism for nationalism, is it not possible that he could subsequently substitute a form of "realism" or just war morality for pacifist convictions? Perhaps this is precisely what Bonheoffer had in mind when writing his 1944 letter to Eberhard Bethge. The most influential study of Bonhoeffer's pacifism suggests that this is what happened: Bonhoeffer found himself unable to sustain his pacifism in the midst of conspiratorial involvement implicating him in the use of force and as a result found it necessary to jettison his pacifist convictions in favor of a more realistic moral calculus.[4]

There are a number of problems with this viewpoint, however, and the work of the previous chapters goes a long way in highlighting its shortcomings. One of the biggest problems with the received Bonhoeffer tradition, as it were, is to what degree it is dependent upon Bonhoeffer's moral philosophy's having been dependent on absolute principles. The notion that Bonhoeffer possessed a position called pacifism, a position he later discarded as unrealistic, is a narrative dependent on the disparity of *ideal* and *real* to be coherent. In other words, it presupposes as true precisely what it ought to question. Bonhoeffer's ethical thought, from the very beginning until its final expressions, never depended on

3. For matters of sequence and dating in this and the following chapter, we rely on the analysis of the editors of the German DBW *Ethics* translated and included as appendices to the DBW English edition of *Ethics*.

4. Larry Rasmussen, *Dietrich Bonhoeffer: Reality and Resistance* (1972; repr., Louisville: Westminster John Knox, 2005), 94–126. Also see David M. Gides, *Pacifism, Just War, and Tyrannicide: Bonhoeffer's Church-World Theology and His Changing Forms of Political Thinking and Involvement* (Eugene, OR: Pickwick, 2011).

such a duality. This leads to another, related problem with the usual accounts of Bonhoeffer's ethical development. Because of the nature of Bonhoeffer's ethics, it is not really possible to chart its evolution by attending primarily to one discreet moral category or issue. Bonhoeffer's ethical reflection, precisely because it is so consistently antiprincipled, problematizes such an analysis. Thus the attempt to isolate Bonhoeffer's "pacifism" and track its development through time, though a part of the interpretive task, produces data insufficient to decide when or to what degree his ethics shifted basic categories. Only once the primary categories of Bonhoeffer's thought are ascertained can any judgment be made upon the existence or degree of change his thought underwent.

The work of the last two chapters shows the basic dynamics of Bonhoeffer's ethical program: God's command and humanity's obedience. This dynamic pairing is consistently employed as the basis of Bonhoeffer's reflection, both before and after his shift from the "phraseological to the real," the shift that prepared the way for *Discipleship*. The *Ethics* manuscripts will prove no exception to this generalization, for there too the primary dynamic exists between God's command and humanity's response. We can note, for instance, that in one of the latest manuscripts destined to be included in *Ethics*, which was titled "The 'Ethical' and the 'Christian' as a Topic," Bonhoeffer questions whether ethics really is the right category at all. This manuscript was probably written in the first few months of 1943, and in it Bonhoeffer expresses a concern that reflection on ethics as a standalone entity gives the impression that human life somehow coheres through obedience to principles or deliberation about extreme cases and moral quandaries. Against this Bonhoeffer holds that God's command is "the sole authorization for ethical discourse."[5] Yet noting this consistency alone does little to determine whether *Ethics* represents a significant departure from *Discipleship*. This is the case because, as we have seen, Bonhoeffer's ethical reflection evinces both consistency and innovation; therefore it is only natural to expect that *Ethics* will demonstrate something of the same phenomenon. The only question is whether what is "new" in *Ethics* is a development from or a repudiation of the distinctive marks of *Discipleship*.

The one constant across the breadth of Bonhoeffer's reflection is the divine/human relationship as the prime locus of moral action. This relationship takes place through an encounter between God's subjectivity and the human creature's own divinely bestowed receptivity. Freedom is the primary effect of God's redemptive encounter with the human. This effect must be caused by the source of infinite freedom itself in order to be free at all, because the tendency

5. Dietrich Bonhoeffer, *Ethics*, ed. Clifford J. Green, trans. Reinhard Krauss, Charles C. West, and Douglas W. Scott, vol. 6 of *Dietrich Bonhoeffer Works* (Minneapolis: Fortress, 2005), 378.

of human action as human action is not toward freedom but bondage. Thus the consistent dynamic of Bonhoeffer's ethics is the interaction between God as subject and the human subject, which happens as a super-added donation from God with its source in God's own freedom, and with the freedom of the human to act in obedience to God's command as its end.

In addition to these constant dynamics there are innovations, the most significant of which is found in the shift that took place to make *Discipleship* possible. As we have seen, only one basic theological factor explains the differences between the ethics of the Barcelona lecture and the ethics of *Discipleship*—a redefinition of divine freedom animated by placing the person of Jesus Christ at the center. Thus a central question for determining the relationship between *Ethics* and *Discipleship* relates to the model of divine freedom employed in *Ethics*. Nevertheless, it is also clear in *Discipleship* that the redefined notion of divine freedom has many other subsidiary consequences for the practical substance of Bonhoeffer's ethics. Foremost among these are the distinctive themes of *Discipleship* itself. The emphases upon the necessity of personal transformation for proper insight into reality, a rehabilitation of New Testament law, simple and paradoxical obedience, the possibility of an embodied life of obedience, and the church/world relationship are a few examples. These distinctive themes of *Discipleship* should be kept in mind as we seek to understand what the *Ethics* manuscripts do and do not imply about the development of Bonhoeffer's thinking. Of course, we cannot offer an in-depth analysis of all the *Ethics* manuscripts in this way. Instead, in the rest of this chapter we will focus on the three manuscripts Bonhoeffer seems to have intended, as of 1943, to be the foundational chapters of *Ethics*: "God's Love and the Disintegration of the World"; "Christ, Reality, and Good: Christ, Church, and World"; and "Ethics as Formation." Though these would form the first chapters of Bonhoeffer's book, they were not written at the same time but span Bonhoeffer's work and thought from 1940 to 1942.[6]

"God's Love and the Disintegration of the World"

In all likelihood Bonhoeffer intended "God's Love and the Disintegration of the World" to be the opening chapter of *Ethics*. The manuscript was probably written late in 1942, and in it Bonhoeffer outlines the basic orientation of his ethical program. His imagined readers would have been prepared for the foundational nature of an opening chapter, but they might not have been prepared for Bonhoeffer's opening lines: "The knowledge of Good and Evil

6. See the appendixes in *Ethics*, 447, 471.

appears to be the goal of all ethical reflection. The first task of Christian ethics is to supersede that knowledge. This attack on the presuppositions of all other ethics is so unique that it is questionable whether it even makes sense to speak of Christian ethics at all."[7] Bonhoeffer's approach exemplified in these opening lines clearly reflects the influence of Søren Kierkegaard. Both Bonhoeffer and the Dane advocate the "teleological suspension of the ethical"—a critique of ethics emphasizing that right action must be directed toward an end beyond the ethical system itself.[8] But why—why is it questionable to speak of Christian ethics?

Bonhoeffer argues this possibly unnerving proposition because Christian ethics does not offer a distinctive form of ethics in competition with others; rather, it undermines the foundations of all ethics as ethics. It undermines the attempts of all human action to be and to strive for the good. Bonhoeffer contrasts Christian ethics—though the very term undoes itself—with all other ethical systems for several reasons. The most obvious is that for Bonhoeffer Christian ethics is singular and distinctive. It is not meant to be one form of systematic reflection upon human morals among others, but the critique and reformation of all ethical reflection. The other reason, inextricably linked with the first, is rooted in Bonhoeffer's insistence that self-transformation precedes true knowledge of reality, and that such transformation can only come about through God's own confrontation of the knowing human subject.

A key step of Bonhoeffer's argument in "God's Love and the Disintegration of the World," then, is to problematize autonomous moral knowledge. To do so, he relies upon his theological exegesis of the second chapter of Genesis, especially the incident where Adam and Eve partake of the "tree of the knowledge of good and evil."[9] Unlike some other interpretations of the myth, Bonhoeffer sees this incident not as an inevitable or salutary advance in human knowledge and maturity but as a tragic fall from communion. The knowledge of good and evil introduces a duality into human perception that frustrates its original, single-minded obedience to God and its uncorrupted relationship with God. This is because true knowledge is, in fact, knowledge of God alone and of all others things—self, world, and others—in light of this. Thus partaking of the tree of the knowledge of good and evil is an inversion

7. Bonhoeffer, *Ethics*, 299.

8. Matthew D. Kirkpatrick, *Attacks on Christendom in a World Come of Age: Kierkegaard, Bonhoeffer, and the Question of "Religionless Christianity,"* Princeton Theological Monograph Series (Eugene, OR: Pickwick, 2011), 111–38.

9. Here Bonhoeffer is drawing on his previous work. See Dietrich Bonhoeffer, *Creation and Fall: A Theological Exposition of Genesis 1–3*, ed. John W. de Gruchy, trans. Douglas Stephen Bax, vol. 3 of *Dietrich Bonhoeffer Works* (Minneapolis: Fortress, 1997), 80–93.

of humanity's knowledge of God as origin. It introduces a veil of estrangement between humanity and God and between humans themselves. Rather than understanding himself as a person insofar as he relates to God and God relates to him, Adam now understands himself as the judge of good and evil and thus as the judge of himself and others.[10]

The second stage of Bonhoeffer's argument is his insistence that although humanity, not God, is responsible for this estrangement, human creatures are unable to overcome it on their own. Bonhoeffer observes a number of existential signs of humanity's impotence vis-à-vis its fallen situation. For instance, he suggests that shame is the result of human beings suffering disunion from God and others. The most penetrating of his observations, however, is his discussion of conscience. According to Bonhoeffer, conscience is a fallen human attempt to reclaim wholeness and communion. However, in the end the phenomenon of conscience actually perpetuates the very problem it seeks to overcome. "Conscience," says Bonhoeffer, "is the voice of fallen life that seeks to preserve unity at least with itself. It is the call to the human being to preserve the unity of the self."[11] Because the self cannot possibly overcome all estrangement, it finds small comfort in "at least" living up to its own conceptions of being good, just, or moral. That is to say, though it lacks the power to bring itself into communion with the larger social wholes of which it is a part, the self can at least bring itself into unity and communion with its own highest expectations. Yet this striving to be good is where the vanity of moral strife shows itself most plainly. It produces a self that is its own judge and jury, as well as the judge and jury of all other people; and it is this act of moral judgment that perpetuates isolation and spreads alienation.

Bonhoeffer's account focuses heavily upon the subject. He works from the assumption that the "objective" vision of what is, or what is good, is already rooted in the subject itself. Bonhoeffer takes it for granted that self-knowledge and perception of the good impinge upon one another. Indeed, he points out that the history of ethics, and of human perception broadly speaking, indicates to what degree subjective human alienation writes itself out, so to speak, on the canvas of reality. The effort of human beings to maintain self-consistency through conscience simply displaces their own internal estrangements onto everything other than themselves. Bonhoeffer writes, "Everything splits apart—is and ought, life and law, knowing and doing . . . the individual and the collective; and even truth, justice, beauty, and love conflict with one another just as do desire and aversion, happiness and sorrow—one could

10. Bonhoeffer, *Ethics*, 300–301.
11. Ibid., 307.

continue this list at length, and the course of human history adds items continually. All of these disunions are variations of the state of disunion that is intrinsic to the knowledge of good and evil."[12] As is obvious from the nature of this list, it is not only the one reflecting but also what that one perceives as reality that is affected by the fall. Both the human subject and the worlds it objectifies are powerless to overcome the human dilemma. Neither human action, construed as morality, nor human reflection, construed as knowledge, can redeem humanity.

It is in the third stage of "God's Love and the Disintegration of the World" that Bonhoeffer comes round to the problem's solution. Because of humanity's powerlessness in this respect, a solution outside the limits of human moral reflection is required. It is found in nothing other than God's action to reconcile the world to himself in Jesus Christ. Because estrangement between God and humanity could not be ameliorated by human effort, it was overcome by God's effort in becoming human. Thus Jesus Christ is the redemption of the world and the restorer of communion.

The fact that Bonhoeffer sees Jesus Christ as the solution to humanity's basic dilemma is not particularly surprising. This is the answer—really just a reworking of the traditional doctrine of justification—that one would expect from Bonhoeffer the Christian theologian.[13] What is surprising is that Bonhoeffer does not stop here. While not wanting to undermine the objectivity of the atonement in any way, Bonhoeffer is really interested in the story of Jesus Christ and the effect of Jesus's life on the believing subject. It is important to note the characteristic manner in which Bonhoeffer portrays Jesus, for it is precisely this portrayal that demonstrates how Jesus transforms the person who sees him. Bonhoeffer's description of Jesus Christ focuses on the contrast, rooted in the Gospel portrayals, between Jesus and the Pharisees. The Pharisees are the quintessential moral persons. Thus their depiction in the Gospels is a narrative characterization of the way "conscience" functions. The Pharisees are, therefore, not primarily hypocrites; they are authentic, consistent, and conscientious people. Yet it is precisely these persons, "admirable to the highest degree," who represent "the epitome of the human being in the state of disunion."[14] The Pharisees are those who know good and evil and categorize

12. Bonhoeffer, *Ethics*, 308–9.

13. Philip Ziegler writes: "What Bonhoeffer said of *Discipleship* [that it was basically an exposition of the doctrines of justification and sanctification] is no less true of the *Ethics* that followed it. Here too justification shows itself to be central to the proceedings. Bonhoeffer distinctly expounds the doctrine through the interplay of three central categories—*revelation*, *reconciliation* and *reality*." Philip G. Ziegler, "Dietrich Bonhoeffer—An Ethics of God's Apocalypse?" *Modern Theology* 23 (2007): 583 (original italics).

14. Bonhoeffer, *Ethics*, 310.

all people upon that basis. Thus they are purveyors of fundamental disunion. We must acknowledge that Bonhoeffer's portrayal of the Pharisees here is capable of perpetuating a form of the anti-Judaism he detested. Nevertheless, Bonhoeffer was conscious of the importance of Jesus's Jewishness, and his work here does not depend on ignoring it.

The manner in which Jesus responds to the Pharisees, seemingly ignoring their distinctions and alternatives, is rooted in his divine Sonship. Jesus Christ is not a moralist entering into debate with other moralists. He is not bringing a new twist on the knowledge of good and evil. Rather, he is overcoming it through his own sovereign act of freedom. "Jesus," says Bonhoeffer, "speaks out of a total freedom that is not even bound by the laws of logical alternatives."[15] It is a freedom in which Jesus "rises above all laws."[16] But this freedom of Jesus is not an act of Jesus's own autonomy; it is an act of obedience to the divine other, God the Father. Jesus Christ's knowledge proceeds from the deep concordance between God's will and his own. Furthermore, it is this knowledge of God's will that forms the basis of Christ's divine freedom. It is this freedom in Christ that gives his example its power and authority. As Bonhoeffer notes, "The freedom of Jesus is not the arbitrary choice of one among countless possibilities. Instead, it consists precisely in the complete simplicity of his action, for which there are never several possibilities, conflicts, or alternatives, but always only one. . . . He lives and acts not out of knowledge of good and evil, but out of the will of God."[17] Thus, according to Bonhoeffer, Christ's action is rooted, not in alienation, but in unity and communion—the unity and communion between the Son and the Father. Or rather, it is the fact of communion between the Father and the Son that makes Christ's obedience to the Father Christ's own free action, and the Father's own incarnate freedom Christ's act of obedience. The knowledge Christ possesses, which is the knowledge of the Father and of the Father's will, transcends and surmounts the knowledge of good and evil stemming from the fall.

Bonhoeffer does not speak only of Christ's knowledge and action, which would fail to address the question of ethics. He also describes the effects of Christ's action upon the actions and knowledge of those who know him. Just as Christ's own knowledge transcends good and evil by being grounded in God's will, so also *knowledge of Jesus Christ* effects both an analogous transcendence of good and evil and a corresponding knowledge of God's will

15. Ibid., 312.
16. Ibid.
17. Ibid., 313.

in the believing disciple. In other words, knowledge of Christ's reconciliation is the source of a Christian's own reconciling knowledge. Furthermore, this knowledge makes possible a genuine type of moral discernment, a discernment that, because of its basis in reconciliation, will produce reconciling action. As Bonhoeffer says,

> Just as there is a false human activity that is itself a judging, so now there is also, surprisingly enough, a judging that is a genuine human activity, that is, a "judging" that springs from the accomplished unity with the origin, with Jesus Christ. There is a "knowledge" that springs from knowing Jesus Christ as the reconciler. . . . This judging and knowing springs from unity, not from disunion. It therefore creates not further disunion but reconciliation.[18]

Judgment has been replaced with knowledge of Jesus Christ, abstract morality with faith in Jesus Christ. And because the object of disciplined attention is now Jesus, rather than any one of countless conflicting ideals, the human creature finds Jesus Christ to be the source of her own freedom and obedient action. In *Ethics* we see the challenge this sets for Bonhoeffer in his manuscript titled "The Concrete Commandment and the Divine Mandates." This was intended to be one of the final chapters in *Ethics*, and perhaps one of its most concrete. In it we see Bonhoeffer applying this same christological realism to the traditional doctrine of the orders of creation. Instead of speaking of "orders" or "estates," Bonhoeffer switches to "mandates" explicitly because he wants to emphasize the "concrete divine commission grounded in the revelation of Christ and the testimony of scripture."[19] He believes that a mandate connotes an ongoing link between these institutions and the command of God. The language of "orders" or "estates" can imply, for Bonhoeffer, that these institutions have a static, standalone character detached from ongoing divine authorization.

Returning to "God's Love and the Disintegration of the World" we see that the fourth step of Bonhoeffer's argument is where he spells out what Christian obedience looks like. Not surprisingly, the first thing Bonhoeffer has to say about Christian obedience is that it is not an autonomous human action; rather, obedience comes about solely through the call of Jesus Christ. This is because humans in their own power cannot overcome their knowledge of good and evil. Christ's call must do that to them and for them. The call of Jesus Christ "overcomes the old knowledge resulting from the fall and instead instills the new knowledge of Jesus, that knowledge which consists entirely

18. Ibid., 316.
19. Ibid., 389.

in doing the will of God."[20] In other words, obedience comes about first and foremost through Christ's action upon the disciple, not by the disciple's own grasping of an idea or moral principle. In this is God's love, and this is the posture to which the biblical witness points.

Bonhoeffer insists that dependence upon Christ overcomes fallen morality precisely because he does not want his discussion of "discernment" to become disconnected from obedience to God's will in Christ. He does not want discernment of any given possible action in the midst of life's circumstances to become merely an exercise in autonomous moral categorization. But this does not mean that all human reflection is to be discarded and that one is to wait and act only on the basis of divine inspirations before doing anything. In fact, Bonhoeffer is quite adamant about the importance of analyzing the actual life situations that force us to decide between one or more courses of action. Thus it is important to include all the reflection that is usually categorized as constituting moral casuistry, for example, "attentive perception of the context," comparison of the present dilemma to "past experiences," foresight into the "possibilities and consequences" of any given situation, and consideration of human "abilities to be employed."[21] And yet, though these analyses must be employed, they are neither final nor ultimate. For, from the Christian perspective, this sort of reflection must conclude with humility, with asking God for illumination and looking to Christ alone for justification. As Bonhoeffer says, "Our self-examination will therefore always consist precisely in surrendering ourselves completely to the judgment of Jesus Christ."[22] One of the most important things to note about "God's Love and the Disintegration of the World" is how its problematization of morality serves to support, rather than undermine, the narration of God's command in Jesus Christ. Though the opening sally directed against all systems of good and evil uses language identical to that of Bonhoeffer's Barcelona lecture, it now functions differently. The Barcelona lecture does not direct the reader to the person of Jesus as the means by which the knowledge of good and evil is overcome. This is because at that point Bonhoeffer utilized a model of divine command averse to specification. The fact that the opening chapter of *Ethics* suggests that dialectic knowledge of good and evil is only overcome in Jesus Christ, the perception of which is obtainable only through the narrative account of Christ in the Gospels, demonstrates a strong continuity between the *Ethics*

20. Ibid., 318.
21. Ibid., 324.
22. Ibid., 325–26.

manuscripts and *Discipleship*. There can be little doubt of this continuity, furthermore, when Bonhoeffer explicitly describes the Christ event in terms of freedom—God's freedom in Christ, Christ's own human freedom, and the freedom he imparts to those who faithfully see him.

Just as *Discipleship* and the opening chapter of *Ethics* share the same model of divine freedom, they also share the same essential moral anthropology. The fundamental problem of fallen humanity according to *Discipleship* is the egocentricity of its individuals. This egocentricity manifests itself as selfishness prompting alienation. It is precisely this model of fallen human subjectivity that is assumed in "God's Love and the Disintegration of the World." In fact, this model of fallen human subjectivity is the primary rationale for rejecting ethics and morality. Moral perception and action in accord with the results of that perception, according to Bonhoeffer, are bound to further isolate the ego from others. This is especially clear in Bonhoeffer's discussion of conscience.

Discipleship and *Ethics* share the same moral anthropology, and therefore they share the same soteriology. The problem with human subjectivity is its fundamental egocentricity manifested as selfishness, isolation, and reflexivity. This can only be overcome through the action of another subjectivity impinging upon it from without. The self-enclosed human subject must be confronted by the divine subject in order to be led out of itself and toward others. In both the *Ethics* manuscripts and *Discipleship* it is the divine subjectivity narrated in Jesus Christ that makes this confrontation possible. It is true that *Discipleship* focuses more obviously upon the *call* of Christ as the source of liberation from self than does *Ethics*. Nevertheless, when *Ethics* sees Jesus Christ as the embodiment of divine freedom as well as the source of human freedom, the logical question is the mediation between the two; the clear answer is the call and command of God in Jesus Christ. In both *Discipleship* and *Ethics* the appropriate human response is not reflection, not a utilitarian weighing of cost and benefit, but simple, immediate obedience.

That both *Discipleship* and the first chapter of *Ethics* share models of divine freedom, moral anthropology, and soteriology certainly suggests that what is written in *Ethics* has more in common with *Discipleship* than it does with the Barcelona lecture on ethics. The Barcelona lecture does presume a moral anthropology and soteriology similar to what is found in *Discipleship* and *Ethics*, but it articulates a model of divine freedom that does not survive Bonhoeffer's own critical scrutiny in *Act and Being*. However, the fact that *Ethics* agrees with *Discipleship* with respect to divine freedom strongly suggests that between *Discipleship* and *Ethics* there is no dramatic break or shift but, instead, basic continuity and logical development.

"Christ, Reality, and Good: Christ, Church, and World"

Bonhoeffer's second intended chapter for *Ethics* was probably begun in the first phase of his work on the project, during the summer or fall of 1940. It opens with the question of reality. What is reality? What is the world? In the opening chapter, just discussed, Bonhoeffer focused upon Jesus Christ as a judgment upon and transformation of the knowledge of good and evil. What this means, however, is that it is precisely our perceptions of reality that come under judgment and are in need of transformation. Stated differently, because our alienation from God irrevocably distorted our conceptions of reality, it is through reconciliation with God that our vision of reality is made clear. It is in "Christ, Reality, and Good" that Bonhoeffer outlines what reality looks like in Christ.

Bonhoeffer begins by suggesting that all ethical questions are inextricably linked to the question of the nature of reality. For instance, to presume that the primary goal of ethical inquiry is the improvement of the world or the moral growth of the self, "the decision has already been made that the self and the world are the ultimate realities."[23] Bonhoeffer, in posing the question of reality, is only beginning where all ethics begins, whether or not this is recognized explicitly by the ethicist. Bonhoeffer is also asking about reality in order to show that this question, too, like the question of the good, is a contested one. He is asking about ultimate reality in order to render questionable the very realities that most ethical systems presume to be the only or at least the primary reality. From the perspective of Christian ethics, at least, it is not the self or the world that is ultimate, but God. If God is the ultimate reality, then the self and the world are not ultimate but penultimate. This does not mean that the world and the self are unreal, a sort of acosmism, but that "these realities, myself and the world, are themselves embedded in . . . the reality of God the Creator, Reconciler, and Redeemer."[24]

Bonhoeffer intends nothing less than bringing metaphysics itself under the lordship of Christ, the particularity of God's freedom expressed in Jesus. The extent of Bonhoeffer's intent is elucidated in a manuscript written shortly after the one we are currently considering. This later one, called "Ultimate and Penultimate Things," was intended to appear near the middle of *Ethics*. In it Bonhoeffer expounds on the "origin and essence" of the Christian life—the doctrine of justification. Justification is, in Bonhoeffer's words, "something ultimate." But God's word of justification presupposes a temporal context,

23. Ibid., 47–48.
24. Ibid., 48.

what Bonhoeffer calls the "penultimate."[25] Theologically, the risk is that one obliterates the other—creation in time hedging out the transcendent, or vice versa. The challenge is resolved through God's entering into created reality in Jesus Christ. Jesus's existence as a human creature, crucified and resurrected, both judges the penultimate and upholds it. This relates to issues of justice and political stability. For example, Bonhoeffer writes, "Slaves who have been so deprived of control over their time that they can no longer hear the proclamation of God's word cannot be led by that word of God to a justifying faith."[26] The penultimate must be preserved for the ultimate, even as the ultimate upholds the value of the penultimate.

This, in part, is where Bonhoeffer's thinking in "Christ, Reality, and Good" is headed. As we further track the structure of his logic in the formative manuscript, we see that since God is the ultimate reality, the purpose of Christian ethics is not moral growth or "making the world a better place," as some ethical systems would have it, but witness to God's ultimate goodness, even if such a witness comes at the expense of improvement.[27] This does not mean, of course, that the pursuit of theocentric goals will inevitably lead to demoralization, guilt, or neglect of the world's needs, but it does at least radically transform the rationale for pursuing these penultimate ends even as it may call them into question more broadly. It may not be clear how Bonhoeffer's theocentric reorientation will bring about the unifying effect noted in the previous section. It is, after all, more than possible that "God" and "reality" could be played one against the other in a way that would only serve further bifurcation of ethical categories. In such a scenario, God and world could function in the same way the ideal and the real do in some ethical frameworks. Such idealism is, of course, the exact opposite of Bonhoeffer's intent here, just as it opposes his lifelong aversion to principle-based ethics. But rather than attack the problem of idealistic ethics with reference to God's command, as he does in *Discipleship*, in this manuscript Bonhoeffer offers a more formal and a more foundational theological solution.

The reason that God and the world, or God's will and reality, cannot be played off each other is rooted in the incarnation. In the incarnation of God "the reality of God has entered into the reality of this world."[28] Just as it would be theologically inappropriate to understand God without reference to God's becoming real in the midst of the world, so also it is inappropriate to understand the nature of the world without reference to God's becoming

25. Ibid., 146, 149, 150, 157.
26. Ibid., 160.
27. Ibid., 48.
28. Ibid., 54.

real in its midst. It is by virtue of the indivisibility of the two natures of Christ's person that world and God are inextricably related to and reconciled with one another. In other words, to oppose God's will and worldly reality in some sort of formal ethical dialectic analogous to the ideal/real distinction is tantamount to heresy of the highest order. Bonhoeffer believes it teaches and maintains a false ethical dichotomy that subverts the truth about God and the reality of the world.

Defining the real of the world in reference to God in Christ has far-ranging consequences for Bonhoeffer's moral thought. Foremost among these is an aversion to abstract formal antinomies in moral reasoning. These polarities include the dialectics between "ought and is, idea and realization, motive and work," but also the distinction popularized by Reinhold Niebuhr between "moral man and immoral society."[29] These dualistic moral frameworks are superseded by another dynamic entirely. They are replaced with a more theologically coherent dynamic relationship between God's past action accomplished in Christ and our present participation in that same reality through the Holy Spirit.[30] What this means, more concretely, is that action according to reality is our participation in what reality is shown to be in Christ. Just as the world and God are reconciled and made whole in Christ, so also participation in that reality addresses the self and the world as wholes. It is in this way, by seeing and participating in the Christ event, that erroneous abstract dichotomies are overcome and replaced. It is no longer appropriate to divide the person from her work, the private from the public, the will from the accomplishment, or the intention from the result, and identify one as "good" or as the criterion for good action at the expense of the other. Such identifications split the person in two and bifurcate the world that the self perceives as real. In place of these divisions, Bonhoeffer offers the whole Christ, who assumes the whole world in himself.

One of the most important conclusions Bonhoeffer draws from his holistic account of reality in Christ relates to the "two-kingdoms" legacy of his Lutheran heritage. This schema, though it has many different historical permutations, revolves around a dichotomy between the church and the world. The primary target of Bonhoeffer's denunciation is the "pseudo-Lutheran" versions of this dualism articulated by many of his contemporary German theologians.[31] When reality as a whole is divided into a churchly realm and a worldly realm, the tendency is to envision each realm as mutually exclusive and

29. Ibid., 50–51.
30. Ibid., 50.
31. Ibid., 56.

self-contained. This is problematic because it contributes to the autonomy of both realms. Thus there develops a notion that the world behaves according to laws of its own, while the church is supposed to live according to another, wholly different set of laws. The more definite and absolute the lines are drawn between church and world, the greater the alienation of the church from the world and the world from the church. Bonhoeffer suggests as much when he says, "Realm thinking as static thinking is, theologically speaking, legalistic thinking. . . . Where the worldly establishes itself as an autonomous sector, this denies the fact of the world's *being accepted* in Christ, the grounding of the reality of the world in revelational reality, and thereby the validity of the gospel for the whole world." Similarly, when the Christian realm is understood as autonomous, the world is cut off from the community of God formed in Christ. Bonhoeffer concludes, "A Christianity that withdraws from the world falls prey to unnaturalness, irrationality, triumphalism, and arbitrariness."[32] Bonhoeffer's language is quite insistent on this particular point because the more absolutely one distinguishes between "church" and "world," the more damage one does to the church, the world, and ultimately to the perceived efficacy of Christ. The church becomes alienated from the world, preoccupied with its own internal order, or, alternatively, it becomes increasingly hostile to the world of unbelief. The world, on the other hand, is left entirely to its own devices and to its own self-understanding. In this way the universal scope of the incarnation is undermined, and reality is no longer reality from, in, and toward Christ. Rather, a totalizing definition of the world is articulated in which Christ is simply one parochial element among others. In dogmatic terms, justification is aborted.

Only after emphasizing the unified nature of all reality as assumed by God in Christ does Bonhoeffer introduce the idea of the "divine mandates" of "work, marriage, government, and church."[33] That is to say, only after speaking of the problems with splitting reality into two mutually incompatible realms does Bonhoeffer introduce his own distinctions in the form of divine mandates. These mandates are divinely given tasks for human beings to undertake. They are not separable "realms," because by their very nature as tasks they can be undertaken by any given person severally at a time. The theory of divine mandates, as explained here in "Christ, Reality, and Good" and later expanded in "The Concrete Commandment and the Divine Mandates," is curious. As we said earlier, it is clearly a destabilizing of the more traditional "orders" or "estates" of creation, concepts that Bonhoeffer believes are too static. To

32. Ibid., 60–61.
33. Ibid., 68.

speak of orders of creation gives the impression that the existing social order is decisive. However, as others have noted, it is strange that Bonhoeffer should only discuss these four mandates. Nevertheless, what he is trying to do is allow for necessary conceptual distinctions without undermining the overarching unity of reality in Christ. In Bonhoeffer's view, "the Christian is at the same time worker, spouse, and citizen."[34] Such a person would, then, be undertaking the mandates of church, work, and marriage throughout his or her life, and often simultaneously. And yet it is possible, and often necessary, to distinguish between the mandates for the purpose of ethical clarification. Work as work is obviously distinguishable from marriage as marriage, and so one mandate should not be collapsed into another. They are different ethical phenomena and deserve their own distinct analyses.

One aspect of "Christ, Reality, and Good" that seems to stand in tension with *Discipleship* is the critique of two-kingdoms theology described above. Bonhoeffer's holistic view of reality in Christ allows for a distinction between the mandates but not an antagonistic dualism between church and world. This much is obvious. What is highly debatable is how Bonhoeffer's insistence upon the holistic nature of reality compares with his earlier understanding in *Discipleship*. It has been suggested, for instance, that Bonhoeffer's opposition to a church/world dualism in *Ethics* constitutes a repudiation of *Discipleship*. Larry Rasmussen, for one, claims that "with this dissolution of two spheres [in *Ethics*] Bonhoeffer relinquishes the necessarily parasitic dependence of his own theological pacifism in *The Cost of Discipleship*. He also opens the way to legitimizing the use of violence by the disciple."[35] In other words, Bonhoeffer's supposed repudiation of two-sphere theology constitutes a fundamental moral shift. Though it may be true that the *Ethics* manuscripts share with *Discipleship* many foundational assumptions about Christian ethics, it is argued that the change in how the church/world relationship is construed is significant enough to entail radically different practical moral outcomes. This reading of *Ethics* is so prominent that it must be engaged here in some depth.

Rasmussen's account does possess a kernel of truth. Ernst Feil, for instance, is probably correct to point out that in *Discipleship* the "world" has more negative connotations than it does in *Ethics*.[36] Nevertheless, this does not necessarily mean that *Discipleship* is basing these judgments upon a formal two-sphere theology of the sort Bonhoeffer will later critique.

34. Ibid., 73.

35. Rasmussen, *Dietrich Bonhoeffer*, 122.

36. Ernst Feil, *The Theology of Dietrich Bonhoeffer*, trans. Martin Rumscheidt (Philadelphia: Fortress, 1985), 125–52.

The negative valuations attached to the notion of "world" in *Discipleship* could just as well be due to *Discipleship*'s nature as a work of theological exegesis of the New Testament. Or it could be due to the more polemical style of the volume generally. It is also possible that though *Ethics* was not written to repudiate any aspect of *Discipleship*, its more positive evaluation of the "world" was seen by Bonhoeffer as offering a necessary corrective to the former work's less-guarded statements. This could partly explain why Bonhoeffer would make the sorts of statements about *Discipleship* recounted at the beginning of this chapter. But even if the shift is an intentional corrective, the fact that the later work amends the earlier does not mean Bonhoeffer is *repudiating* his prior perspective. Correction does not entail repudiation unless that which is correcting and that which is corrected are logically incompatible.

One of the reasons it may be difficult to see the continuities between *Discipleship* and *Ethics* regarding church/world relations is due to the nuanced nature of Bonhoeffer's critique in the latter volume. Despite his refutation of a strong church/world dualism in *Ethics*, as has already been seen, Bonhoeffer has no difficulty in distinguishing the church from the other divine mandates. Furthermore, in *Ethics* Bonhoeffer has no qualms distinguishing "church" from "world." This is clear from chapter headings such as "Church and World" and "On the Possibility of the Church's Message to the World." These two proposed chapters present nuanced treatments of the complex interrelationship of church and world, but they do so by maintaining the distinction between them. Furthermore, even a cursory examination of other writings by Bonhoeffer from the same time period demonstrates that the naming of "church" in apposition to "world" is still quite possible for his thinking.[37] He is not, therefore, advising the abolition of the distinction between church and world in his insistence upon the unitary nature of reality in Christ in "Christ, Reality, and Good." His primary concern is with the possibly misleading uses of this distinction. The distinction itself is valid. With respect to the current discussion, this means that finding a distinction between church and world in *Discipleship* does not necessarily imply that *Ethics* opposes *Discipleship*. *Ethics* itself contains the same distinctions.

Bonhoeffer insists that reality is one in Christ. But because this assertion does not prevent him from making distinctions between church and world, it is logical to assume that Bonhoeffer has something very specific in mind when

37. Dietrich Bonhoeffer, "A Study on 'Personal' and 'Objective' Ethics," in *Conspiracy and Imprisonment: 1940–1945*, ed. Mark Brocker, trans. Lisa E. Dahill and Douglas W. Stott, vol. 16 of *Dietrich Bonhoeffer Works* (Minneapolis: Fortress, 2006), 540–51.

he denounces thinking in terms of two kingdoms. The primary problem with two-kingdoms theology for Bonhoeffer lies in its tendency to interpret the distinction between church and world such that, by implication, there are in fact two ontological realities with which Christian ethics must concern itself. This ontological dualism is created and maintained by the tendency to derive normative ethical or moral values for the "world" that are unaddressed by the claim of Christ's lordship. This is evident when Bonhoeffer says, "Thinking in terms of two realms understands the paired concepts worldly-Christian, natural-supernatural, profane-sacred, rational-revelational, as ultimate static opposites that designate certain given entities that are mutually exclusive." The problem is that such thinking "fails to recognize the original unity of these opposites in the Christ-reality and, as an after-thought, replaces this with a forced unity provided by a sacred or profane system that overarches them."[38] Thinking in terms of two spheres leads to the definition of norms that are opposed to each other. Thus without necessarily intending to do so, some uses of two-kingdoms theology can define the world in such a way that Christian action is completely ineffectual and irrelevant a priori. In such a "world," obedience to Jesus Christ is impossible not because of sin or rebellion but because Christ's lordship exists only inside the walls of a church building. In sum, two-kingdoms thinking is dismissed by Bonhoeffer primarily because it takes the world's recalcitrance too seriously.

The question is whether *Discipleship* presupposes the sort of two-kingdoms thinking with which Bonhoeffer later takes issue. Does *Discipleship* articulate a dualistic split in the nature of reality? Does it presume that the church and world should function under completely antagonistic and mutually exclusive sets of laws?

In both *Discipleship* and *Ethics* Bonhoeffer bases his ecclesiology on a nuanced Christology that enables him to articulate the necessary distinctions between church and world without losing sight of the unity of reality. Basing his judgment on long-established church teaching, Bonhoeffer understands the incarnation to entail the assumption not only of one human individual but also of the entire human race. As Bonhoeffer says in *Discipleship*:

> When contemplating [the incarnation], the early church fathers insisted passionately that while it was necessary to say that God had taken on human nature, it was wrong to say that God had chosen a single, perfect human being with whom God would then unite. [Rather] God became human. This means God took on the whole of our sick and sinful human nature. . . .

38. Bonhoeffer, *Ethics*, 58–59.

> The incarnate Son of God was thus both an individual self and the new humanity. Whatever he did was at the same time also done on behalf of the new humanity which he bore in his body.[39]

What this means is that Jesus Christ, precisely in being particular, has a universal impact upon the nature of humanity and of reality as a whole. Because Jesus Christ lived, died, rose again, and ascended to the Father, all of human nature has lived, died, risen, and ascended in and with him. What is reality in Christ is also reality for the whole world he encompasses. And yet Christ was and continues to be a particular human being. One cannot abolish the universality of Christ without also abolishing his particularity, or vice versa, for it is precisely in the particularity that the universal is assumed.

This Christology funds Bonhoeffer's ecclesiology. So it should come as no surprise that the distinction-within-unity between God's assumption of the individual human and the whole of human nature in Christ has its parallel in the church. The church is, after all, the *body* of Jesus Christ. Because Jesus Christ is both a particular human being and the one in whom all humanity has been adopted, the church participates in both of these dual realities at the same time. The church is a concrete, particular, and discreet social phenomenon in time and space. But it also simultaneously participates in the entirety of the human race as assumed in the person of Christ. In this way Bonhoeffer's ecclesiology stresses two seemingly different things, the particularity of the church and the universality of Christ's humanity in which it participates. At one discreet moment in his argument Bonhoeffer may stress one aspect of this distinction over the other, but a patient and careful reader of the texts will eventually find the other emphasized as well.

When it is suggested that *Ethics* represents a repudiation of *Discipleship*, the unspoken insinuation is that the parochialism and naive, ecclesiastical sentimentality of *Discipleship* is replaced by a more mature recognition of the unified nature of all reality. This is a misreading of *Discipleship*. It is not difficult, however, to see how such an error can be made. *Discipleship* is primarily focused on the church—its nature, its order, and its mission—while *Ethics* situates the church within a broader framework of the other divine mandates. This difference in format, combined with the polemical voice of some portions of *Discipleship* in comparison with the more considered tone of the *Ethics* manuscripts, could well lead one to the conclusion that *Discipleship* rests upon a harsh ontological dualism between church and world,

39. Dietrich Bonhoeffer, *Discipleship*, ed. Geffrey B. Kelly and John D. Godsey, trans. Barbara Green and Reinhard Krauss, vol. 4 of *Dietrich Bonhoeffer Works* (Minneapolis: Fortress, 2000), 214–15.

while *Ethics* sees the unitary nature of all reality. But such an interpretation does not pay close enough attention to the fact that in *Discipleship*, just as in *Ethics*, Bonhoeffer's ecclesiology simply does not permit him to establish an ontological disjunction between church and world. There is a difference between the two entities, and it is appreciable; but that does not constitute an ontological dualism, neither does such a differentiation stand in contrast to *Ethics*. Both *Ethics* and *Discipleship* share the same unified vision of reality in Christ that allows them to differentiate church and world without tearing them apart.

Though it is incorrect to posit a strong disjunction between *Discipleship* and *Ethics* regarding the church/world relationship, the fact that this error is made by otherwise discriminating readers may indicate the potential "dangers" Bonhoeffer saw in *Discipleship*. Although it is impossible to prove, it is likely that the "dangers" Bonhoeffer saw in *Discipleship* lie in the possibility of its being pressed into the service of an ontological dualism and an ethical dichotomization between church and world. Though *Discipleship* does not, in fact, assume such dualisms, it is easy to see how it could be understood that way. With this danger in mind, then, it is possible that Bonhoeffer intended *Ethics* to contextualize the ecclesiocentrism of *Discipleship*, not by shifting his fundamental theological ethics or ecclesiology, but by writing a formal work of Christian ethics meant to deal not only with the church but also with vocational life, the nature of government, and the nature of marriage, as well as the value, rights, and duties of the human person. This is not to say that *Discipleship* does not speak of some of these very same topics. *Discipleship* does indeed speak of marriage, vocational life, and government. But a formal treatment of these mandates is not its primary emphasis. Thus it is only natural that the *Ethics* manuscripts should examine these in more detail, albeit from the same fundamental premises.

"Ethics as Formation"

The proposed third chapter of Bonhoeffer's *Ethics*, "Ethics as Formation," was probably written in the second half of 1940. It rests upon the very same assumptions as the two previous chapters, only here the implicit becomes explicit: Bonhoeffer speaks about the *form* of Christ and the *formation* of those who faithfully see him. The notion that Christ possesses a form and that this form stands over against abstract human principles was clearly present from the very first chapter of *Ethics*. Similarly, the idea that Christ's form acts to shape human identities is also clearly presupposed. But it is not until the third chapter that form and formation are named as constituting the particular type of Christian ethics Bonhoeffer endorses.

Bonhoeffer sets up this discussion by considering several alternatives, each of which he surely saw enacted. One option was to rely on what appeared reasonable. But Bonhoeffer quickly states that the failure of "reasonable people is appalling; they cannot manage to see either the abyss of evil or the abyss of holiness."[40] They try to be fair to everyone and are overrun by opposing forces. They resign themselves to an "unreasonable world" and accomplish nothing. Even more appalling, however, "is the bankruptcy of all ethical *fanaticism*." Fanatics believe that purity and moral fortitude are enough to conquer evil. But they lose sight of the big picture and charge ahead blindly until they tire and are defeated.[41] Still others rely on their conscience or retreat into the world of their own private virtuousness. Bonhoeffer writes, "Men of *conscience* fend off all alone the superior power of predicaments that demand decision. But the dimensions of the conflicts in which they have to choose, counseled and supported by nothing but their own conscience, tear them to pieces."[42] Those who rely on their consciences fail to realize their own vulnerability to deception. Those who retreat from public life in an attempt to preserve their private virtue are ultimately selfish. Bonhoeffer asserts, "Only at the cost of self-deception can they keep their private blamelessness clean from the stains of responsible action in the world."[43] In good Teutonic fashion, Bonhoeffer admits that the "way of duty" seems to offer a path through moral uncertainty, but passing off responsibility to others by appealing to duty demonizes the self. Those who choose this path "limit themselves to duty [and] never venture a free action that rests solely on their own responsibility. . . . People of duty must finally fulfill their duty even to the devil."[44] Lastly, Bonhoeffer rejects the alternative of relying on personal freedom. The radical takes this option when she values the necessity of an action above her own piety. This person is willing to "consent to the bad, knowing full well that it is bad, in order to prevent the worse."[45] As noble as each of these alternatives appears, Bonhoeffer dismisses each one. None will endure. None can chart a way through the confusion. None can see to the essence of things. Instead, only the person who combines wisdom and simplicity will stand. And this can be grasped only through the reconciliation of the world by God in Jesus Christ.

40. Bonhoeffer, *Ethics*, 78.
41. Ibid.
42. Ibid., 79.
43. Ibid., 80.
44. Ibid., 79.
45. Ibid.

God's revelation in Jesus happened in time and space. Because human beings exist and perceive in time and space, God's revelation was perceivable. It was perceivable as an object of human attention and awareness. It was also a particular and distinct object, a particular human in time and space—Jesus Christ. Jesus Christ had a particular form as the subject who disclosed the truth of God and God's world. Bonhoeffer directs faithful moral vision to Christ's form in order to draw moral inferences to serve as guides for moral discernment in his particular context of social upheaval. When Bonhoeffer speaks of the form of Jesus Christ, he is not talking about an idea but about the flesh-and-blood Jesus Christ whose life is narrated in the Gospels. The effect of the Jesus of the Gospels upon humanity can be understood in the fashion of a triptych with panels for the incarnation, crucifixion, and resurrection. These three distinct pictures disclose the reality about the world in which we live and act, and just so they can shape us and guide our action.

The first panel of the christological drama that Bonhoeffer explores is the incarnation. Here Bonhoeffer emphasizes how God entered into real humanity. God did not unite with an isolated, morally perfect human individual but with all of humanity, with its sin and relative virtue. From this theological fact Bonhoeffer speaks against twin errors: idealization of humanity and disgust for humanity. Both represent a disguised hatred of the real humanity that Christ assumed.[46]

The second panel is that of Christ the crucified one. Jesus Christ was judged by God on the cross through his death. Human beings can be reconciled to God only in and through death. This divine judgment against all sin and unrighteousness leads Bonhoeffer to exclude two opposing criteria of ethical judgment: the view that success is its own justification and the moralist view that the good is entirely independent of success or failure. The backdrop for Bonhoeffer's thoughts here is most likely the surrender of France in the early summer of 1940, which was an overwhelming success for Germany.[47] Yet Bonhoeffer rejects both absolute ethical criteria because neither can escape God's judgment. Both the successful and the good are destined to death, and thus both success and moral goodness are unsuitable substitutes for the cross as criteria for assessing history.[48]

The third panel of the christological drama is that of the resurrection. The overcoming of death through the resurrection means that humanity has been liberated from death's absolutism. We can now live as ones liberated from

46. Ibid., 84–87.
47. Ibid., 89n55.
48. Ibid., 88–91.

either a desperate clinging to all life's pleasures or an immoderate carelessness. The resurrection dethrones the ultimate power of death so that an appropriate affirmation of life can be made, one that neither denigrates nor absolutizes earthly existence.[49]

In the description of these three panels that together constitute the form of Christ, Bonhoeffer has already drawn certain moral inferences. In so doing he suggests how obedient human life can be formed in Christ's image. These inferences are meant to describe the true essential nature of reality and therefore possess a universal descriptive scope. Yet, though these descriptions of humanity are universally valid, Bonhoeffer believes that it is only in the church that real human beings are given their humanity. He claims, "He who bore the form of *the* human being can only take form in a small flock; this is Christ's church." What formation means, then, is primarily "Jesus Christ taking form in Christ's church."[50] The church is not a religious community, an aggregate of the like-minded. It is "the human being who has become human, has been judged, and has been awakened to new life in Christ."[51] Though all humanity has been described in the form of Christ, it is only those who are part of the church who come to claim that true humanity. This means that Bonhoeffer's ethics, though universal in scope or intent, recognizes that not all humanity will necessarily find truth in Christ.

The most practical consequence of Bonhoeffer's discussion of the church in this context is that it specifies the context of formation. The formation of those addressed by the form of Christ takes place in and through the church. Christ's form summons or addresses all of human nature, though only some respond. Christ's form illuminates all of human reality, though only some perceive the form and receive illumination. The entire world has been accepted, judged, reconciled, and redeemed, but not all know that this is the case. Thus one way to think of the church is as an epistemologically privileged community that exists for all of humanity. The knowledge given and the formation undergone enable the church to act as a "vicarious representative" for all humanity, a concept that can be traced the whole way back to Bonhoeffer's first dissertation.[52] To act otherwise would be to neglect the very form of Christ that is its basis.

Throughout the entirety of *Ethics* Bonhoeffer opposes moral idealism of any kind. Much of the discussion above has already demonstrated this. The emphasis upon reality in Christ is meant to subvert the dialectic between "ought" and "is" or between the "ideal" and the "real." In these various

49. Ibid., 91–92.
50. Ibid., 96.
51. Ibid., 97.
52. Ibid., 97.

instances—and many more could be cited—Bonhoeffer demonstrates the most consistent facet of his moral thought, the aversion to principle-based ethics and moral absolutes. The "Ethics as Formation" manuscript is no exception. This is not only due to Bonhoeffer's consistency as a writer and thinker. It is also because "formation" is Bonhoeffer's name for his particular account of Christian morality.

In "Ethics as Formation" Bonhoeffer is holding up the person and action of Jesus Christ as a moral archetype or example that should subsequently shape Christian behavior. Therefore Bonhoeffer finds it especially important to ward off a possible idealizing misreading of his views. He vehemently denies, for instance, that what are sometimes called "Christian principles" ought to be developed into a program for reforming the world or ourselves. This denial is carried through to the end of the manuscript, where Bonhoeffer writes, "The following text will not develop a program for the formation of the Western world. But it will speak of how the form of Christ takes form in this Western world."[53] Instead of being a program that we can run, "formation occurs only by being drawn into the form of Jesus Christ, by being conformed to the unique form of the one who became human, was crucified, and is risen. This does not happen as we strive 'to become like Jesus,' as we customarily say, but as the form of Jesus Christ himself so works on us that it molds us, conforming our form to Christ's own (Gal. 4:9). Christ remains the only one who forms."[54] Bonhoeffer's point is that Christians do not remake the world with ideas distilled from Scripture or even Christ's teachings. After all, Jesus did not come to teach a revised form of piety, but to form human creatures anew. The reason Bonhoeffer rejects a view of Christ as "essentially" a teacher is rooted in this central concern: if Christ is primarily a teacher, then it is what he teaches rather than who he is that is of central importance. Bonhoeffer suggests that when this occurs, inevitably a moral ideal or a system of moral principles stands as substitute for Jesus Christ.

Bonhoeffer is also concerned about how moral idealism misconstrues a proper account of human action. When an abstract ideal has taken the place of Jesus Christ, human action takes on another form altogether. It is no longer formation in and by Christ; it is autonomous moral attainment. Central to Bonhoeffer's account of obedience is the axiom that formed action comes only as a result of having been formed. Humans are formed by "being drawn" into and "being formed by" the form of Jesus Christ. The form of Jesus Christ "forms us" in his image. We do not form ourselves, nor do we form the world.

53. Ibid., 101.
54. Ibid., 93–94.

Jesus Christ is the form who forms the world and especially those to whom he is revealed.

This third intended chapter of Bonhoeffer's *Ethics* articulates a type of Christian ethics that is almost identical to that of *Discipleship*. This is most obviously the case when he juxtaposes formation with moral idealism, but the concentration upon formation itself—not to mention the centrality of the church in formation—also suggests a strong affinity with *Discipleship*. The whole second part of *Discipleship* is nothing other than an extended theological meditation upon both the form of Jesus Christ and the subsequent formation of the believing community.[55] The last chapter makes the emphasis upon formation especially clear, dealing as it does with the "image of Jesus Christ" and the believer's likeness to that image. The language is slightly different from *Ethics*, but the point is essentially the same. The form of Jesus Christ is seen and described in the church through faith so that through Christ's form, the believer is conformed to his likeness.[56] There is even a focus in *Discipleship* on the threefold nature of Christ's form—incarnate, crucified, and transfigured.[57] Just as in *Ethics*, each of these aspects shapes human identity. The changes in language or the inferences drawn from the form of Christ in *Ethics* may serve slightly different purposes, but these variances are not caused by some sort of drastic rethinking. Rather, in focusing upon formation in the "Ethics as Formation" manuscript, Bonhoeffer is building upon, if not simply borrowing from, what he said in his earlier book.

In *Discipleship* the correct form of Christ's authority grounds the commandments in Christ's person. Christ's personal authority to command is both absolute and trustworthy because God freely wills to be in this way. The commandments are true and valid because Christ is true and valid—an order that should not be reversed. When the commandments are, however, abstracted from their grounding in Christ's person and made into absolute moral principles, the person of Christ is made subservient to these moral standards. The correct form of moral anthropology, precisely because it grounds the commandments in Christ's person, envisions the action of the moral agent as dependent upon Christ's action in the commanding event. This is the only way moral agents can be obedient to and empowered by Christ's own person, which is to say, by the graciousness of God.

It should be evident, after examining his account of formation above, that in *Ethics* Bonhoeffer continues to hold to these same insights related to the

55. Bonhoeffer, *Discipleship*, 201–88.
56. Ibid., 281–88.
57. Ibid., 285–86.

authority of Christ and moral anthropology. No part of *Ethics* would suggest the autonomy of any certain moral value gleaned from the New Testament or elsewhere. Bonhoeffer does not begin with an ideal such as responsibility, love, duty, reason, or freedom and then analyze the application of this concept to specific cases or ethical scenarios. This entire form of moral reasoning is foreign to *Ethics*, just as it is foreign to *Discipleship*. What this means, then, is that when Bonhoeffer subjects moral idealism to critique in *Ethics*, especially its supposed Christian form as "Christ as teacher," he cannot have anything he wrote in *Discipleship* in mind. *Discipleship* contains the identical critique, directed against the same misleading portrayal of Christ's authority. Related here is the way Bonhoeffer's direct condemnation of private virtuousness leads some of Bonhoeffer's contemporary readers to see in *Ethics* a rejection of the peace ethic of *Discipleship*. However, it is difficult to see how Bonhoeffer shows more self-critique at this point than at others. What Bonhoeffer is rejecting is a selfish piety, one that holds one's moral purity as more important than the lives and welfare of others. Some bellicists might consider this an argument against pacifism, and perhaps it would hold against some types of pacifism, but in this context it is entirely unrelated to the Christ-centered peace ethic embraced by Bonhoeffer.

The grounding of formation in Christ's form has implications not only for the nature of moral action but also for the relationship between the church and the world. One of the hallmarks of the Barthian revolution in theology, with which Bonhoeffer largely agrees, is a rejection of unaided human reason as the means to truth about God and God's world. Bonhoeffer extends this insight about the necessity of God's revelation for theological knowledge to theological ethics. This is especially evident when it comes to the formation of the church. Because the form of Christ is revealed, it creates a distinct community called the church. In the church the form of Jesus Christ is both made known and acknowledged. This epistemological exclusivity cannot be juxtaposed to a more inclusive universality, because it is precisely in the church alone that the whole of the world is made known. On the other hand, because Christ's form already implies the truth about the entire world, it is applicable not only in the church but everywhere. There is no place where Christ's form cannot work or become effective, including life within the mandates of work, marriage, and government.

Because of the central place of the church in *Ethics*, it would be a mistake to suggest that Bonhoeffer's experience in political resistance led him to back down from the "exclusivist claims" of *Discipleship*. Rasmussen has claimed that it was precisely the experience of making common cause with non-Christian humanists that led Bonhoeffer to a new vision of "Christo-universalism."

This universalism, claims Rasmussen, was one that broke with Bonhoeffer's earlier propensity, demonstrated in *Discipleship*, "to locate Christ's [formation] solely in the Church."[58] The preceding analysis shows that this cannot be entirely accurate. Bonhoeffer's Christo-universalism is always rooted in a prior Christo-particularism, in both *Discipleship* and *Ethics*. Though it may be true that *Discipleship* focuses centrally upon the particularity of Christ and the exclusivity of the church, this should not be interpreted as a formal rejection of Christ's universal applicability or of the manner in which the church already includes the world. At most it can be said that the particularism of *Discipleship* becomes more obvious in the light of the universal focus of Bonhoeffer's work in his *Ethics*. As has already been seen, though, this does not entail a rejection of the church's centrality for formation. *Ethics* too, like *Discipleship*, upholds the church in particular as the mandate within which Christ's form is made most fully known.

A better description than Rasmussen's of the relationship between *Discipleship* and *Ethics* is provided by Clifford Green. Green offers the image of two concentric circles as a helpful model for interpreting Bonhoeffer's theology and ethics.[59] The outer circle is best understood as representing the world, while the inner circle represents the church. At the center of both lies God's revelation in Christ. Now, in consideration of all the evidence, it seems appropriate to suggest that while *Discipleship*'s primary concern is the inner circle, *Ethics* is concerned with both. In other words, the relationship between *Discipleship* and *Ethics* is in some ways that of part to whole. The subject matter of *Discipleship* is primarily related to the church and articulated from the perspective of the church looking outward to the world. The subject matter of *Ethics* includes a discussion of the whole of which the church is a part. But because both see the whole of reality from the center of reality, we must go further and suggest that if *Discipleship* is looking from inside the first circle toward the circumference of the outer circle, *Ethics* is looking from the edge of the outer circle inward toward the center. Both works have the same center in Christ, and because this is the case, both also presuppose the same holistic reality. The differences between them are best explained by their differences in perspective.

Any work of systematic reflection is bound to contain undeveloped or underdeveloped themes and dynamics. A work of thought is less like an isolated mechanism of clockwork and more like a work of art. Just as the work of art is singular and self-consistent without being final—it could have turned

58. Rasmussen, *Dietrich Bonhoeffer*, 33.
59. Green, "Editor's Introduction," in Bonhoeffer, *Ethics*, 5.

out differently than it did without contradicting its own consistency—so also any work of the human spirit contains both consistency and potential for further development and growth. When true development occurs in someone's thinking, it is only natural to expect there to be differences between works considered in and of themselves and in comparison with one another. If there were no differences between one work and a subsequent work, there could hardly have been any development. Yet if there were no continuity, there could hardly have been any development either. Development, as the term is being used here, presupposes both continuity and differentiation. Absolute contradiction between one work and another obviously means repudiation of the former on the basis of the latter. Thus far our examination of *Ethics* and *Discipleship* has not found sufficient evidence to suggest that *Ethics* was meant to contradict *Discipleship* in either part or whole. And yet the obvious differences between the two works, in both form and content, compel one to assume that *Ethics* represents a development of *Discipleship*. Such a model of the relationship between the two works, one finished and the other cut short, allows for both continuity and differentiation without implying essential contradiction. Bonhoeffer's thought displayed in the *Ethics* manuscripts is logically dependent upon the *Discipleship* foundation, even as it comes to conclusions that retrospectively expose shortcomings of the latter. Stated in the obverse, the lacunae in *Discipleship* are noted as such, reflected upon, and thus filled and developed in *Ethics* on the basis of essentially the same fundamental convictions that created them in the first place.

7

"Everyone Who Acts Responsibly Becomes Guilty"

Contested Themes in Ethics

In 2003, amid an ongoing international debate about the invasion of Iraq, Jean Bethke Elshtain published a book titled *Just War against Terror*. Elshtain was then and still remains a respected scholar and public intellectual. In the context of that protracted war, her book received significant attention. Elshtain's argument is wide ranging and many fronted, yet it is her reference to the legacy of Dietrich Bonhoeffer that catches our attention here. With the fears of Americans after the events of September 11, 2001, in mind, she wrote: "But to do nothing as people are slaughtered makes one complicit in injustice. The anti-Nazi theologian and martyr Dietrich Bonhoeffer, for example, writing as one dedicated to overthrowing Hitler, judged harshly those who retreated into the 'sanctuary of private *virtuousness*' when confronted with hideous injustice."[1] For her, Bonhoeffer's example was most

1. Jean Bethke Elshtain, *Just War against Terror: The Burden of American Power in a Violent World* (New York: Basic Books, 2003), 24–25. Elshtain refers to Bonhoeffer's example numerous times throughout her book. It is not apparent that any of these subsequent references treat Bonhoeffer more carefully than the one cited here. This is particularly ironic in light of a review article she wrote before September 11, 2001, titled "Dietrich Bonhoeffer *Ethics*" (1949), in which she reminds readers that Bonhoeffer's theology of government cannot be understood outside of

prescient because he recognized the need for a violent response to a world plagued by terror. Elshtain goes on to argue that Americans themselves, as powerful and wealthy as they might have seemed to outsiders, were in such a position. In the world of Elshtain's nationalist security concerns, Bonhoeffer is a saint because he was involved in assassination attempts. As we saw in the last chapter, where we dealt with the foundational *Ethics* manuscripts, Bonhoeffer does denounce the temptation to keep one's hands pure at the expense of the suffering of others. Yet it is far from clear that Bonhoeffer would think a massive preemptive attack could be a proper alternative to the preservation of private virtue.

Elshtain was not alone in her views at the outset of that war, and she remains far from alone in her reading of Bonhoeffer. However, in our view, Elshtain's remarks exemplify a flawed reading of Bonhoeffer, one that is far too common. We part ways with such interpretations at two important points: First, focusing on Bonhoeffer's involvement in the conspiracy to undermine the Nazi government gives the appearance that this action was central to Bonhoeffer's witness. Second, such a focus trades on a fundamental assumption this book questions—that Bonhoeffer was determinatively involved in attempts on Hitler's life. Some contemporary interpreters of Bonhoeffer give the impression that his involvement in plots on Hitler's life is his primary redeeming characteristic. Bonhoeffer did clearly oppose the Nazi regime, but more fundamentally than being an "anti-Nazi" theologian, he was a *Christian* theologian whose care for the world was demonstrated by his deep concern for the church and its witness. This did cause him to oppose Nazism, but it also prompted his opposition to the bourgeois character of the church, deontological ethics, nationalism, the racism and flabby theology he encountered in the United States of America, and the continued division of the Christian community. More central to Bonhoeffer's subversive work was his role as the head of the underground seminary at Finkenwalde and his subsequent mentorship of pastors of the Confessing Church. These activities employed his theological training and ministry experience, both of which were crucial to Bonhoeffer's identity.

Perhaps it is out of shame for the church's support for many deplorable nationalist causes that contemporary commentators lift Bonhoeffer up as proof that Christians are not always caught up in the ideology of nationalism. Or perhaps Bonhoeffer's conspiracy activity is made central in an effort to prove that theologians and academics are not merely talkers and writers but

---

its origin in the New Testament. In the same article she laments the fact that Bonhoeffer is too often turned into an "all-purpose resister." See *First Things*, March 2000, 43.

are also intrepid people of action. However, in describing Bonhoeffer as the quintessential employer of redemptive violence, we risk making his memory a martyr for our own causes. Such vivid misrepresentations of Bonhoeffer often feed on his employment of two significant ideas in *Ethics*: guilt and responsibility. In this chapter we will examine both of these ideas and argue that the way Bonhoeffer develops them is not congruent with the narrative that *Ethics* represents a turn from naive pacifism to mature "realism." We turn our attention first to the place of guilt and responsibility in the *Ethics* manuscripts and then more briefly to several points of comparison between Bonhoeffer's thought and that of the champion of "realism," Reinhold Niebuhr.

Acknowledging Guilt

Scholars of Bonhoeffer and his German context note that few theologians in that period took up the theme of guilt (*Schuld*) with the directness and political relevance that he did.[2] This is part of what makes Bonhoeffer a distinctive theologian of the period. It is not surprising, then, that in her book *Everyone Who Acts Responsibly Becomes Guilty* Christine Schliesser demonstrates that this theme runs the length of Bonhoeffer's body of work.[3] The presence of the theme of guilt in the *Ethics* manuscripts does not represent something radically new in Bonhoeffer's thought. Indeed, Schliesser's in-depth study shows that even though Bonhoeffer's use of the concept in *Ethics* is not identical to its use in *Discipleship*, the function of guilt in the later text is far from novel. As we consider the theme here, many readers will realize that portions of Bonhoeffer's writing have a familiar ring. The fact is that Bonhoeffer's poignancy and frankness have led to his being often quoted on this topic. Such quotations often connect with us on a visceral level, but they become even more significant when we understand how they fit within Bonhoeffer's thought in the early 1940s. This means that we will revisit several of the key themes discussed in the previous chapter. In fact, it is within the christological context of "ethics as formation" that Bonhoeffer intends the concept of guilt to become intelligible. In the last chapter we approached this objective side of Bonhoeffer's ethics through an analysis of three manuscripts that Bonhoeffer intended to frame his approach. Here we will focus initially on a manuscript he intended as a later chapter, "Guilt, Justification, Renewal," which probably

2. Renate Wind, *A Spoke in the Wheel: The Life of Dietrich Bonhoeffer*, trans. John Bowden (London: SCM, 1991), 101.

3. Christine Schliesser, *Everyone Who Acts Responsibly Becomes Guilty: Bonhoeffer's Concept of Accepting Guilt* (Louisville: Westminster John Knox, 2008).

was written in the summer or fall of 1941. This chapter was intended to follow one begun almost a year later called "Church and World." In that manuscript Bonhoeffer argues that publicly acknowledged goods such as reason, justice, culture, humanity, truth, and freedom find their ultimate justification in Jesus Christ. The disruption of these cultural goods forces a reexamination of the relationship of church and world. Therefore followers of Christ find common cause with others who pursue such goods. During this period that he believed was characterized by the inordinate justification of chaos, wickedness, and sin, Bonhoeffer wrote, "Jesus cares for those who suffer for a just cause even if it is not exactly for the confession of his name; he brings them under his protection."[4] The opening paragraph of "Guilt, Justification, Renewal," then, marks a change of perspective, turning once again from a look outward to a consideration of the center. It begins this way: "The issue is the process by which Christ takes form among us."[5] The paragraph concludes with the assertion that falling away from Christ is to fall away from true human nature. This notion of falling away sets up Bonhoeffer's discussion of what it means to return, a process that can only happen through repentance and an acknowledgment of guilt.

Bonhoeffer posits that a genuine acknowledgment of guilt presupposes a relationship to the form of Christ. Guilt is not an emotional, sensory, or experiential category for Bonhoeffer. It does not result from an experience of degradation or moral breakdown.[6] Instead, the concept of guilt functions relationally, and can be acknowledged only by truly encountering the form of Christ. This encounter occurs in the church, which is the place where acknowledging guilt, as Bonhoeffer says, "becomes real."[7] The confession of guilt is part of the very being of the church, and through Christ's leading, the church is the community of the repentant. In this acknowledgment of guilt, Christ takes form in the world. The church is defined by confession in and through each penitent individual who recognizes that even his or her personal sin harms the community. By way of example, Bonhoeffer writes:

> I cannot pacify myself by saying that my part in this is slight and hardly noticeable. There is no calculating here. I must acknowledge that my own sin is to blame for all of these things. I am guilty of inordinate desire; I am guilty of cowardly silence when I should have spoken; I am guilty of untruthfulness

4. Dietrich Bonhoeffer, *Ethics*, ed. Clifford J. Green, trans. Reinhard Krauss, Charles C. West, and Douglas W. Scott, vol. 6 of *Dietrich Bonhoeffer Works* (Minneapolis: Fortress, 2005), 346–47.
5. Ibid., 134.
6. Ibid., 135.
7. Ibid.

> and hypocrisy in the face of threatening violence; I am guilty of disowning without mercy the poorest of my neighbors; I am guilty of disloyalty and falling away from Christ. Why does it concern me if others are also guilty? Every sin of another I can excuse; only my own sin, of which I remain guilty, I can never excuse.[8]

The sort of personal, even individual, examination demonstrated here echoes the fifth chapter of *Discipleship*, where Bonhoeffer writes, "Jesus' call to discipleship makes the disciple into a single individual. Whether disciples want to or not, they have to make a decision; each has to decide alone. Each must follow alone."[9] In neither book does the personal piety that is evident exclude systemic concerns, though it mitigates against the reduction of justification to a theory.

In "Guilt, Justification, Renewal" Bonhoeffer unfolds the theme of guilt to encompass the church's corporate acts, even its inaction. Bonhoeffer wants the church to acknowledge its failings, not because it could have prevented whatever atrocities are in view—those of the Nazi government, for instance—but on the conviction that it did not truly take the form of Christ. Bonhoeffer's words of confession on behalf of the church are dirge-like:

> The church confesses that it has not professed openly and clearly enough its message of the one God, revealed for all times in Jesus Christ and tolerating no other gods besides. The church confesses its timidity, its deviations, its dangerous concessions. It has often disavowed its duties as sentinel and comforter. Through this it has often withheld the compassion that it owes to the despised and rejected. The church was mute when it should have cried out, because the blood of the innocent cried out to heaven. The church did not find the right word in the right way at the right time. It did not resist to the death the falling away from faith and is guilty of the godlessness of the masses.[10]

Bonhoeffer goes on to confess that the church did not protest while misdeeds were carried out under the name of Christ. It allowed the day set apart for worship and rest to be co-opted. It did not speak out against the cult of youth and allowed families to be destroyed. The church did not raise its voice when it witnessed the cruel oppression of those without defense. The church had nothing useful to say about the disruption in the right relationship of the sexes. It did nothing as the poor were taken advantage of. The church wanted

8. Ibid., 137.

9. Dietrich Bonhoeffer, *Discipleship*, ed. Geffrey B. Kelly and John D. Godsey, trans. Barbara Green and Reinhard Krauss, vol. 4 of *Dietrich Bonhoeffer Works* (Minneapolis: Fortress, 2000), 92.

10. Bonhoeffer, *Ethics*, 138–39.

security, quiet repose, and respect it had not earned.[11] In Bonhoeffer's view the church is guilty of breaking the whole of the Decalogue. For Bonhoeffer this "free confession of guilt" is not peripheral—it is not an abnormal act of heroism. It is merely, as he says, "the form of Jesus Christ breaking through in the church."[12] The church is a community of those who confess their guilt before God and the world.

Through confession, the Christian community participates in the shame of the cross. Only in this can the individual or the church be justified and find new life. It is important to emphasize here that the goal of this justification is not the glory of a small, pious community; instead, Bonhoeffer avers that the "renewal of the West lies completely in God's renewal of the church."[13] As Christ renews the church, so the West as a particular historical and political community can be renewed vicariously through the church's action. This would require the return to a just order that would once again allow the church to proclaim the gospel and facilitate the encounter of individuals with Christ, through which true forgiveness and healing could be found. This is how Bonhoeffer's manuscript "Guilt, Justification, Renewal" ends—not on a note that would sound the call for personal virtuousness but on one as tentative as it was expansive. It ends on a note of hope for a society fractured by war.

Two observations about Bonhoeffer's discussion of guilt in this part of *Ethics* are apparent. The first is that the use of this concept is not tantamount to the rejection of the high ethical standards demonstrated in Bonhoeffer's earlier writing. If this were the case, his ownership of guilt would be far less poignant. If Bonhoeffer's understanding of Christian ethics has changed since his writing of *Discipleship*, it certainly has not been watered down. He has not now reduced morality to making the best of a terrible situation. The second observation is that the doctrine of Christology remains central to Bonhoeffer's ethical deliberation. He has not rejected the norm or authority of Christ's command and form for something more "realistic." But this brings us to an important juncture. Up to this point our discussion of guilt has implied what we might call a passive or indirect orientation, the carrying of guilt for either the misdeeds of others or for one's inaction. In either case the misdeed is in the past.[14] Yet readers familiar with Bonhoeffer's *Ethics* know that more is at

11. Ibid., 138–40.

12. Ibid., 142.

13. Ibid.

14. For reflections on the similarity between Bonhoeffer's consideration of guilt and the church's confession of guilt in Germany after the war, see Heinz Eduard Tödt, "Dealing with Guilt in the Church's Confession and in the Justice System after 1945," in *Authentic Faith:*

stake. As Christine Schliesser notes, one of the things that makes Bonhoeffer's use of the concept of guilt slightly different in *Ethics* from his previous work is that here he also contemplates taking on guilt actively, directly violating civil and divine law.[15]

It is one thing to look back in a moment of reflection and acknowledge one's culpability for something already finished. It is quite another to carry out actions that one knows are wrong and morally inexcusable. We turn now toward this second scenario to consider how Bonhoeffer employs the concept of guilt in a more active sense. It is within this realm that Bonhoeffer's involvement in the resistance and his ongoing participation, along with that of his friends and family, in Nazi Germany falls. As we have noted several times in this book, we do not know everything there is to know about Bonhoeffer's involvement in the German resistance. It is clear, though, that he acted against his own government. He sought to make a German surrender more feasible and aided a number of Jewish persons to escape the claws of the regime. It is clear that he did his best to avoid military service at a time when being a conscientious objector to military service was punishable by death. These acts were not incidental to Bonhoeffer's life and thought. Surely Renate Wind is correct to say that for Bonhoeffer "the place where Christ would be present . . . was in the political conspiracy, in the perilous praxis of a piety that voluntarily assumed guilt, in the encounter with fellow human beings who had been forsaken by the world in the prison of Tegel and in the hell of the extermination camps."[16] To begin exploring the theme of actively and voluntarily becoming guilty, we turn to yet another of the *Ethics* manuscripts, "History and Good." Bonhoeffer intended this to become his fourth chapter, following "Ethics as Formation." This manuscript is one that Bonhoeffer did manage to revise. The *Dietrich Bonhoeffer Works* edition of *Ethics* includes both a first and a second draft. Here we will work with the revised version that was likely written in the summer of 1942. We will consider the structure of Bonhoeffer's argument at some length since it also has bearing on the concept of responsibility (*Verantwortung*).[17] In fact, we cannot return to the theme of guilt until we understand how Bonhoeffer construes responsibility.

Bonhoeffer's Theological Ethics in Context, ed. Ernst-Albert Scharffenorth and Glen Harold Stassen, trans. David Stassen and Ilse Tödt (Grand Rapids: Eerdmans, 2007), 262–67.

15. Schliesser, *Everyone Who Acts Responsibly*, 91–92, 144, 164–72.

16. Wind, *Spoke in the Wheel*, 101.

17. See the editors' comments in Bonhoeffer, *Ethics*, 254–55, notes 27 and 32, for a description of the relationship between the English term "responsibility" and the German *Verantwortung* and the verb *antworten*, "to answer," from which it is derived.

Responsibility

We noted in the last chapter how Bonhoeffer's approach to ethics begins with his insistence that reality must be understood through God's revelation in Christ. Now in "History and Good" Bonhoeffer joins to this epistemological assumption the recognition that ethics cannot ignore the unique context of the ethical agent. Human beings are creatures. This statement is a platitude of course, but in Bonhoeffer's ethics it serves as a reminder that any thinking about morality that forgets the essential difference between creatures and the Creator is a dead end. When addressing questions about *the good*, we must remember that we do not have the Creator's privilege; our decisions are made despite limited knowledge and judgment. One of the things that this means for Bonhoeffer is that the category of the generic, hypothetical individual, the abstract subject, is of no use in moral deliberation.[18] Since the abstract subject has no biases and no context, a crucial similarity to all real humans is lost.

It would be easy to link Bonhoeffer's antipathy toward abstraction with his consideration of responsibility, since on the face of it both moves seem to emphasize similar pragmatic concerns. Yet we must consider that although Bonhoeffer's initial critical move could lead to an intuitive ethic devoid of consistency and devoid of guidance—in short, an ethic against ethics—"History and Good" does swing in a constructive direction. The hinge, as we have come to expect, is christological. In its simplest form it is the recognition that Jesus is "the life."[19] True human life is found outside the creature's being, in Christ. Thus life is found in the dialectic of the "No" pronounced on our sinful life and the "Yes" given as we find new life in Christ. In this vein Bonhoeffer writes, "We can no longer speak about our life other than in this relation to Jesus Christ."[20] The proper human response, then, is a life that brings together this negation and affirmation. This means that true life is a response to Christ: this is what Bonhoeffer calls the responsible life.[21] In this way the theme of responsibility becomes a dominant line of thought in the "History and Good" manuscript.

Shortly before Bonhoeffer penned "History and Good," he read proofs of Karl Barth's *Church Dogmatics*, volume 2, part 2, the second half of which deals directly with ethics, the "Command of God" in Barth's terms. In this section Barth writes, "We cannot act as if the command of God issued by

18. Ibid., 247–48.

19. Bonhoeffer cites John 14:6 and the Pauline echoes in Philippians 1:21 and Colossians 3:4 (ibid., 249).

20. Ibid., 251.

21. Ibid., 254.

God's grace to the elect man Jesus Christ, and again by God's grace already fulfilled by this man, were not already known to us as the sum total of the good. We cannot act as if we had to ask and decide of ourselves what the good is and how we can achieve it; as if we were free to make this or that answer as the one that appears to us to be right."[22] Barth's basic dogmatic structure is reflected in Bonhoeffer's manuscript.

We might assume that if Bonhoeffer intended his ethics to be useful and practical, as opposed to abstract and generic, then perhaps he might privilege such a seemingly commonsense motif as responsibility. In English, the term "responsibility" is used regularly and carries a great deal of rhetorical weight, even though its casuistic usefulness is surely doubtful. The term connotes moral seriousness and maturity. It can even imply agents' accountability or liability relative to their effective capacity—their ability to influence the outcome of events. In some cases the term implies calculated action taken regrettably at the expense of prior utopian ideals, as in, "Feeling the weight of her *responsibility*, the young woman put aside her hopes for a college education and went to work in order to support her ill mother." Responsibility appears to be in touch with the challenges of reality and to oppose a sort of squishy optimism. However, these connotations are not at all what Bonhoeffer intends the concept to invoke in *Ethics*. At a fundamental level Bonhoeffer's thinking remains committed to advocating actions that are undertaken with a view toward integrity with the incarnation of Jesus Christ.

Bonhoeffer does endeavor to connect his ethics with reality—but only "reality" in its truest sense, that which is revealed in God's incarnation in Christ. Bonhoeffer writes, "Trying to understand reality without the Real One means living in an abstraction, which those who live responsibly must always avoid; it means living detached from reality and vacillating endlessly between the extremes of a servile attitude toward the status quo and rebellion against it."[23] For most of us, though, it seems more realistic to view the world without the Christ lens; the liturgy of our daily lives inadvertently trains us in this practical ignorance. Bonhoeffer's reversal of this fundamental notion shows the epistemological indispensability of his Christian commitment. In this light, Bonhoeffer's thinking bears no more similarity to the ethical contours of so-called realism than it does to religious fundamentalism. In his view, acts in right relationship with the Son adhere neither to views of Christ that only "sanction the status quo" nor to those of "religious enthusiasts" who would

22. Karl Barth, *The Doctrine of God*, part 2, ed. G. W. Bromiley and T. F. Torrance, trans. G. W. Bromiley et al., vol. 2 of *Church Dogmatics* (Edinburgh: T&T Clark, 1957; repr., Peabody, MA: Hendrickson, 2010), 518.

23. Bonhoeffer, *Ethics*, 262.

see in him a revolutionary mandate.[24] Instead, appropriate acts are done in view of Christ as the one who loves humanity and who is both reconciler and judge. Jesus the Christ is not just the answer to a theological problem. Jesus matters for human moral discernment because through him God has remade the world. This aspect of Bonhoeffer's theology is partly why some scholars describe his approach as "apocalyptic." Bonhoeffer's theological ethics is apocalyptic not so much because it is propelled eschatologically but because he follows the lead of the apostle Paul in assuming that the revelation of Christ redefines reality and the moral capacity of the ethical agent.[25]

Bonhoeffer extends his line of thinking to conclude that the Christian's life is—in the crude, geometric sense of the word—eccentric, meaning that such life has its locus outside itself, in Christ.[26] Responsibility is then conceptually dependent. It can be construed only in relation to that which ultimately shapes realty. Only within the structure of what we might call the "Christ-life" can true responsibility take shape. In *Ethics* this follows from Bonhoeffer's programmatic assertion that knowledge of God in Christ must be prior to knowledge of the ethical. To reverse the order perpetuates a fundamental disunity, for the unity of life is found only in its origin.[27] Responsibility cannot be known apart from God's revelatory act of becoming human.

Though responsibility is conceptually dependent in Bonhoeffer's thought, it is an essential part of *Ethics*. Larry Rasmussen, whose views are under some scrutiny in this book, goes so far as to say that it is the "core theme."[28] If we follow Rasmussen's view, we must remember that Bonhoeffer's notion of responsibility is approachable only through his theology more broadly construed, as described in the preceding paragraphs. Bonhoeffer does not use the term generically or with the assumption that it is universally understood. This point about Bonhoeffer's thought can be sharpened through the claim that responsibility in his view could not entail the *necessity* of Christians using violence to right the wrongs of the world, since abstract theories of what might justify or necessitate such bellicosity are fundamentally antithetical to Bonhoeffer's approach. The exceptional character of his construal of responsibility does not escape Bonhoeffer's awareness. Succinctly put, he believes that in the biblical sense "responsibility is primarily a response, given at the

24. Ibid., 263.

25. Philip G. Ziegler, "Dietrich Bonhoeffer—An Ethics of God's Apocalypse?" *Modern Theology* 23 (2007): 579–94.

26. Bonhoeffer, *Ethics*, 249–50.

27. Ibid., 299–317.

28. Larry Rasmussen, "The Ethics of Responsible Action," in *The Cambridge Companion to Dietrich Bonhoeffer*, ed. John W. de Gruchy (Cambridge: Cambridge University Press, 1999), 206–25, here 218.

risk of one's own life, to the questions people ask about the Christ event."[29] Responsibility means to take ownership of one's role in the engagement of Christ and humanity. Responsibility implies the value of other humans in a way that principle-based ethics does not. Bonhoeffer has Kant in mind:

> Treating truthfulness as a principle leads Kant to the grotesque conclusion that if asked by a murderer whether my friend, whom he was pursuing, had sought refuge in my house, I would have to answer honestly in the affirmative. Here the self-righteousness of conscience has escalated into blasphemous recklessness and become an impediment to responsible action. Since responsible action is the entire response, in accord with reality, to the claim of God and my neighbor, then this scenario glaringly illuminates the merely partial response of a conscience bound by principles.[30]

We see, then, a deep qualification to the notion that responsibility is a core theme in *Ethics*. As central as it may be, responsibility still cannot be considered independent of Christology, for in Bonhoeffer's paradigmatic words from "Christ, Reality, and Good," "the question of the good can only find its answer in Christ."[31]

Responsibility is centrally a *response*. It denotes life "lived in answer to the life of Jesus Christ."[32] Bonhoeffer writes, "Responsibility thus means to risk one's life in its wholeness, aware that one's activity is a matter of life and death."[33] This is opposed to the half answers that come from considerations of utility or timeless principles. Bonhoeffer makes abundantly clear the fact that the responsibility he speaks of is not a common concept or a moral strategy for sorting through competing values. It is not a way of establishing new norms that might release one from culpability. Responsibility cannot be used to mobilize Christians or anyone else for every generic cause bearing the appearance of righteousness. This is the case because acting responsibly is not an attempt to achieve the reconciliation already accomplished by Christ. This, of course, stands in opposition to readings of Bonhoeffer that have rashly used his example to support not only tyrannicide but also various wars and forms of vigilantism. Bonhoeffer's version of responsibility is fundamentally a *response* to the agency of Christ. It is nothing if it loses its rootedness in God's taking on human flesh as the Christian Scriptures portray.[34]

29. Bonhoeffer, *Ethics*, 255.
30. Ibid., 279–80.
31. Ibid., 49.
32. Ibid., 254.
33. Ibid., 255.
34. See Christopher Holmes, "'The Indivisible Whole of God's Reality': On the Agency of Jesus in Bonhoeffer's *Ethics*," *International Journal of Systematic Theology* 12 (2010): 283–301.

Bonhoeffer further anchors responsibility in Christology when he describes it as an act of mediation that resembles the incarnation. Speaking in the first person, he depicts the responsible act this way: "I *simultaneously* represent Christ before human beings, and represent human beings before Christ. My answering for Christ before human ears simultaneously reaches the ears of Christ as my answering for human beings."[35] Bonhoeffer cites 1 Peter 3:15, which enjoins hearers to be prepared to respond to the one who asks for an account of their hope. It is curious that in his use of the concept of responsibility some see Bonhoeffer turning away from the expectations of Christian discipleship. We see instead that responsibility is an act of intercession between humans and Christ. It imitates the divine assumption of humanness, though it does not replace it. Responsibility is the Christian being caught up in the reality of God's self-mediation and reconciliatory nature. It is an ongoing, fresh response to God and humanity seeking to live in light of the reconciliation God has already effected. Responsibility is not the result of the intrusion of commonsense upon a utopian ethic—the evolution of the starry-eyed youngster into the world-weary adult. Bonhoeffer's construal of responsibility questions the "reasonable" because Christ has come and because witnesses to this are called to account by it before God and other creatures. Responsibility can exist only "in confessing Jesus Christ in word and life."[36] Without Bonhoeffer's realist Christology, his concept of responsibility utterly collapses.

In *Ethics* Bonhoeffer describes responsibility not only as a concept, a nexus of theological themes; it is also a practice. Bonhoeffer's pastoral work, ecclesial networking, and various other forms of resistance to the Nazi government were acts of Christ-shaped responsibility. The responsible life is structured by two things: the agent's bond to God and the agent's freedom. Freedom is found in selflessness. Bonhoeffer writes: "The *bond* has the form of *vicarious representative action* and *accordance with reality*. Freedom exhibits itself in *my responsibility* for my living and acting, and in the *venture* of concrete decision."[37] The responsible life is one of action on behalf of others.

The motif of "vicarious representative action" (*Stellvertretung*) has sometimes been translated as "deputyship." As we have noted earlier in this book, it is a theologically defined concept central to Bonhoeffer's anthropology and important for grasping his self-understanding as well as the function of responsibility in his ethics. To explain this idea, Bonhoeffer gives examples

35. Bonhoeffer, *Ethics*, 256.
36. Ibid., 256.
37. Ibid., 257.

of the statesman, the parent, and the instructor—people in positions that are required to act on behalf of others, whether it be the nation, the family, or the guild. He points out that this type of responsibility by virtue of position cannot be avoided, but also that the requirements of responsibility are bound up not only in positions of authority. The social embeddedness of every human creature means that even the hermit experiences the demands of vicarious representation. The human in response to others is the proper focus of ethical reflection. It is Jesus's action that undergirds the entirety of this discussion, since Jesus's assumption of human nature means his life was characterized by vicarious representation on behalf of all humanity.[38] Bonhoeffer writes, "Jesus was not the individual who sought to achieve some personal perfection, but only lived as the one who in himself has taken on and bears the selves of all human beings. His entire living, acting, and suffering was vicarious representative action."[39] In living his whole life in this manner, Jesus is the archetype of humanity, and since he is described as life itself, all of life should be vicarious representative action.

Here we might pause to note that precisely at this point Bonhoeffer's theological ethic seems to betray a worrying "messianic complex" in which the human is deputized for far too much. Though this is a vulnerability of *Ethics* as a whole, we should not fail to notice that even as we surely must be wary of Bonhoeffer's aggrandizement of the Christian, Christology remains the controlling doctrine. The expediencies of necessity or optimistic views of the power of humankind, both of which might cut a messianic ethic loose from its proper dogmatic context, are pushed aside. In some ways ethical "realism" assumes an even greater aggrandizement of the ethical agent.

The life of responsibility is selfless. This does not mean that it is ascetic in a strictly negative sense, as though it were a nearly impossible path or special monastic calling chosen by and meant for only a few. Instead, it is to be understood normatively as the only way of truly living. In this light, and taking into account the nationalistic demands of a nation at war, the question naturally arises regarding the propriety of being responsible to a cause, as in National Socialism, or to a principle, as in pacifism. Bonhoeffer says that the idea of being responsible to a cause is "legitimate" only as long as it is recognized that only through Christ is "the world of things and values given back its orientation toward human beings."[40] Bonhoeffer is not arguing for an anthropocentric cosmology in a technical sense. It is more of an indication of

38. Ibid., 257–58.
39. Ibid., 258.
40. Ibid., 260.

the way in which God is deeply for, or in favor of, humanity's flourishing. This was intended in God's original act of creation but was twisted and masked in the fall, only to be regained through Christ, the new Adam. This is the light in which we should observe Bonhoeffer's ongoing concern for the German people. The corruption of this properly ordered responsibility is serious, for it sacrifices human life to the idol of the cause. Bonhoeffer says that the behavior of responsible people is not fixed in advance, as it might be if bound to specific principles or ideologies. Against such allegiances, he argues that the actions of responsible individuals do not use their contexts as "raw material" from which to fashion the furthering of their own causes or programs.[41] We might say that responsible people are not like the political ideologues who troll the newswires for opportunities to argue their point. Instead, responsible individuals act with sensitivity to their context; they do not disregard it as ones selfishly adhering to principles or seeking to further a cause. This rejection of selfishness and deontological ethics is not an endorsement of a pure intuitionalism, egoism, or situationalism. Instead, it is a manifestation of radical christological commitments.

Acting in responsibility is limited in two key ways. First, Bonhoeffer realizes that one individual's responsibility might be limited by that of another.[42] The sphere within which one's representative action is to take place is restricted. Second, responsibility is refined by the inherent limitations of human creatures.[43] This concession, though—as I will more fully argue later—is not the sin-induced tragedy found in the thought of Reinhold Niebuhr. The uniqueness in Bonhoeffer's conceptualization of human finitude is expressed well in the following:

> Because it was *God* who became human, responsible action, although conscious of the human character of its decision, can never prematurely judge its own origin, essence, and goal, but must completely surrender such judgment to God. Whereas all action based on ideology is already justified by its own principle, responsible action renounces any knowledge about its ultimate justification. The deed that is done after responsibly weighing all personal and factual circumstances, in light of God becoming *human* and *God* becoming human, is completely surrendered to God the moment it is carried out. Ultimate ignorance of one's own goodness or evil, together with dependence upon grace, is an essential characteristic of responsible historical action.[44]

41. Ibid., 261.
42. Ibid., 269.
43. Ibid., 267.
44. Ibid., 268.

We see in this quotation several additional important characteristics of responsible action. First, we see a continuation of the point being made about the finite nature of human life. Bonhoeffer acknowledges the limited character of human moral decision making while at once holding fast to God's grace and the importance of God's free act in the incarnation. The second limitation to responsibility is seen in Bonhoeffer's insistence that the ultimate judgment of one's action must be surrendered to God. The above quotation continues,

> The deed that is done after responsibly weighing all personal and factual circumstances, in light of God becoming *human* and *God* becoming human, is completely surrendered to God the moment it is carried out. Ultimate ignorance of one's own goodness or evil, together with dependence upon grace, is an essential characteristic of responsible action. Those who act on the basis of ideology consider themselves justified by their idea. Those who act responsibly place their action into the hands of God and live by God's grace and judgment."[45]

Individuals possess no complete knowledge of the goodness or evilness of their actions. This does not lead Bonhoeffer down a nihilistic trail; it does not denigrate the moral agent to the point of inaction. The effect is that in Bonhoeffer's schema moral agents cannot, and need not, stand outside God's grace. They are not assumed to be ideal humans free from limits and flaws who are capable of generating their own justification. Bonhoeffer's understanding of freedom is such that the normal parameters of moral decision making, choosing between right and wrong, are surpassed. Bonhoeffer assumes that the Christian will choose what is right. However, action becomes a "free venture" because the agent must sometimes choose between right and right.[46] The challenge for the free and responsible agent is that modern society has stunted our ability to act in this way.[47]

One of the key lines of argument in our book has been that Bonhoeffer's readers should not see a sharp disjuncture between his *Discipleship* and *Ethics*. Important to this discussion, then, is how obedience as emphasized in *Discipleship* can be reconciled with this emphasis on freedom in *Ethics*. Bonhoeffer asserts that obedience and freedom are interwoven by arguing that the two concepts should be laid alongside each other. In "History and Good" he writes, "Obedience without freedom is slavery, freedom without obedience is arbitrariness. Obedience binds freedom and freedom ennobles obedience. Obedience binds the creature to the Creator, freedom places the creature,

45. Ibid., 268–69.
46. Ibid., 284.
47. Bonhoeffer actually uses the phrase "ethically emasculated" (ibid., 286).

made in God's image, face-to-face with the Creator. . . . Obedience knows what is good and does it. Freedom dares to act and leaves the judgment about good and evil up to God."[48] This is a noteworthy claim. In bringing together two seeming opposites, freedom and obedience, Bonhoeffer tries to point to something beyond both. It is in responsibility that the two poles of this dialectic are actualized. In fact, Bonhoeffer argues that trying to have either freedom or obedience without the other would destroy one's ability to act in responsibility. He writes, "Responsible action is bound and yet creative."[49] The response of the ethical agent is developed through this tension, or as Bonhoeffer says:

> Responsible human beings, who stand between obligation and freedom and who, while bound, must nevertheless dare to act freely, find justification neither by their bond nor by their freedom, but only in the One who has placed them in this—humanly impossible—situation and who requires them to act. Responsible human beings surrender themselves and their action to God.[50]

It is striking, then, that we do not need to roam very far afield to find the answer to one of the questions underwriting the inquiry of this chapter. Bonhoeffer has laid out very directly how the obedience of *Discipleship* aligns itself with the freedom of *Ethics*. Chastened by obedience and liberated into action by freedom, the individual follows Christ into the complexity of the world.

Bonhoeffer concludes his reflections on responsibility in "History and Good" by delineating the place of the responsible life. His goal is to outline the relationship of this theme to vocation. In short, Bonhoeffer is wary of the practice of responsibility being controlled by the duties of vocation: "People do not fulfill the responsibility laid on them by faithfully performing their earthly vocational obligations as citizens, workers, and parents, but by hearing the call of Jesus Christ that, although it leads them also into earthly obligations, is never synonymous with these, but instead always transcends them as a reality standing before and behind them."[51] Christian ethics must not be subverted by the ethical parameters of a given office, because the command of God stands in judgment of all other obligations. However, we must quickly note that vocation is far from a useless concept for Bonhoeffer. It is within the context of one's vocation that the Christian responds to Christ's call. Vocation does not control or limit the individual's response, but such a response—the life of responsibility—cannot be outlined without the specifics of one's place in

48. Ibid., 287–88.
49. Ibid., 288.
50. Ibid.
51. Ibid., 291.

the world. Thus responsibility is lived out within one's participation in the world. Here Bonhoeffer echoes *Discipleship*, where he explores the dynamics of the church's visibility. Even in that more ecclesially focused book Bonhoeffer insists that even though there must be points at which the church community is clearly separate, it remains involved in the world. He argues, "Whether in the world or separated from it, Christians in either case seek to obey the same word: 'Do not be conformed to this world, but be transformed into a new form by the renewing of your minds, so that you may discern what the will of God is.' . . . There is an illegitimate way of remaining in the world, just as there is an illegitimate way of escaping from it."[52] In "History and Good" Bonhoeffer presses more broadly that to participate responsibly in one's vocation means to have an awareness of the whole of realty, yet he insists, "Responsibility in a vocation follows the call of Christ alone."[53]

Becoming Guilty

It is along the spine of the theme of responsibility in "History and Good" that Bonhoeffer pushes the concept of guilt into an active mode. For instance, Bonhoeffer observes that in extraordinary times the law of the state clashes with the basic necessities of life. This leads him to the tortured conclusion that if the actions of Christians are to take the form of Christ, those actions that are "appropriate" and "responsible" will depart from the "domain governed by laws and principles"; these actions have to step beyond the "normal and the regular."[54] Unfortunately it is here that some readers of Bonhoeffer fail to notice even this basic context of the extraordinary situation, and see in Bonhoeffer the historical actor a codified approval of violence. Such a reading risks what Bonhoeffer describes as turning *necessitá* into technique.[55] It is also important to recognize, as Clifford Green directs, that for Bonhoeffer civil law is linked to the law of God.[56] Civil law is not just a function of the will of the masses expressed in something like a national constitution or charter of rights and freedoms. This does not mean that Bonhoeffer collapses civil law into divine law or naively identifies the will of God with the criminal code, but that the two are of a piece in a way that is foreign to many contemporary North American readers.

In "The Concrete Commandment and the Divine Mandates" Bonhoeffer's high view of social order is expressed clearly when he writes, "God's

52. Bonhoeffer, *Discipleship*, 247.
53. Bonhoeffer, *Ethics*, 293.
54. Ibid., 272–73.
55. Ibid., 273.
56. Green, "Introduction," in *Ethics*, 22, 35.

commandment therefore always seeks to encounter human beings within any earthly relationship of authority, within an order that is clearly determined by above and below."[57] This social order is created by divine mandate, and through it individuals encounter God's commandment. Understandably, Bonhoeffer's reworking of the traditional Lutheran perspective here does not always sit well with readers. Even Karl Barth thought it risked setting another word alongside the Word of God, even wondering if Bonhoeffer's doctrine of the mandates does not suggest at least a bit of "North German patriarchalism."[58] At any rate, the guilty verdict that Bonhoeffer has in mind for breaking laws and principles is ultimately both conventional and reflective of the judgment of God. This illumines the gravity of the issues at stake for Bonhoeffer. He is wrestling not only with the guilt of breaking laws bound to the contingencies of human society but also with the guilt of breaking the law of God.

We have already encountered the seeds of Bonhoeffer's position in the way he discusses Jesus vis-à-vis the Pharisees in what was intended to be the foundational *Ethics* chapter, "God's Love and the Disintegration of the World." Jesus, when responding to the many challenges of the Pharisees, spoke in ways that were free even from the constraints of the religious principles they assumed. To the Pharisees, Jesus's action appeared to be "the destruction of all order, all piety, and all faith."[59] Bonhoeffer's sense of free responsibility is a contextually conscious ethic indelibly linked to a particular situation. It implies the rebellious creativity of the ethical agent answering without calculation only to the judgment of God. Only in the space opened through God's reconciliation in Christ can responsible action take the form of Christ in the world. We have seen that to be responsible means to risk one's life, not in half measures, but in its integrated totality. It is important to remember that free responsible action, for Bonhoeffer, is not ultimately a judgment on the rightness or wrongness of the law that is being broken; rather, such an action upholds the law by acknowledging that it *is* being broken. It is on this basis that the action "involves the willingness to become guilty."[60] This echoes the life of Jesus, and on this topic it is helpful to attend to Bonhoeffer's words directly:

> Jesus' concern is not the proclamation and realization of new ethical ideals, and thus also not his own goodness, but solely love for real human beings.

57. Bonhoeffer, *Ethics*, 391.

58. Karl Barth, *The Doctrine of Creation*, part 4, ed. G.W. Bromiley and T. F. Torrance, trans. A. T. Mackay et al., vol. 3 of *Church Dogmatics* (1961; repr., Peabody, MA: Hendrickson, 2010), 22. For a helpful comparison of Barth and Bonhoeffer on this subject, see Holmes, "On the Agency of Jesus in Bonhoeffer's *Ethics*," 297–300.

59. Bonhoeffer, *Ethics*, 312.

60. Ibid., 275.

> This is why he is able to enter into the community of human beings' guilt, willing to be burdened with their guilt. Jesus does not want to be considered the only perfect one at the expense of human beings, nor, as the only guiltless one, to look down on a humanity perishing under its guilt. He does not want the idea of a new human being to triumph over the wreckage of a humanity defeated by its guilt.[61]

It is the example and the love of Christ that leads Bonhoeffer's ethic to endorse becoming guilty by breaking the law. Christ broke the Sabbath laws; he left his parents; he ate with sinners. In the end he was even forsaken by God. Christ did all this not out of a desire for moral purity or as service to some abstract notion of justice or equality, but out of a unified love for God and human creatures.

Christ's selfless love is an example of actively taking guilt upon oneself. Thus, like Christ, the individual engaging in free responsible action is guilty in one sense and sinless in another.[62] Whether or not this is ultimately intelligible, Bonhoeffer believes that following Christ in this way sets the conscience free for service. The freed conscience aligns itself with responsibility—response to God and to humanity—and willingly bears guilt.[63] Bonhoeffer famously writes, "Because Jesus took the guilt of all human beings upon himself, everyone who acts responsibly becomes guilty."[64] It is impossible to act in true responsibility and avoid becoming guilty. In fact, attempts to avoid becoming guilty cuts one off from true reality as it is known in Jesus and the justification that comes through his bearing of guilt. While people cannot claim Christ's essential sinlessness, their responsible action can lead to a kind of "relative sinlessness."[65] In the end free responsibility ignores righteousness to find it. It is knowingly tenuous. Bonhoeffer emphasizes this by saying that those who freely act in responsibility, though they might not be condemned by their own conscience and vindicated by others on account of circumstance, can before God "hope only for grace."[66] To hope for grace is no small thing. Wrapped up in this hope is an acknowledgment of breaking God's law. Bonhoeffer knew that his acts of resistance and maybe even the compromises of those he deeply cared for involved stepping over lines drawn by moral absolutism and breaking divine precepts, but he believed that to do so in taking the form of Christ was to boldly hope to walk in the shadow of the cross.

61. Ibid.
62. Ibid.
63. Ibid., 279.
64. Ibid., 275–76.
65. Ibid., 279.
66. Ibid., 283.

It is difficult to consider this part of *Ethics* without wondering what Bonhoeffer might have had in mind. What are the specific deeds that lead to such culpability?[67] Many read this section of Bonhoeffer's unfinished work and assume he was wrestling with his own involvement in attempts to assassinate Hitler. In this volume we have endeavored to show that this is less likely than has often been presumed. Of course, we cannot know for sure. However, there is also the possibility that Bonhoeffer was less self-absorbed than such a hypothesis would imply. After all, this very manuscript describes responsibility as "selfless."[68] What if Bonhoeffer did not have only himself in mind as he reflected on the character of obedience to the command of God; what if he was thinking about his friends, family, and former students? Heinz Eduard Tödt, a German Bonhoeffer scholar who experienced Hitler's Germany, points out that Hans von Dohnanyi was deeply troubled by the way his work in the civil service contributed to the Nazi project. Bonhoeffer's brother-in-law could not, in Tödt's words, "avoid a considerable amount of cooperation with convinced National Socialists."[69] Of course, Dohnanyi was not alone: "All oppositionals shared the basic problem of how far the unavoidable cooperation with the National Socialists was already a guilty complicity."[70] We also know that many of Bonhoeffer's former students served in the German military, even though they opposed war in general and the German cause specifically. Their only other option was death. It may well be that Bonhoeffer was reflecting on their choice when he wrote about responsibility and guilt. There is some evidence to suggest that this was the case. In "History and Good" itself, Bonhoeffer mentions the case of the military recruit in his discussion of the relationship of responsibility and obedience.[71] In the pages that follow, he refers again to the challenge faced by soldiers in war. Bonhoeffer mentions soldiers, alongside students and employees, as examples of persons under authority who must nevertheless live responsibly.[72] We know that Bonhoeffer regularly received letters from his former students telling him about the difficulty of maintaining

67. Throughout the preparation of this volume Mark Thiessen Nation both pressed this question and provided the alternative sketched here. He elaborates further in "'A Blanket License to Commit Evil Acts?': A Fresh Examination of Bonhoeffer's Christological Framing of *Ethics*," in *Perspectives in Religious Studies* 40 (2013): 143–53.

68. Bonhoeffer, *Ethics*, 259.

69. Heinz Eduard Tödt, "The Bonhoeffer-Dohnanyi Circle in Opposition and Resistance to Hitler's Regime of Violence: Interim Report on a Research Project," in *Authentic Faith: Bonhoeffer's Theological Ethics in Context*, ed. Ernst-Albert Scharffenorth and Glen Harold Stassen, trans. David Stassen and Ilse Tödt (Grand Rapids: Eerdmans, 2007), 206.

70. Ibid., 208.

71. Bonhoeffer, *Ethics*, 285.

72. Ibid., 287.

their ministerial practice in the midst of their soldier's duties. They worried about the tasks they were required to carry out; they worried about death and about the future. Bonhoeffer endeavored to respond as a pastor to these former students.[73] They had few options. In a letter to Winfried Maechler, Bonhoeffer expresses regret that the young man would no longer be allowed to serve as a medical orderly: "It is hard for someone when every kind of choice is taken away."[74]

Early in 1942 Bonhoeffer received a letter from Russia. It was from a former student named Erwin Sander, who was serving in the German army. He relates the despicable situation in blunt terms: "In mid-January a unit of our division had to shoot fifty prisoners in one day because we were on a march and were not able to take these prisoners along. In partisan areas, children and women who are suspected of supplying partisans with provisions are disposed of with a shot through the base of the skull." Further along in the letter he writes, "We have had to burn down many a village in the last three weeks out of military necessity."[75] These young men whom Bonhoeffer cared deeply for, whom he had taught and whom he had prayed with, bore the guilt of participation in the Nazi war machine.

Bonhoeffer and "Realism"

It is logical that drawing specific conclusions from a complex and unfinished book should be difficult. Nevertheless, with respect to the thesis of this chapter, several conclusions are already obvious. First, this analysis has shown that Bonhoeffer in no way checked his rigorous ethics at the door of World War II or his involvement in the resistance. Bonhoeffer held to an ethic centered on Christ—uncompromised, though not unaffected, by his circumstances. His continued avoidance of absolutes and ongoing involvement in the resistance against Nazism, which it must be remembered began long before the *Ethics* manuscripts were written, need not mean that he compromised the central dogmatic structure of his approach to the Christian life. Second, it is also apparent that Bonhoeffer's rationale for his longstanding involvement in the resistance was because of—not in spite of—his theology. Bonhoeffer believed that responding to God's command necessitates being wholeheartedly in the

73. Bonhoeffer's circular letters from the period evidence this; for example, see *Conspiracy and Imprisonment: 1940–1945*, ed. Mark Brocker, trans. Lisa E. Dahill and Douglas W. Stott, vol. 16 of *Dietrich Bonhoeffer Works* (Minneapolis: Fortress, 2006), 44–48, 205–9, 237–40, 253–55, 264–65.

74. Ibid., 324.

75. Ibid., 251–52.

world and taking up real problems. Following the example of Christ, Bonhoeffer concerned himself with the lives and the suffering of real people. Third, Bonhoeffer believed that breaking the law was cause for incurring guilt. He did not set up a new norm or redraw ethical lines in order to give permission for his proposed action. His thought and action proceeded, instead, in free responsibility that accepted guilt for his actions on behalf of those who suffered. He was never sure that he would even be vindicated before God, since such surety would imply a knowledge of good and evil beyond God's reconciling action. Finally, it must be acknowledged that Bonhoeffer's involvement in the resistance was not a utilitarian choosing of the lesser of two evils. Bonhoeffer clearly states that this sort of reflection, which presumes to know good and evil, is not Christian but is rather the result of humanity's disunion from its origin in God.[76]

What, then, are we to make of Renate Wind's statement in *A Spoke in the Wheel*: "It had become clear for [Bonhoeffer] that his own ethical rigorism no longer worked; that it was too much bound up with his own personal search for perfection"?[77] Surely this seems to be something of a misstatement, for it is far from clear that Bonhoeffer came to believe his "ethical rigorism no longer worked" or that he was ever searching for "perfection." With the concept of guilt standing as one of the central themes of *Ethics*, it is difficult to understand how we might conclude that he rejected a rigorous Christian ethic—even one that privileged nonviolence. In a similar well-worn track in Bonhoeffer studies, Wind also states that Bonhoeffer "faced the question which was the greater guilt, that of tolerating the Hitler dictatorship or that of removing it."[78] I'm not convinced that this is how Bonhoeffer would have described his involvement in the resistance. Bonhoeffer's theology framed the way he understood the world. It did not simply aid a utilitarian response to a war that had rudely imposed upon his utopian faith. Furthermore, and more generally, it is not clear how an ethic that justifies killing and bellicism is any less interested in moral purity than one that consistently rejects it.

Here, though, is where Bonhoeffer's concept of guilt and his nonabsolutism set him apart. At a fundamental level, a Christian peace ethic is a particular orientation to the teachings of Jesus that takes at face value the admonition in the Sermon on the Mount to love even our enemies; it is not essentially a particular relationship to absolutes or principles. The reality that Bonhoeffer may have been associated with people who planned to end Hitler's life likewise

76. Bonhoeffer, *Ethics*, 299–338.
77. Wind, *Spoke in the Wheel*, 100.
78. Ibid.

does not require Bonhoeffer's modern interpreters to assume a drastic shift or maturation between the writing of *Discipleship* and *Ethics*. There remains little reason to assume a move from a puritanical ethic to an absolute justification of violence. If a nonabsolute or nonlegalist pacifism is as central to Bonhoeffer's ethics in *Discipleship* as it appears to be, then Clifford Green is right to say that "the *Ethics* book does not represent a conversion from nonviolence to violence."[79] Thus Bonhoeffer's involvement in the resistance, in whatever way it might have been related to the various modes of conspiracy, does not mean that he embraced the idea that killing is redemptive or that those who carry it out are free from sin. If Green is right to say, "'Pacifism' for Bonhoeffer did not mean adopting nonviolence as an absolute principle," then surely the theory of substantial discontinuity in the last decade of Bonhoeffer's life is overdrawn.[80] Thus it seems reasonable to conclude that Bonhoeffer's resistance to the Hitler government, whether or not he was involved in any significant way in the violent attempts on Hitler's life, came about not from some radical maturation of his theology—some sort of reckoning with reality—but rather from the commitment to the living Christ at the very heart of his Christian faith. Willem A. Visser 't Hooft writes that the "very conviction which had made [Bonhoeffer] a man of peace, led him into active resistance."[81] In an essay written in 1943 titled *After Ten Years*, we can see how Bonhoeffer did not even then wish to redraw the lines around what he considered normative, if penultimate:

> There is clearly no historically significant action that does not trespass ever again against the limits set by [the abiding laws of human communal life]. But it makes a decisive difference whether such trespasses against the established limit are viewed as their abolishment in principle and hence presented as a law of its own kind or whether one is conscious that such trespassing is perhaps an unavoidable guilt that has its justification only in that law and limit being reinstated and honored as quickly as possible. . . . The world *is*, in fact, so ordered that the fundamental honoring of life's basic laws and rights at the same time best serves self-preservation, and that these laws tolerate a very brief, singular, and, in the individual case, necessary trespass against them. But those laws will

79. Clifford Green, "Introduction," in Bonheoffer, *Ethics*, 16. Green gives a nuanced description of Bonhoeffer's peace ethic that fits in a number of ways with the argument of this volume in "Pacifism and Tyrannicide: Bonhoeffer's Christian Peace Ethic," *Studies in Christian Ethics* 18, no. 3 (2005): 31–47.

80. Green, "Introduction," 15–16.

81. Willem A. Visser 't Hooft, "An Act of Penitence," in *I Knew Dietrich Bonhoeffer*, ed. Wolf-Dieter Zimmerman and Ronald Gregor Smith, trans. Käthe Gregor Smith (New York: Harper & Row, 1966), 193–95, here 194.

> sooner or later—and with irresistible force—strike dead those who turn necessity into a principle and as a consequence set up a law of their own alongside them.[82]

This quotation further shows Bonhoeffer's belief that he can take action that is at once appropriate and unlawful. His attempt to uphold the law or norm parallels his perspective on the continued relevance of the hard teachings of Jesus.

For Bonhoeffer the challenge facing those who would act as Christians is to combine simplicity and wisdom within a singularity of focus that seeks to accept the form of Christ within the messiness of the world. Bonhoeffer's consideration of the active assumption of guilt in "History and Good" reminds us of the way Bonhoeffer interprets Jesus's dictum about acting in such a way that our right hand should not know what our left is doing. Obedience occurs without a second guess, without evaluation against criteria external to God's command. This, Bonhoeffer says in "God's Love and the Disintegration of the World," is "the liberating call to single-mindedness" that "overcomes the old knowledge resulting from the fall." This call also "instills the new knowledge of Jesus," which itself "consists entirely in doing the will of God."[83] This call to single-mindedness frees the Christian to cling to God's commandments, to God's judgment, and to the mercy that proceeds anew every day from God.[84]

By now it should be apparent that Bonhoeffer's positive account of responsibility in *Ethics* is not symptomatic of a new positive assessment of violence at odds with his previous peace ethic. Nevertheless, this precise assumption is widely held. At the root of this misunderstanding is a hasty identification of Bonhoeffer's later thought with the ethics of Reinhold Niebuhr. In 2004 the editor of *The Christian Century* wrote, "One of Niebuhr's students at Union, Dietrich Bonhoeffer, would return to Germany, and gradually move to the Niebuhrian conclusion that the evil of Nazism should be opposed on Christian ethical grounds."[85] We are not always given such an obvious tip that Bonhoeffer's thought is being linked with Niebuhr's, but in more subtle form the basic evidences in this quotation are far from uncommon. Suppositions about Niebuhr's influence are compounded in this case by the facts that Bonhoeffer studied under Niebuhr at Union Theological Seminary and that the Union professor was instrumental in facilitating Bonhoeffer's second sojourn

82. Dietrich Bonhoeffer, *Letters and Papers from Prison*, ed. John W. de Gruchy, trans. Isabel Best, Lisa E. Dahill, Reinhard Krauss, and Nancy Lukens, vol. 8 of *Dietrich Bonhoeffer Works* (Minneapolis: Fortress, 2009), 46.

83. Bonhoeffer, *Ethics*, 318.

84. Ibid., 81.

85. John M. Buchanan, "In Adversity," *The Christian Century*, April 6, 2004, 3.

to the United States of America. We cannot pursue a thorough comparison of Bonhoeffer and Niebuhr here; however, a brief exploration of several key themes will demonstrate the problem of the quick association that regularly drives misreadings of Bonhoeffer's later work.

As a Christian ethicist, Niebuhr regularly explores in his work how Jesus and traditional Christianity relate to politics and social ethics. At the risk of being glib, we can say Niebuhr's conclusion is that ethics driven by direct application of Jesus's teaching is simply too unconnected to the real world to be of much use. In his book *An Interpretation of Christian Ethics*, which was published several years after Bonhoeffer's first stay in New York, Niebuhr describes the Christian faith in sociological and subsequently mythical terms.[86] Central to Niebuhr's concern in this book is his belief that Jesus opposes what is "natural"—the basic concerns stemming from physical existence.[87] Niebuhr draws this conclusion from the fact that Jesus's teaching reins in "natural" desires. He explains, "Jesus' attitude toward vindictiveness and his injunction to forgive the enemy reveals more clearly than any other element in his ethic his intransigence against forms of self-assertion which have social and moral approval in any natural morality."[88] Yet since these basic desires are necessary for survival, the follower of Jesus is caught on the horns of a dilemma between obedience to Jesus and the basic instincts of survival. Therefore it is not surprising that when speaking in a more pastoral mode, Niebuhr suggests that modern sermons should "contain some suggestions of the impossibility of these ethical demands for natural man in his immediate situations."[89] With this recommendation the dilemma evaporates, and the practical force of Jesus's teaching in the Sermon on the Mount is kept at bay.

Niebuhr's general orientation parallels the assessment of some Bonhoeffer interpreters that Bonhoeffer's early theology is essentially apolitical.[90] Yet the contrast to Bonhoeffer's thought could hardly be sharper. Not only is the ecclesially accessed anthropology and epistemology of Bonhoeffer's dissertations

86. See Reinhold Niebuhr, *An Interpretation of Christian Ethics* (New York: Harper & Brothers, 1935), 12, 25–34. On June 22, 1939, Bonhoeffer said: "Read in the afternoon, Niebuhr: *Interpretation of Christian Ethics*. Filled with wrong and superficial statements." Later in the same letter he says, still about Niebuhr: "This thinking does not come from the Bible, for that reason deeply unproductive. His essay in *Beyond Tragedy* about 'as deceivers yet true' is pure modernism" (Bonhoeffer, *Theological Education Underground: 1937–1940*, ed. Victoria J. Barnett, trans. Claudia D. Bergmann, Scott A. Moore, and Peter Frick, vol. 15 of *Dietrich Bonhoeffer Works* [Minneapolis: Fortress, 2011], 229–30).

87. Niebuhr, *Interpretation of Christian Ethics*, 41.

88. Ibid., 44.

89. Ibid., 46.

90. See, for example, Kenneth E. Morris, "Bonhoeffer's Critique of Totalitarianism," *Journal of Church and State* 26 (1984): 255–72.

inherently political, but *Discipleship* is built around the practicality of the hard teachings of Jesus. In the latter work, a rejection of the rigorous demands of discipleship is labeled cheap grace.[91] The core of this christocentric realism is ardently maintained in *Ethics*, where Bonhoeffer writes:

> People say that it is utopian to regard the Sermon on the Mount as a basis for historical-political action. This view has become so widespread, especially in Germany but also far beyond its borders, that historical-political action and Christian action have been completely torn apart. However, it is not difficult to prove that this view is in conflict with reality, unrealistic, and false.[92]

Bonhoeffer is primarily concerned not with the apparent naturalness of an ethic anchored in the New Testament narrative of Jesus but with a form of discipleship that assumes it to be an appropriate response to the call of God. Again we see the specter of acosmism, but that only goes to further prove the point. Perhaps this difference between Niebuhr and Bonhoeffer is starkest with respect to pacifism. In *Moral Man and Immoral Society*, published in 1932, the acerbic Niebuhr writes, "Tolstoian pacifists and other advocates of non-resistance, noting the evils which force introduces into society, give themselves to the vain illusion that it can be completely eliminated, and society organized upon the basis of anarchistic principles."[93] The disjuncture here between Niebuhr and Bonhoeffer is twofold. First, while Bonhoeffer—as we have argued throughout this volume—embraces a peace ethic and is not afraid of the label "pacifism," Niebuhr rejects it outright. Furthermore, what Niebuhr understands pacifism to be bears little relationship to the substance of Bonhoeffer's ethic. Bonhoeffer has no reason to be convinced by Niebuhr of the impropriety of this type of Christian pacifism. Along with the previous points, this two-layered disjuncture makes it difficult to see how Bonhoeffer could have taken up a Niebuhrian ethic late in life. Bonhoeffer would have needed to misread Niebuhr to find his views as the target of the American public intellectual.

These distinctions notwithstanding, the Niebuhrian interpretation of Bonhoeffer's later work has of course become influential. One way to demonstrate

91. Incidentally, Jean Bethke Elshtain hijacks Bonhoeffer's language to criticize Tony Campolo's concern with the term "Crusades" in relation to the "War on Terror." She says, "'The Crusades' now functions as a loaded term that conjures up guilt in the absence of concrete responsibility. It becomes a form of what Dietrich Bonhoeffer called 'cheap grace'—or 'cheap guilt' in this case" (Elshtain, *Just War Against Terror*, 118). Her opinion on "the Crusades" notwithstanding, the logic of her parallel to Bonhoeffer's concern with cheap grace remains a mystery.

92. Bonhoeffer, *Ethics*, 240. This occurs in the first version of "History and the Good." The logic works somewhat differently in the second version.

93. Reinhold Niebuhr, *Moral Man and Immoral Society: A Study in Ethics and Politics* (Louisville: Westminster John Knox, 2001), 20.

this is with a comparison. Niebuhr says that the significance of asceticism is in its "symbolic character." He continues,

> Since the ascetic saint is, economically speaking, a parasite on the sinful world, and since disavowal of the natural relationships and responsibilities of ordinary life leads to the destruction of life itself, his devotion to the absolute ideal can be no more than a symbol of the final ideal of love, under the tension of which all men stand.[94]

It would seem that to be committed to nonviolence as a disciple of Christ—an ascetic practice in Niebuhr's eyes—is to become a parasite. But what does it mean when in 1972 Rasmussen describes Bonhoeffer's position on the use of violence as "parasitic"? Rasmussen believes this is the case because Bonhoeffer held that the use of violent coercion was necessary for some but forbidden for disciples.[95] Rasmussen's employment of Niebuhrian categories to evaluate Bonhoeffer is indisputable. The former writes,

> While some of the [Bonhoeffer] literature of the 1930s seems to infer occasional legitimate use of violence against the State, the student of Bonhoeffer must nevertheless come to terms with the categorical nonviolence taught in *The Cost of Discipleship*. On that count, two modifications in Bonhoeffer's theology were necessary, the abandoning of strains of asceticism and parasitism. Biographically traced, these are left behind when Bonhoeffer analyzes the structure of responsible life (especially the acceptance of guilt) and when he overcomes two-sphere thinking.[96]

No highlighting is needed to show how Rasmussen borrows the powerful rhetoric of Niebuhr. Certainly from a normative perspective there is little easier than agreeing that if abandoning asceticism and parasitism means moving nonviolence to the attic of quaint ideas, then all is gain. Yet in the context of Christian ethics, and particularly the work of Bonhoeffer, such logic is faulty for several reasons.

First, the belief that the ascetic saint is parasitic on a sinful world violates central tenets of the Christian faith and ignores a significant stream of the Christian tradition that believes it is evil that is actually parasitic upon all that is good and righteous. Second, though it is understandable that the view attributed to Bonhoeffer may *appear* parasitic under the probing of Rasmussen's

94. Niebuhr, *Interpretation of Christian Ethics*, 187.

95. Larry Rasmussen, *Dietrich Bonhoeffer: Reality and Resistance* (1972; repr., Louisville: Westminster John Knox, 2005), 121.

96. Ibid., 125.

Niebuhrian instruments, surely these Niebuhrian calipers measure Bonhoeffer's thought unfairly. It is far too simple to say he believes violent coercion is necessary for some and prohibited for the disciple. Bonhoeffer's reasoning in *Discipleship* is thicker than Rasmussen recognizes. For instance, in the volume under dispute, Bonhoeffer writes,

> God's chosen people of Israel did exist in a political form in which, according to the divine will, retribution consisted of returning a blow for a blow. For the community of disciples, which makes no national or legal claims for itself, retribution means patiently bearing the blow, so that evil is not added to evil. That is the only way community can be established and preserved.[97]

A few paragraphs further down the page, Bonhoeffer avers: "Our voluntary renunciation of counterviolence confirms and proclaims our unconditional allegiance to Jesus as his followers, our freedom, our detachment from our own egos."[98] In these two statements we see that Bonhoeffer's thinking about violence differs dramatically from Rasmussen's caricature of isolation and inactivity.

On a final note here, it is hard to understand how Rasmussen believes that Bonhoeffer's use of the concept of responsibility might help him evade charges of asceticism or parasitism. It is not only the case that Bonhoeffer's rejection of violence never was parasitic as the Niebuhr-Rasmussen alliance would have it; it is also the case that Bonhoeffer's construal of responsibility has little relationship to either charge. If, on the other hand, Bonhoeffer was parasitic and ascetic before his writing of *Ethics*, the book shows few signs of moving beyond these difficulties. This is the case because Bonhoeffer does not juxtapose responsibility to obedience. The two concepts are knit together under a christological rendering of response to the divine command. Responsibility modifies obedience only in its recognition of the freedom of the individual. As I have argued above, this does not lower the ethical bar. Instead, it proposes that through Christ believers have not only the mandate and the resources for a higher level of ethical discernment but also the freedom to act upon such discernment.

Reinhold Niebuhr deeply influenced modern theology through his insistence that social ethics must take sin seriously. The neo-orthodox Niebuhr is under no illusions with respect to the evil nature of certain aspects of modern society, and here he and Bonhoeffer do share something significant. They both have come to the realization that sin and evil are such that education and optimism

97. Bonhoeffer, *Discipleship*, 132–33.
98. Ibid., 133.

are insufficient for their banishment. Like Niebuhr, Bonhoeffer does not believe that the evils of the world can be cured by goodwill and simple nonresistance.

Niebuhr argues that it is impossible to realize the kingdom of God, because real people can never get beyond their own "egoism." This leads him to conclude that the eschatology of Jesus must go beyond a this-worldly existence.[99] While Bonhoeffer's theology agrees with this in part, there are important differences. First, Bonhoeffer does not accept an easy separation of Jesus from the world and thus sidesteps related eschatological dualisms. Bonhoeffer wants to understand the world *through* the eschatologically enmeshed person of Jesus, the apocalypse of God. The epistemological upshot is that he refuses to give a "this-worldly" existence priority over the world he knows through Jesus. Second, regardless of the specifics of Bonhoeffer's ecclesiology, his early academic work, specifically *Sanctorum Communio*, demonstrates his belief that the social reality of the church is necessary and its Christo-form character quite possible in the providence of God. Bonhoeffer believed that in God's grace the communion of saints is given the resources necessary to move beyond the inherent limits of individualism.

For Niebuhr, loving one's neighbor as one's self is impossible, yet paradoxically the command remains necessary.[100] The law of love is impossible because, as he says, "no party to the conflict has a perspective high enough to judge the merits of the opponent's position. Every appeal to moral standards thus degenerates into a moral justification of the self against the enemy."[101] In contrast to Niebuhr's realism, we have already noted Bonhoeffer's belief that responsibility is "selfless" and is the only true way of living.[102] The arc of this contrast can be scribed further when we observe Niebuhr's argument in *Moral Man and Immoral Society* that links reason to justice and then concludes that since society will never be wholly reasonable, it will also never be wholly just.[103] Bonhoeffer was skeptical of the reasonable individual. Far too many reasonable people had acquiesced to complicity with the Nazi regime, but that did not change the calling of the Christian.

Another example of a similar distinction between Niebuhr and Bonhoeffer is their response to the ethical dilemma. In *An Interpretation of Christian Ethics* Niebuhr acknowledges the initial merit of an argument for pacifism based on the axiom that all life is sacred. Upon further analysis, however, Niebuhr rejects this line of reasoning. He says that it "becomes less convincing

99. Niebuhr, *Interpretation of Christian Ethics*, 31–32.
100. Ibid., 117.
101. Ibid., 126.
102. Bonhoeffer, *Ethics*, 259.
103. Niebuhr, *Moral Man and Immoral Society*, 34–35.

when it is recognized that life is in conflict with life in an imperfect world, and therefore no one has the opportunity of supporting the principle of the sanctity of life in an absolute sense."[104] There is no need to deny the truth of Niebuhr's insight. It does, however, show an orientation distinct from much of Bonhoeffer's ethics. Though Bonhoeffer acknowledges similar ethical dilemmas, unlike Niebuhr, he is primarily concerned with the difficulty of choosing between two good options, not the tragic necessity of choosing between two wrong ones.[105] Fundamentally, it seems that Bonhoeffer emphasizes the world's existence not in tragedy but in grace.

Despite Niebuhr's early Marxist sentiment and labor advocacy, his social ethics assumes a position of power. As an opponent of the Nazi regime and a critic of the national church, Bonhoeffer lived his last several years in relative subjugation. Although he was mindful of and concerned for the future of Germany, and even more broadly civil society, his writing does not betray the pretension of being able to steer it. Niebuhr, while recognizing the irony of trying to control history, is preoccupied with making policy for the whole of a nation, even for all of Christendom. This points to one of the most profound differences between Bonhoeffer and Niebuhr: the distinction of the church from the world is important for Bonhoeffer's thought in a way that it is not for Niebuhr's.

Niebuhr rejects pacifism because he believes it is impossible, unrealistic, and, in a vicious world, even harmful. When Niebuhr says that the principle of the sanctity of life cannot be held absolutely, he moves to rationalize not an ethic oriented toward peace, which might be recognized in classic justified war thinking, but supports instead a seemingly endless cycle of armaments deterring armaments and wars opposing wars. In the development of Niebuhr's thought, this does represent an abandonment of an earlier utopianism, but this is Niebuhr, not Bonhoeffer. For Niebuhr this means that pacifism, or any willingness to achieve a just peace through suffering, gets thrown out with the absolutism of the ascetic. Bonhoeffer rejected absolutism, to be sure, but he did not embrace a Niebuhrian realism. This is why bellicose political leaders are much more frequently drawn to Niebuhr's work than to Bonhoeffer's. Bonhoeffer always interpreted his world through the (un)realistic apocalypse of Christ. In this way he sought to continue apprehending reality anew. In contrast, Niebuhr says this: "What is lacking among all these moralists, whether religious or rational, is an understanding of the brutal character of the behavior of all human collectives, and the power of self-interest and collective egoism

104. Niebuhr, *Interpretation of Christian Ethics*, 196.
105. For example, see Bonhoeffer, *Ethics*, 284.

in all inter-group relations."[106] This is not lacking in Bonhoeffer the moralist. Bonhoeffer understands the "brutal character" of at least one human collective; yet he does not, as Niebuhr advises, turn to choosing the lesser of two evils; he does not believe that all human collectives were bound to act with brutality. Bonhoeffer expected more of the church and demanded more of himself. His use of the concept of responsibility in *Ethics* was not an admission of the inevitability of egoism and self-interest.

Niebuhr has been called a "priest of the present order."[107] The moniker sticks because his work offers few ways out of the violence and evil of the world that in his construal seem so inevitable. He says, "The limitations of the human mind and imagination, the inability of human beings to transcend their own interests sufficiently to envisage the interests of their fellowmen as clearly as they do their own makes force an inevitable part of the process of social cohesion."[108] Stanley Hauerwas has argued that Bonhoeffer sought to regain the visibility of the church.[109] Though Bonhoeffer's approach to the issue of nationalism is not that of Hauerwas, his work in the field of theological ethics does seek to address the distinct community of those who follow Christ. The comparison to Niebuhr's state-directed ethics highlights this.[110] Bonhoeffer came to reject two-sphere thinking, but he still recognized that the ethical rigorism he expected from Christians could not necessarily be expected from the culture at large or from the state. As a member of a traditional German society, and one who loved his homeland dearly, this was strange ground for Bonhoeffer to tread. He does so in *Ethics* rather tentatively. It is true that Niebuhr also assumes a division in moral expectations when he writes the following: "As individuals, men believe that they ought to love and serve each other and establish justice between each other. As racial, economic and national groups they take for themselves, whatever their power can command."[111] Niebuhr draws the line of ethical demarcation not between social entities but within individuals as they are torn between acts of personal self-giving and collective selfishness. On their own, individuals can be expected to obey the teachings of Christ, yet as collectives they should not. This is distinct from Bonhoeffer's conviction that the church ought to take the form of Christ. It is distinct from Bonhoeffer's belief that the Christian view of reality is

106. Niebuhr, *Moral Man and Immoral Society*, xxx.

107. Bill Kellermann, "Apologist of Power," *Sojourners*, March 16, 1987, 20.

108. Niebuhr, *Moral Man and Immoral Society*, 6.

109. Stanley Hauerwas, *Performing the Faith: Bonhoeffer and the Practice of Non-Violence* (Grand Rapids: Brazos, 2004), 47–48.

110. Niebuhr, *Moral Man and Immoral Society*, 3.

111. Ibid., 9.

particularly shaped by its theological assumptions and therefore would not be easily considered common or reasonable.[112] Neither in *Ethics* nor in *Discipleship* does Bonhoeffer propose that the individual should be bifurcated in the way Niebuhr does. For Niebuhr and many other Christians, however, the individual/collective distinction, not the church/world distinction, holds the most practical power. Niebuhr's primary concern is for the actions of countries and societies.[113] Many Bonhoeffer interpreters make a significant mistake when they employ the churchman Bonhoeffer to do the statesmen-advising work of Niebuhr. Only a twisted and bent Bonhoeffer can do such work.

The difference between Bonhoeffer's prophetic voice and that of Niebuhr is that the life to which Bonhoeffer calls his hearers is to be directly and fully shaped by Jesus. Where Niebuhr is drawn to the more generic concept of prophetic religion, Bonhoeffer relies on the life, teaching, death, and resurrection of a specific prophet—one attested to as the very revelation of God. Bonhoeffer's "living-for-others" view of Christ and Christianity is radically different from "realism," and Bonhoeffer's concept of responsibility bears little resemblance to the ways the concept is employed in the Niebuhrian tradition. Responsibility, for all its practical-sounding nature, is not a change or a weakness in Bonhoeffer's rigorously Christ-centered ethic of discipleship.[114] Neither does the presence of guilt in Bonhoeffer's *Ethics* manuscripts mark a radical shift in his thought. Both concepts must be understood as extensions of Bonhoeffer's ethic of formation in Christ. We do Bonhoeffer, the church, and ultimately the world a great disservice when we employ Bonhoeffer's legacy to underwrite our contemporary proclivity toward war.

112. Bonhoeffer, *Ethics*, 266.

113. Among other places, this is demonstrated clearly in the beginning of his chapter "The Law of Love in Politics and Economics," in Niebuhr, *Interpretation of Christian Ethics*, 139.

114. While I sympathize with Bonhoeffer's christological construction of responsibility, I ultimately do not find the term to be the most helpful for careful ethical reasoning. It has become far too elastic and far too imprecise. Writing in 1954, John Howard Yoder cautions readers about the "ethically ambiguous" nature of responsibility. See his early essay in the *Concern* pamphlet series: "The Anabaptist Dissent: The Logic of the Place of the Disciple in Society," *Concern*, no. 1 (June 1954): 64.

Conclusion

We are the ones to be converted, not Hitler.
—Dietrich Bonhoeffer

"There are no acts that are bad in and of themselves; even murder can be sanctified."[1] These are words from the twenty-three-year-old Dietrich Bonhoeffer in a lecture on ethics given in Barcelona. Ferdinand Schlingensiepen, in a recent biography, says that these words may have seemed strange coming from a pastoral assistant in 1929 Barcelona. However, by the beginning of the 1940s "they had become appallingly true and had to be put into action."[2] That is to say, after witnessing the gross injustices and acts of violence perpetrated by the Hitler regime, Bonhoeffer saw that to be responsible he must become involved, if not in "murder," at least in tyrannicide—knowing that such acts "can be sanctified." In fact, in retrospect, says Schlingensiepen, one could say that "the central decision of his life, *to which everything else had been leading*, had finally been taken."[3] And once he had made this momentous decision, "every other consideration had to be subjected to the plans for the assassination."[4]

1. As quoted in Ferdinand Schlingensiepen, *Dietrich Bonhoeffer 1906–1945: Martyr, Thinker, Man of Resistance*, trans. Isabel Best (London: T&T Clark, 2010), 286.

2. Ibid., cf. 50.

3. Ibid., 285, emphasis added.

4. Ibid., 281. This seems quite similar to what Eric Metaxas, in his much more popular biography, implies. Another common approach, as above in the previous chapter, is to name Bonhoeffer's shift by borrowing Niebuhrian "Christian realism" language. See, for example, Geffrey B. Kelly and F. Burton Nelson, *The Cost of Moral Leadership: The Spirituality of Dietrich Bonhoeffer* (Grand Rapids: Eerdmans, 2003), 108. Not only is there no indication that

Schlingensiepen's way of putting it may be more bold and straightforward than most commentators on Bonhoeffer's life, theology, and legacy. However, it seems to me he has really honestly named what many accounts suggest. Bonhoeffer may have in fact been a pacifist earlier in his short theological life, say the standard accounts, but by the early 1940s—when he had decided to be involved in the attempts to kill Hitler—he had to rethink his whole theological ethic. Bonhoeffer's decision to become involved in the attempts to assassinate Hitler was indeed "the central decision of his life," the culmination of his life and thought. It was that "to which everything else had been leading." Therefore, of course, we view his previous life and thought in light of his involvement in the conspiracy and the attempts on Hitler's life. And then we comb through the unfinished manuscript of his book *Ethics*, as well as his *Letters and Papers from Prison* (and now also volumes 15 and 16 in the collected works), in order to find passages that make sense of some dramatic shifts in Bonhoeffer's thought, shifts that provide a theological warrant and justification for his turn to become, effectively, "an assassin." For, as Larry Rasmussen says, "All the twisting possible cannot make the author of *The Cost of Discipleship* a volunteer for assassinating even Adolf Hitler."[5]

The only problem with this interpretation—despite its dominance as a paradigm for understanding Bonhoeffer—is that it flies in the face of the most obvious interpretation of Bonhoeffer's own words and of the facts about his life, including his life and writings beyond 1939. I hope that has been made obvious by the detailed arguments of this book. But let me rehearse the heart of the argument in outline here.

Before naming particulars, it is good to be reminded of the way in which Bonhoeffer claimed there was continuity in his life and thought, with only one major disruption. From prison, on April 11, 1944, Bonhoeffer wrote to Eberhard Bethge: "I am wholly under the impression that my life—strange as

---

Bonhoeffer ever resonated very deeply with the basic ethical approach of his former teacher, but Bonhoeffer did also on occasion offer specific critiques of Niebuhr's approach. See, for example, Bonhoeffer, *Theological Education Underground: 1937–1940*, ed. Victoria J. Barnett, trans. Claudia D. Bergmann, Scott A. Moore, and Peter Frick, vol. 15 of *Dietrich Bonhoeffer Works* (Minneapolis: Fortress, 2011), 229–30.

5. Larry Rasmussen, *Dietrich Bonhoeffer: Reality and Resistance* (1972; repr., Louisville: Westminster John Knox, 2005), 120. This book was rereleased, with no revisions, by Westminster John Knox in 2005. For an interesting exchange around the 2005 rerelease of this book, see Clifford Green, "Review of *Dietrich Bonhoeffer: Reality and Resistance*," *Conversations in Religion and Theology* 6 (2008): 155–65; and Larry Rasmussen, "Response to Clifford Green," *Conversations in Religion and Theology* 6 (2008): 165–73. Now also see David M. Gides, *Pacifism, Just War, and Tyrannicide: Bonhoeffer's Church-World Theology and His Changing Forms of Political Thinking and Involvement* (Eugene, OR: Pickwick, 2011).

it may sound—has gone in a straight line, uninterrupted, at least with regard to how I've led it."[6] Eleven days later he writes another letter to Bethge in which he says: "I don't think I have ever changed much, except perhaps at the time of my first impressions abroad, and under the first conscious influence of Papa's personality. It was then that a turning from the phraseological to the real ensued."[7] Thus by his own account in 1944—with the second letter being the day after an attempt was made on Hitler's life—Bonhoeffer is saying that he turned toward "the real" and away from the ideal or "phraseological," not after 1939, but between 1928 and 1932.[8]

Thus Bonhoeffer turned toward "the real" during his time in New York City, 1930–31. By his own account he became a Christian during this time; he experienced "a grand liberation." It was especially the Bible—and within the Scriptures, the Sermon on the Mount—that freed him. He became a daily reader of the Psalms and a man of serious prayer. He came to see that "everything depended on the church and of the ministry." And "Christian pacifism, which I had previously fought against with passion, all at once seemed perfectly obvious." Bonhoeffer is naming these dramatic changes in his life not in 1931, perhaps in the emotional afterglow of his extraordinary experiences in the Abyssinian Baptist Church, but rather in January of 1936, almost five years later and after almost three years of living with the reality of Adolf Hitler as Reich Chancellor and then Führer. For Bonhoeffer, this turning toward reality—this embracing of true Christian realism—meant that there were things "worth standing up for without compromise." "To me," says Bonhoeffer, "it seems that peace and social justice are such things, as is Christ himself."[9] In fact, in the letter of January 14, 1935, where Bonhoeffer says this, he acknowledges to his physicist brother, Karl-Friedrich, that he is sometimes perceived as fanatical. However, he also informs his brother that if he were to become more "reasonable," he would have to "chuck [his] entire theology."[10] His "fanaticism" is most fully articulated in his book *Discipleship* and then lived out in the community of seminarians, shaped with deliberation by Bonhoeffer and

6. Dietrich Bonhoeffer, *Letters and Papers from Prison*, ed. John W. de Gruchy, trans. Isabel Best, Lisa E. Dahill, Reinhard Krauss, and Nancy Luken, vol. 8 of *Dietrich Bonhoeffer Works* (Minneapolis: Fortress, 2009), 352.

7. Ibid., 358.

8. See Bonhoeffer's cousin's account of this: Hans Christoph von Hase, "Turning Away from the Phraseological to the Real," in Dietrich Bonhoeffer, *Barcelona, Berlin, New York: 1928–1931*, ed. Clifford Green, trans. Douglas W. Stott, vol. 10 of *Dietrich Bonhoeffer Works* (Minneapolis: Fortress, 2008), 591–604.

9. Dietrich Bonhoeffer, *London: 1933–1935*, ed. Keith W. Clements, trans. Isabel Best, vol. 13 of *Dietrich Bonhoeffer Works* (Minneapolis: Fortress, 2007), 285.

10. Ibid., 284.

reflected on in his book *Life Together*. He very specifically affirms *Discipleship* in a letter to Bethge from prison on July 21, 1944.[11] He had also, in prison, told Maria, his fiancée, that he would like to read *Life Together* with her when he was out of prison.[12]

His affirmations of these particular writings less than a year before his execution are significant. For if he had come to see his earlier writings as wrong, there is no reason he could not have said so. In fact, it would have garnered respect for him to have chucked at least key tenets of some of his earlier lectures and published writings. It would have increased his stature to make it clear that he had by now abandoned the commitments implied by the passages in *Discipleship* that seem to reflect what he had on occasion referred to as pacifism. Virtually no one would have been bothered by his distancing himself from the "new monasticism" practiced at Finkenwalde, from this "naïveté." But this is not what we see. Rather, we see an affirmation of his earlier writings. And on occasion we see clear reiteration of some of his key themes—such as love of enemies and sharing possessions generously—even in writings in prison.[13] Additionally, of course, we see fresh formulations and creative, honest wrestling with some of the most painful and difficult questions humans can pose—from a brilliant theologian living through the horrors perpetrated by the Nazi regime.[14]

Now let me summarize in five points the conclusions of the arguments presented in this book. First, it is highly unlikely that Bonhoeffer was involved in any assassination attempts. Chapter 3 explored Bonhoeffer's work in the Abwehr, the military intelligence agency, and discussed in some detail the five assassination attempts between 1938 and 1944 that are most relevant to Bonhoeffer's life. It should be clear from these discussions that Bonhoeffer had no involvement in any of them. I won't attempt to recount the details presented there that nuance this claim. My hope is that this book will cause more and more writers about Bonhoeffer to discontinue the all-too-frequent

11. Bonhoeffer, *Letters and Papers from Prison*, 486.

12. Maria von Wedemeyer-Weller, "The Other Letters from Prison," in *Letters and Papers from Prison*, enlarged ed., ed. Eberhard Bethge (New York: Macmillan, 1971), 416. I would also note that Bonhoeffer seemed quite pleased, in late December 1940, when his books *Life Together* and *Discipleship* were being read at the Ettal monastery. Dietrich Bonhoeffer, *Conspiracy and Imprisonment: 1940–1945*, ed. Mark Brocker, trans. Lisa E. Dahill and Douglas W. Stott, vol. 16 of *Dietrich Bonhoeffer Works* (Minneapolis: Fortress, 2006), 113.

13. See, for example, "Thoughts on the Day of Baptism of D. W. R, May 1944," in Bonhoeffer, *Letters and Papers from Prison*, 383–90, esp. 389–90; and "Outline for a Book," *Letters and Papers from Prison*, 499–504.

14. For one helpful set of reflections on some of Bonhoeffer's more provocative writings from prison, see John W. Matthews, *Anxious Souls Will Ask . . . : The Christ-Centered Spirituality of Dietrich Bonhoeffer* (Grand Rapids: Eerdmans, 2005).

vague references to Bonhoeffer's "involvement in assassination attempts."[15] Moreover, I hope more than a few will concede, as Sabine Dramm has argued, that it appears that the central reason why Bonhoeffer began employment with the Abwehr was to avoid military service on the front lines, killing in the name of Hitler—that is, effectively being a conscientious objector—not to gain access to conspirators attempting to kill Hitler.

Second, in January 1936 Bonhoeffer himself claimed that he had, sometime before 1933, come to see "Christian pacifism" (*Der christliche Pazifismus*) as "self-evident" (*Selbstverständlichkeit*), a conviction that he had "previously fought against with passion." Earlier, in July 1932, in the midst of passionate statements against the affirmation of war by Christians, Bonhoeffer told those listening to his lecture that "we should not balk here at using the word 'pacifism.'" And yet it seems that ever since he uttered these words, his interpreters have done precisely this. In fact, even as I, Mark, write this, I am well aware that many readers of this book will likely think that I, as a Mennonite, have skewed this discussion because of my own commitments (as if other perspectives are neutral). So, what is to be said about Bonhoeffer's self-proclaimed "pacifism"?[16]

First, I think one of the central reasons many have been unwilling to accept Bonhoeffer's self-designation is that they assume he shifted in perhaps the last five or six years of his life to something more akin to a position of

15. I want to acknowledge here Clifford Green's encouragement only to use the term "tyrannicide" when speaking of Bonhoeffer and attempts to kill Hitler. I think he means what I said, in chapter 3, when reflecting on conspirators such as Hans von Dohnanyi—namely, that those who were morally serious would have only contemplated killing a leader if they were truly convinced, with substantive knowledge, that such a person was a tyrant who was exceedingly dangerous and destructive. I affirm the concern. Then I would say that (1) I don't believe Bonhoeffer was involved in any such efforts, and thus it is really only a hypothetical exercise in relation to him; (2) the common term that is used, including by most Bonhoeffer scholars, is "assassination"; and (3) "tyrannicide" is a moral concept that requires argumentation to establish its validity as a moral category. This is true even if it is obvious to us now that Hitler was a tyrant. Moreover, we should remember that the case would have had to have been made to establish the claim that he was a tyrant in 1938 or even in 1944. It was not obvious to everyone then.

16. For my earlier attempts at naming Bonhoeffer's "pacifism," see Mark Nation, "'Pacifist and Enemy of the State': Bonhoeffer's 'Straight and Unbroken Course' from Costly Discipleship to Conspiracy," *Journal of Theology for Southern Africa* 77 (December 1991): 61–77 (abridgement of a 49-page essay); and Mark Thiessen Nation, "Discipleship in a World Full of Nazis: Dietrich Bonhoeffer's Polyphonic Pacifism as Social Ethics," in *The Wisdom of the Cross: Essays in Honor of John Howard Yoder*, ed. Stanley Hauerwas, Chris K. Huebner, Harry J. Huebner, and Mark Thiessen Nation (1999; repr., Eugene, OR: Wipf & Stock, 2005), 249–77. My views have evolved. I now have a deeper knowledge of Bonhoeffer's theology and certain dimensions of his life as well as facts regarding the resistance movements and assassination attempts. I have also become more deeply committed to framing the issues through Bonhoeffer's own language and categories.

Niebuhrian "realism" or a just war sort of approach that then could lend itself to a justification of tyrannicide. I hope this book has raised serious questions about this sort of claim.

Second, there are two things related to Bonhoeffer's self-designation that seem clear. Bonhoeffer was consistently—from 1932 to the end of his life (thus before and after Hitler assumed power)—strongly opposed to nationalism. His clear teachings against nationalism were rooted in the Sermon on the Mount and his belief that God commanded peace, as well as in his strong sense of the unity of the church and his belief that war among Christians was a violation of such unity. Connected to this, he was a strong advocate for conscientious objection for Christians. Beginning in 1932, Bonhoeffer would often make sure that conscientious objection was a topic of discussion at ecumenical gatherings he was involved with. On at least one occasion, in August 1934, when asked what he would do if war broke out, he said that he hoped he would have the strength not to take up arms. In 1935, when military conscription returned to Germany, Bonhoeffer urged his seminary students to consider conscientious objection. In 1939, when he knew that he would be receiving orders to enter military service, Bonhoeffer left Germany for the United States, largely to avoid serving in the military. After returning to Germany a few weeks later, he explored alternatives to killing in the military. He first applied to be a military chaplain; his application was denied. He then became an employee with the Abwehr. A key reason he did so, as Dramm suggests, was to avoid military service. As both Dramm and Bethge point out, Bonhoeffer's superiors in the Abwehr repeatedly made arguments to the authorities that his work with the Abwehr was essential to the welfare of Germany, thus helping him retain his "uk" status (which meant he was not eligible for military service on the front lines). The central issue of Bonhoeffer's trial was his refusal to do military service, as well as encouraging others in the same refusal. He was therefore imprisoned because, as the judge could see, his work with the Abwehr was truly a cover to allow him to be, effectively, a conscientious objector.

Third, one of the complicating issues in relation to referring to Bonhoeffer as a pacifist is that he was in principle opposed to reducing ethics to principles. And yet as normally understood, pacifism means *as a matter of principle* being committed to never killing. There are several issues to be named here. We cannot simply say because of this conundrum that Bonhoeffer was never a pacifist and leave it at that, for at least two reasons. Bonhoeffer was clearly opposed to a "principled" approach to ethics when he referred to himself as a pacifist and yet employed the term anyway (knowing what the term meant). Moreover, if we are going to say he was not a pacifist then we have to name fairly specifically what he *was*. Somehow we have to name what distinguishes him from virtually all Germans who were Christians and/or theologians of his time—namely, his strong emphasis on discipleship and specifically on peace, his call for Christians to be conscientious objectors, and his strong critique of nationalism. (Normally those who held together this set of issues were, then as now, pacifists.)

We could see Bonhoeffer as being similar to Karl Barth in this regard. This is in several ways quite appropriate. It was, in fact, partly from Barth that he acquired his distaste for principles in ethics. Moreover, like Barth, Bonhoeffer was committed to keeping ethics theological. But, of course, this means not only refusing to be committed to an abstraction like pacifism but also refusing to use a principled approach to ethics, period.[17] Barth, in his mature theology, said that "we cannot be pacifists in principle, only in practice. But we have to consider very closely whether, if we are called to discipleship, we can avoid being practical pacifists, or fail to be so."[18] It seems to me that at the very least we should also see Bonhoeffer as this sort of practical pacifist.

Linking Bonhoeffer with Barth in terms of the peace ethic of both is much better than most approaches to Bonhoeffer. This seems to me to be a way to name the approach taken in Clifford Green's essay "Pacifism and Tyrranicide," mentioned earlier in this book. Green sees, as we do, that central to Bonhoeffer, as with Barth, was the commitment to keeping ethics tethered to God—the living God known especially in the revelation of Jesus Christ. Peace is for both very much integrated into their theology as a whole. This is what led both Barth and Bonhoeffer to oppose reducing ethics to abstract principles. It is also what led them to know that the Prince of Peace and his call for all of his followers to be peacemakers and to love their enemies entailed a strong emphasis on peace in ways that matter for how we live our lives in the world.

However, there are also some differences between the two. Bonhoeffer specifically referred to himself as a pacifist; Barth, even in his later, mature theology, very specifically said he was not a "pacifist" per se but rather a practical pacifist. Second, there are the differences between the two named by Bonhoeffer in *Act*

17. For an appreciation and critique of Barth on this, see John Howard Yoder, *Karl Barth and the Problem of War and Other Essays on Barth*, ed. Mark Thiessen Nation (Eugene, OR: Cascade Books, 2003), esp. 46–60. Also, see chapters 4 and 5 in the present book.

18. Karl Barth, *The Doctrine of Reconciliation*, part 2, ed. G. W. Bromiley and T. F. Torrance, trans. G. W. Bromiley, vol. 4 of *Church Dogmatics* (1958; repr., Peabody, MA: Hendrickson, 2004), 550. On Barth on war and peace, see Yoder, *Karl Barth and the Problem of War*; also see Arne Rasmusson, "Church and Nation-State: Karl Barth and German Public Theology in Early 20th Century," *Ned Geref Teologiese Tydskrif* 46 (2005): 511–24; and Arne Rasmusson, "Church and War in the Theology of Karl Barth," in *Living Theology*, ed. Len Hansen et al. (Wellington, South Africa: Bible Media, 2011), 386–98.

and Being.[19] As discussed in chapter 5, this work allowed Bonhoeffer to have clarity about the person of Jesus as vital to the transforming revelation of God in our life together. This theological shift, joined to Bonhoeffer's transforming experiences in New York City at the beginning of the 1930s, led not only to a change in his approach to peace but also to the clarion call issued in *Discipleship* and the formation of the community at Finkenwalde.

Let me say a few things briefly and directly about the use of the word "pacifist" in relation to Bonhoeffer. I sometimes refer to him as a pacifist. I do so partly for purposes of brevity. There is no other one- or two-word descriptor that comes closer to naming Bonhoeffer's approach to violence than this word. And after all, it was a word he used to refer to his own commitments. However, I mostly try to use some of Bonhoeffer's specific theological/ethical language or give biographical narrative to show what he taught and how he lived. It does seem to me that his life and thought come closer to pacifism than any other already-known category. However, I've come to believe that Barth and Bonhoeffer both were right to make theological claims—especially regarding the God known in Jesus Christ—central. And then their instinct was right that if we substitute *any* abstraction for this central theological claim—even pacifism, peace, or social justice—we are likely to skew a proper understanding of our faith and call to faithfulness. And then, in the midst of attending to this theological carefulness, we still must use specific, contextually relevant language to call for faithfulness. This leads us to the next main point.

The fourth main point is that, in addition to being against nationalism and for peace, Bonhoeffer also had come to believe that Christians needed to be attentive to the needs of the most vulnerable in society—whether African Americans in the United States or Jews in Nazi Germany. I know there are those who believe that Bonhoeffer did not do as much as he should have for Jews in Germany; perhaps that is true. However, considering the times and typical views during Bonhoeffer's era, I am impressed by his clarity regarding the issues from early in the Hitler reign. In addition, when I read through the collected works and realize how busy this theologian was—and that he seemed not, by nature, to be an activist—I am also impressed that he wrote documents calling for action, took bold stands, and acted in specific ways to help the marginalized and then persecuted Jews (baptized and unbaptized). He also seemed in general to empathize, in ways unusual for his class, with those who were poor.

19. These differences were softened as Barth himself matured and on some subjects drew from Bonhoeffer in his later writings.

Finally, let me state one of my central hopes for what this book will accomplish. Repeatedly I see writings about Bonhoeffer that imply that what truly sets him apart is that he was a theologian—a former pacifist and trainer of pastors—who then became involved in plots to kill Hitler. However, as a way of centrally defining the ongoing legacy of Dietrich Bonhoeffer, this is seriously distorting. Even those who are not fully convinced by some arguments of this book might agree with this claim. Clifford Green has said in various places that we can't truly understand Bonhoeffer unless we have read his first doctoral thesis, *Sanctorum Communio*.[20] Michael DeJonge, in his recent book on Bonhoeffer, has made it clear that we also don't understand Bonhoeffer as a serious theologian unless we have read *Act and Being*.[21] Both of these claims are true. But then it should also be said that these serious academic works are the building blocks for what is refashioned by Bonhoeffer, after his transformative experiences in the United States in 1930–31 and after living with the reign of Hitler for four years, into his book *Nachfolge*, *Discipleship*. For this book depends upon the constructive work of these two dissertations. The call to follow Jesus, discipleship, is about the revelation of God made known to us in the person of Jesus Christ—being present with us, empowering us, commanding us to be his body in the midst of the world. And let me make something clear: just as the Sermon on the Mount is not mostly about "pacifism," so *Discipleship* is neither mostly about the Sermon on the Mount nor mostly about pacifism. No, it is a provocative call to serious, holistic discipleship, drawing upon both the Gospels and the Pauline material in the New Testament. This call entails many specifics, including love of enemies. Bonhoeffer, in this 1937 book, is attempting to offer a provocative challenge, a word from God for the Christian community in Nazi Germany. Similarly, at Finkenwalde, Bonhoeffer was attempting to shape a disciplined community of church leaders that could lead churches in this challenging context. His reflections on this short-lived experiment were summarized in the book *Life Together* in 1938. Both books have continued powerfully to convey the challenging word of God to many over the past seventy-five years.

These things, positively stated, make Bonhoeffer virtually unique within the context of Nazi Germany. Negatively stated, it is precisely what he said to his grandmother in a letter in August 1933, as he worked on the Bethel Confession of Faith: "Our choice is Germanism or Christianity." Bonhoeffer saw that

20. See, for example, Clifford J. Green, *Bonhoeffer: A Theology of Sociality*, rev. ed. (Grand Rapids: Eerdmans, 1999).

21. Michael P. DeJonge, *Bonhoeffer's Theological Formation: Berlin, Barth, and Protestant Theology* (Oxford: Oxford University Press, 2012).

theologically (and thus for him also ethically) so many within the Protestant church, including most within what was becoming the Confessing Church, were willing to redefine the Christian faith from the center out according to "Germanism," what it meant to be German, at least as understood by most Germans during the reign of Hitler. It is so difficult for many of us—certainly Americans—truly to attempt to imagine ourselves in Germany in, say, 1933 or even much later. Richard Steigmann-Gall has shown that more than a few Nazi leaders were not cynically "using" the Christian faith to bring fellow Germans along.[22] They were quite sincerely articulating a "positive Christianity" and "Christian values" that they hoped would be embraced by most Germans, which of course meant fellow Christians. Along with Steigmann-Gall, Claudia Koontz has shown how the Nazis integrated a particular understanding of what it meant to be "virtuous" Germans with the Christian faith—replete with, among other things, anti-Semitism and militarism.[23] All of this is a backdrop for what Bonhoeffer means by "Germanism and Christianity" as alternatives. It also helps us see why some specifics are named in the Bethel Confession that he helped to formulate—specifics that in many ways were what set him apart from most in the Confessing Church, not to mention the larger Protestant church in Germany. There were, as Bonhoeffer saw it, vitally important—classic, doctrinal—issues at stake here, as well as the need contextually to distinguish faux Christian claims from genuine ones, thus naming false ways of stating apparent Christian claims.[24] Bonhoeffer was quite conscious of all this when he wrote *Discipleship*. Within that context, this was truly a revolutionary book. The radicality of this book—a tract for the times and really all times—is what sets Bonhoeffer apart from others. It is what makes him unique.

As the son of a World War II veteran, I, Mark Thiessen Nation, cannot approach the topic of Nazi Germany—and the horrible realities of World War II and the Holocaust of the Jews—with dispassion. The "But what about Hitler?" question is a question with which I have lived for more than thirty years.[25] The

22. Richard Steigmann-Gall, *The Holy Reich: Nazi Conceptions of Christianity, 1919–1945* (Cambridge: Cambridge University Press, 2003).

23. Claudia Koontz, *The Nazi Conscience* (Cambridge, MA: Belknap Press of Harvard University Press, 2003).

24. It is interesting—and disturbing—for example, to see how some Nazi leaders invoked Jesus in apparently serious theological terms but also employed his teachings, including the Sermon on the Mount, for their purposes. See Steigmann-Gall, *Holy Reich*, on this.

25. On this, see Robert W. Brimlow, *What About Hitler?* (Grand Rapids: Brazos, 2006). Though our readings of Bonhoeffer differ, I continue to believe his book is quite important.

pain and suffering endured because of the war Hitler started—including the more than fifty-five million people who died—was horrendous.[26] I do not take the question lightly. And then, I am well aware that there are various responses to this set of harsh realities.[27]

André Trocmé, a Reformed pastor in southern France, as a pacifist, led his parish in the midst of the Holocaust in the saving of the lives of five thousand Jews.[28] Martin Niemöller, a central leader within the Confessing Church—and a former officer in the German navy during World War I—after having been a personal prisoner of Adolf Hitler for eight years (1937–45), became a lifelong peace and justice activist.[29] And then there is Franz Hildebrandt, a Jewish Christian who Eberhard Bethge said was Bonhoeffer's "best-informed and most like-minded friend."[30] In July 1937 Hildebrandt was arrested. The Bonhoeffer family realized that as a Jew his life would be in danger; thus they helped him to escape from Germany and emigrate to England. Hildebrandt then lived through World War II as an immigrant in the United Kingdom. In 1984 he was one of a number of Germans to speak at a conference in Seattle, Washington, commemorating the fiftieth anniversary of the Barmen Confession of faith. In an extemporaneous comment he said, "If there is any one book that every pastor should read, it is *The Politics of Jesus* by John Howard Yoder" (knowing Yoder was in the audience).[31] Twenty-five years

---

His extremely brief seventh chapter—"The Christian Response"—puts one of the offenses of the gospel squarely, nakedly, on the table.

26. To begin to deal with the complexities, I would suggest Andrew Roberts, *The Storm of War: A New History of the Second World War* (New York: Harper, 2011); Michael Burleigh, *Moral Combat: Good and Evil in World War II* (New York: Harper, 2011); Nicholson Baker, *Human Smoke: The Beginnings of World War II, the End of Civilization* (New York: Simon & Schuster, 2008); A. C. Grayling, *Among the Dead: The History and Moral Legacy of the WWII Bombing of Civilians in Germany and Japan* (New York: Walker, 2006); and Jacques Semelin, *Unarmed Against Hitler: Civilian Resistance in Europe, 1939–1943* (Westport, CT: Praeger, 1993).

27. My wrestling with this set of issues and naming some tangible, redemptive acts within Nazi Germany is reflected in Mark Nation, "The Politics of Compassion: A Study of Christian Nonviolent Resistance in The Third Reich" (master's thesis, The Associated Mennonite Biblical Seminary, 1981). I focused on ideology, euthanasia, the Jewish question, and war. I also wrote a seventy-one-page paper on the Confessing Church about the same time.

28. See Philip Hallie, *Lest Innocent Blood Be Shed* (1979; repr., New York: HarperPerennial, 1994). Also see the film documentary *Weapons of the Spirit*.

29. For a biographical account, see James Bentley, *Martin Niemöller* (New York: Free Press, 1984). Also see Martin Niemöller, "'What Would Jesus Say?': An Interview with Martin Niemöller," *Sojourners*, August 1981, 12–14; and Martin Niemöller, "Bringing the Beatitudes Down to Earth," *Sojourners*, August 1981, 15–16.

30. Eberhard Bethge, *Dietrich Bonhoeffer: A Biography*, rev. ed., ed. Victoria J. Barnett (Minneapolis: Fortress, 2000), 565.

31. This is my memory of what he said. In the published version of his lecture, Hildebrandt simply lists *The Politics of Jesus* as "essential literature" in a footnote to a comment affirming

earlier Hildebrandt had said in a foreword to John Yoder's booklet "Peace without Eschatology":

> What is commonly said from the pulpits about [peace], if it is mentioned at all, would . . . "be just as possible, if Christ had never become incarnate, died, ascended to heaven, and sent His Spirit." We are ineffective precisely because we are disobedient. In a theological and ecclesiastical climate . . . where any literal application of the Gospel is suspect of "Schwärmertum" and where only the ex-pacifist is respectable, it will take some time and not a little humility to admit, especially for those trained in the school of the great Reformers, that at this point in question the Mennonite minority has been, and still is right: "not because it (nonresistance) works, but because it anticipates the triumph of the Lamb that was slain."[32]

Is it possible that, in fact, almost forty years after Bonhoeffer's death, Hildebrandt was still his "most like-minded friend"?

Fabian von Schlabrendorff, a man who was directly involved in attempting to kill Hitler, was in prison with Bonhoeffer and yet himself escaped execution. He offered brief reflections on his relationship to Bonhoeffer. He ended with this short, intriguing paragraph: "When after several months I returned to my home, which had been destroyed by bombs, I at first saw nothing but rubble. Anything which the bombs had spared had been stolen. Only one book lay undamaged among the bricks and mortar: Dietrich Bonhoeffer's *Cost of Discipleship*."[33]

In September of 1934 Bonhoeffer mentioned that he had heard that some in the Oxford movement were trying to convert Hitler. Bonhoeffer referred to this as "a ridiculous failure to recognize what is going on. *We* are the ones to be converted, not Hitler."[34] Perhaps to be preoccupied with Bonhoeffer's supposed affirmation of killing Hitler is also "a ridiculous failure to recognize what is going on." Still living in a world racked by violence and gross injustice, we continue to need Bonhoeffer's provocative challenge. Perhaps we—like Bonhoeffer in 1929—are still in need of conversion. Amid the rubble of the world, we need to discover *The Cost of Discipleship* "among the bricks and

---

pacifism. See Franz Hildebrandt, "Barmen: What to Learn and What Not to Learn," in *The Barmen Confession: Papers from the Seattle Assembly*, ed. Hubert G. Locke (Lewiston, NY: Edwin Mellen, 1986), 302.

32. Franz Hildebrandt, "Foreword," in *Peace without Eschatology?* by John H. Yoder (Scottdale, PA: Concern Reprint, 1959), 4.

33. Fabian von Schlabrendorff, "In Prison with Dietrich Bonhoeffer," in *I Knew Dietrich Bonhoeffer*, ed. Wolf-Dieter Zimmermann and Ronald Gregor Smith (1966; repr., London: Fontana Books, 1973), 231.

34. Bonhoeffer, *London*, 218.

mortar" so it will help us see that, to paraphrase Bonhoeffer, "we are the ones who need to die, not Hitler." For as he reminds us, "Whenever Christ calls us, his call leads us to death."[35] Only when we have undergone such death and risen with Christ to new life in him will we be able to say, with Bonhoeffer, that "discipleship is joy."[36] Only then will we, like him, come to see concrete forms of love of enemy, to see practical pacifism, as "self-evident."

35. Bonhoeffer, *Discipleship*, 87.
36. Ibid., 40.

Bibliography

Works by Dietrich Bonhoeffer

"Dietrich Bonhoeffer Works" Series

Bonhoeffer, Dietrich. *Sanctorum Communio: A Theological Study of the Sociology of the Church*. Edited by Clifford J. Green. Translated by Reinhard Krauss and Nancy Lukens. Vol. 1 of *Dietrich Bonhoeffer Works*. Minneapolis: Fortress, 1998.

———. *Act and Being: Transcendental Philosophy and Ontology in Systematic Theology*. Edited by Wayne Whitson Floyd and Hans-Richard Reuter. Translated by Martin Rumscheidt. Vol. 2 of *Dietrich Bonhoeffer Works*. Minneapolis: Fortress, 1996.

———. *Creation and Fall: A Theological Exposition of Genesis 1–3*. Edited by John W. de Gruchy. Translated by Douglas Stephen Bax. Vol. 3 of *Dietrich Bonhoeffer Works*. Minneapolis: Fortress, 1997.

———. *Discipleship*. Edited by Geffrey B. Kelly and John D. Godsey. Translated by Barbara Green and Reinhard Krauss. Vol. 4 of *Dietrich Bonhoeffer Works*. Minneapolis: Fortress, 2000.

———. *Life Together* and *Prayerbook of the Bible: An Introduction to the Psalms*. Edited by Geffrey B. Kelly. Translated by Daniel W. Bloesch and James H. Burtness. Vol. 5 of *Dietrich Bonhoeffer Works*. Minneapolis: Fortress, 1996.

———. *Ethics*. Edited by Clifford J. Green. Translated by Reinhard Krauss, Charles West, and Douglas W. Stott. Vol. 6 of *Dietrich Bonhoeffer Works*. Minneapolis: Fortress, 2005.

———. *Fiction from Tegel Prison*. Edited by Clifford J. Green. Translated by Nancy Lukens. Vol. 7 of *Dietrich Bonhoeffer Works*. Minneapolis: Fortress, 2000.

———. *Letters and Papers from Prison*. Edited by John W. de Gruchy. Translated by Isabel Best, Lisa E. Dahill, Reinhard Krauss, and Nancy Lukens. Vol. 8 of *Dietrich Bonhoeffer Works*. Minneapolis: Fortress, 2009.

———. *The Young Bonhoeffer: 1918–1927*. Edited by Paul D. Matheny, Clifford J. Green, and Marshall D. Johnson. Translated by Mary Nebelsick and Douglas W. Stott. Vol. 9 of *Dietrich Bonhoeffer Works*. Minneapolis: Fortress, 2003.

———. *Barcelona, Berlin, New York: 1928–1931*. Edited by Clifford J. Green. Translated by Douglas W. Stott. Vol. 10 of *Dietrich Bonhoeffer Works*. Minneapolis: Fortress, 2008.

———. *Ecumenical, Academic, and Pastoral Work: 1931–1932*. Edited by Victoria J. Barnett, Mark Brocker, and Michael B. Lukens. Translated by Isabel Best, Nicholas S. Humphrey, Marion Pauck, Anne Schmidte-Lange, and Douglas W. Stott. Vol. 11 of *Dietrich Bonhoeffer Works*. Minneapolis: Fortress, 2012.

———. *Berlin: 1932–1933*. Edited by Larry L. Rasmussen. Translated by Douglas W. Stott, Isabel Best, and David Higgins. Vol. 12 of *Dietrich Bonhoeffer Works*. Minneapolis: Fortress, 2009.

———. *London: 1933–1935*. Edited by Keith W. Clements. Translated by Isabel Best. Vol. 13 of *Dietrich Bonhoeffer Works*. Minneapolis: Fortress, 2007.

———. *Illegale Theologenausbildung: Finkenwalde 1935–1937*. Edited by Otto Dudzus and Jürgen Henkeys. Vol. 14 of *Dietrich Bonhoeffer Werke*. Munich: Chr. Kaiser Verlag, 1996.

———. *Theological Education Underground: 1937–1940*. Edited by Victoria J. Barnett. Translated by Claudia D. Bergmann, Scott A. Moore, and Peter Frick. Vol. 15 of *Dietrich Bonhoeffer Works*. Minneapolis: Fortress, 2011.

———. *Conspiracy and Imprisonment: 1940–1945*. Edited by Mark Brocker. Translated by Lisa E. Dahill and Douglas W. Stott. Vol. 16 of *Dietrich Bonhoeffer Works*. Minneapolis: Fortress, 2006.

Other Sources for Dietrich Bonhoeffer's Work

Bonhoeffer, Dietrich. *Reflections on the Bible: Human Word and Word of God*. Edited by Manfred Weber. Translated by M. Eugene Boring. Peabody, MA: Hendrickson, 2004.

———. *A Testament to Freedom: The Essential Writings of Dietrich Bonhoeffer*. Rev. ed. Edited by Geffrey B. Kelly and F. Burton Nelson. New York: HarperCollins, 1995.

———. *The Way to Freedom: Letters, Lectures and Notes 1935–1939*. Translated by Edwin H. Robertson and John Bowden. London: Fount Paperbacks, 1972.

Secondary Sources Related to Dietrich Bonhoeffer and His Context

Arner, Rob. *Consistently Pro-Life: The Ethics of Bloodshed in Ancient Christianity*. Eugene, OR: Pickwick, 2010.

Baker, Nicholson. *Human Smoke: The Beginnings of World War II, the End of Civilization*. New York: Simon & Schuster, 2008.

Balfour, Michael, and Julian Frisby. *Helmuth von Moltke: A Leader Against Hitler*. London: Macmillan, 1972.

Barnett, Victoria. *For the Soul of the People: Protestant Protest Against Hitler.* Oxford: Oxford University Press, 1992.

Barth, Karl. *The Doctrine of Creation*. Part 4. Edited by G. W. Bromiley and T. F. Torrance. Translated by A. T. Mackay, T. H. L. Parker, H. Knight, H. A. Kennedy, and J. Marks. Vol. 3 of *Church Dogmatics*. 1961. Reprint, Peabody, MA: Hendrickson, 2010.

———. *The Doctrine of God*. Part 2. Edited by G. W. Bromiley and T. F. Torrance. Translated by G. W. Bromiley, J. C. Campbell, Iain Wilson, J. Strathearn McNab, Harold Knight, and R. A. Stewart. Vol. 2 of *Church Dogmatics*. 1957. Reprint, Peabody, MA: Hendrickson, 2010.

———. *The Doctrine of Reconciliation*. Part 2. Edited by G. W. Bromiley and T. F. Torrance. Translated by G. W. Bromiley. Vol. 4 of *Church Dogmatics*. 1958. Reprint, Peabody, MA: Hendrickson, 2004.

———. "Fate and Idea in Theology." In *The Way of Theology in Karl Barth: Essays and Comments*. Edited by H. Martin Rumscheidt. Translated by George Hunsinger, 32–42. Allison Park, PA: Pickwick, 1986.

Baumann, Clarence. *The Sermon on the Mount: The Modern Quest for Its Meaning*. Macon, GA: Mercer University Press, 1985.

Bentley, James. *Martin Niemöller, 1892–1984*. New York: Free Press, 1984.

Bergen, Doris L. *Twisted Cross: The German Christian Movement in the Third Reich*. Chapel Hill: University of North Carolina Press, 1996.

Bethge, Eberhard. *Dietrich Bonhoeffer: A Biography*. Rev. ed. Edited by Victoria J. Barnett. Minneapolis: Fortress, 2000.

Bethge, Eberhard, and Renate Bethge, eds. *Last Letters of Resistance: Farewells from the Bonhoeffer Family*. Translated by Dennis Slabaugh. Philadelphia: Fortress, 1986.

Bonhoeffer, Emmi. Interview in *Dietrich Bonhoeffer: Memories and Perspectives*. DVD. Directed by Bain Boehlke. Lansdale, PA: Vision Video, 1983.

Bosanquet, Mary. *The Life and Death of Dietrich Bonhoeffer*. New York: Harper & Row, 1968.

Brimlow, Robert W. *What About Hitler?: Wrestling With Jesus's Call to Nonviolence in an Evil World*. Grand Rapids: Brazos, 2006.

Brunner, Emil. *The Divine Imperative*. Translated by Olive Wyon. Philadelphia: Westminster, 1947.

Burleigh, Michael. *Moral Combat: Good and Evil in World War II*. New York: Harper, 2011.

Busch, Eberhard. *Karl Barth: His Life from Letters and Autobiographical Texts*. Translated by John Bowden. Philadelphia: Fortress, 1975.

Carter, Guy Christopher. "Confession at Bethel, August 1933—Enduring Witness: The Formation, Revision and Significance of the First Full Theological Confession of the Evangelical Church Struggle in Nazi Germany." PhD diss., Marquette University, 1987.

Clingan, Ralph Garlin. *Against Cheap Grace in a World Come of Age: An Intellectual Biography of Clayton Powell, 1865–1953*. New York: Peter Lang, 2002.

Copleston, Frederick. *Modern Philosophy: From the French Enlightenment to Kant*. Vol. 6 of *A History of Philosophy*. 1964. Reprint, New York: Doubleday, 1994.

DeJonge, Michael P. *Bonhoeffer's Theological Formation: Berlin, Barth and Protestant Theology*. Oxford: Oxford University Press, 2012.

———. "The Fact of the Person of Jesus Christ: Dietrich Bonhoeffer's *Act and Being*." PhD diss., Emory University, 2009.

Dorrien, Gary. *The Barthian Revolt in Modern Theology: Theology without Weapons*. Louisville: Westminster John Knox, 2000.

Dramm, Sabine. *Dietrich Bonhoeffer and the Resistance*. Translated by Margaret Kohl. Minneapolis: Fortress, 2009.

Elshtain, Jean Bethke. *Just War Against Terror: The Burden of American Power in a Violent World*. New York: Basic Books, 2004.

Feil, Ernst. *The Theology of Dietrich Bonhoeffer*. Translated by Martin Rumscheidt. Philadelphia: Fortress, 1985.

Fest, Joachim. *Plotting Hitler's Death: The Story of the German Resistance*. Translated by Bruce Little. New York: Metropolitan Books, 1996.

Gellately, Robert. *Backing Hitler: Consent and Coercion in Nazi Germany*. Oxford: Oxford University Press, 2001.

Gerlach, Wolfgang. *And the Witnesses Were Silent: The Confessing Church and the Persecution of the Jews*. Translated and edited by Victoria J. Barnett. Lincoln: University of Nebraska Press, 2000.

Gides, David M. *Pacifism, Just War, and Tyrannicide: Bonhoeffer's Church-World Theology and His Changing Forms of Political Thinking and Involvement*. Eugene, OR: Pickwick, 2011.

Gill, Anton. *An Honorable Defeat: A History of German Resistance to Hitler, 1933–1945*. New York: Henry Holt, 1994.

Gisevius, Hans Bernd. *To the Bitter End: An Insider's Account of the Plot to Kill Hitler 1933–1944*. Translated by Richard and Clara Winston. Boston: Houghton Mifflin, 1947. Reprint, New York: DaCapo Press, 1998.

Grayling, A. C. *Among the Dead: The History and Moral Legacy of the WWII Bombing of Civilians in Germany and Japan*. New York: Walker, 2006.

Green, Clifford J. *Bonhoeffer: A Theology of Sociality*. Rev. ed. Grand Rapids: Eerdmans, 1999.

———. "Bonhoeffer at Union. Critical Turning Points: 1931 and 1939." *Union Seminary Quarterly Review* 62 (2010): 1–16.

———. "Pacifism and Tyrannicide: Bonhoeffer's Christian Peace Ethic." *Studies in Christian Ethics* 18, no. 3 (2005): 31–47.

———. "Review of *Dietrich Bonhoeffer: Reality and Resistance*." *Conversations in Religion and Theology* 6 (2008): 155–65.

Gutteridge, Richard. *Open Thy Mouth for the Dumb: The German Evangelical Church and the Jews, 1879–1950*. Oxford: Basil Blackwell, 1976.

Hallie, Philip P. *Lest Innocent Blood Be Shed: The Story of the Village of Le Chambon, and How Goodness Happened There*. 1979. Reprint, New York: HarperPerennial, 1994.

Hauerwas, Stanley. *Performing the Faith: Bonhoeffer and the Practice of Nonviolence*. Grand Rapids: Brazos, 2004.

———. "The Significance of Vision: Toward and Aesthetic Ethic." In *Vision and Virtue: Essays in Christian Ethical Reflection*, 30–47. Notre Dame, IN: Fides, 1974.

Haynes, Stephen R. *The Bonhoeffer Legacy: Post-Holocaust Perspectives*. Minneapolis: Fortress, 2006.

———. *The Bonhoeffer Phenomenon: Portraits of a Protestant Saint*. Minneapolis: Fortress, 2004.

Helmreich, Ernest Christian. *The German Churches Under Hitler: Background, Struggle, and Epilogue*. Detroit: Wayne State University Press, 1979.

Hildebrandt, Franz. "Barmen: What to Learn and What Not to Learn." In *The Barmen Confession: Papers from the Seattle Assembly*, edited by Hubert G. Locke, 285–302. Lewiston, NY: Edwin Mellen, 1986.

———. Foreword to *Peace without Eschatology?* by John H. Yoder, 3–4. Scottdale, PA: Concern Reprint, 1959.

Hoffman, Peter. *The History of the German Resistance 1933–1945*. 3rd ed. Montreal: McGill-Queen's University Press, 1996.

———. *Stauffenberg: A Family History*. 3rd ed. Montreal: McGill-Queen's University Press, 2009.

Holland, Scott. "First We Take Manhattan, Then We Take Berlin: Bonhoeffer's New York." *Cross Currents*, Fall 2000: 369–82.

Holmes, Christopher. "'The Indivisible Whole of God's Reality': On the Agency of Jesus in Bonhoeffer's *Ethics*." *International Journal of Systematic Theology* 12 (2010): 283–301.

Johnson, Eric A. *Nazi Terror: The Gestapo, Jews, and Ordinary Germans*. New York: Basic Books, 1999.

Johnson, Eric, and Karl-Heinz Reuband. *What We Knew: Terror, Mass Murder and Everyday Life in Nazi Germany*. London: John Murray, 2005.

Jones, Nigel. *Countdown to Valkyrie: The July Plot to Assassinate Hitler*. London: Frontline Books, 2008.

Jones, W. T. *Kant to Wittgenstein and Sartre*. 2nd ed. Vol. 2 of *A History of Western Philosophy*. New York: Harcourt, Brace & World, 1969.

Kanitz, Joachim. Interview in *Dietrich Bonhoeffer: Memories and Perspectives*. DVD. Directed by Bain Boehlke. Lansdale, PA: Vision Video, 1983.

Kant, Immanuel. *Critique of Pure Reason*. Translated by J. M. D. Meiklejohn. 1787. Reprint, New York: Barnes & Noble, 2004.

Kelly, Geffrey B. "An Interview with Jean Lasserre." *Union Seminary Quarterly Review* 27, no. 3 (Spring 1972): 149–60.

Kelly, Geffrey B., and F. Burton Nelson. *The Cost of Moral Leadership: The Spirituality of Dietrich Bonhoeffer*. Grand Rapids: Eerdmans, 2003.

Kerr, Nathan. *Christ, History, and Apocalyptic: The Politics of Christian Mission*. Eugene, OR: Cascade Books, 2009.

Kershaw, Ian. *Luck of the Devil: The Story of Operation Valkyrie*. New York: Penguin Books, 2009.

Kirkpatrick, Matthew D. *Attacks on Christendom in a World Come of Age: Kierkegaard, Bonhoeffer, and the Question of "Religionless Christianity."* Princeton Theological Monograph Series. Eugene, OR: Pickwick, 2011.

Kolb, Robert, Timothy J. Wengert, Charles Arand, Eric Gritsch, William Russell, James Schaaf, and Hane Strohl, trans. and eds. *The Book of Concord: The Confessions of the Evangelical Lutheran Church*. Minneapolis: Fortress, 2000.

Koontz, Claudia. *The Nazi Conscience*. Cambridge, MA: Belknap Press of Harvard University Press, 2003.

Marsh, Charles. "Bonhoeffer on the Road to King: 'Turning from the Phraseological to the Real.'" In *Bonhoeffer and King: Their Legacies and Import for Christian Social Thought*, edited by Willis Jenkins and Jennifer M. McBride, 123–38. Minneapolis: Fortress, 2010.

———. *Reclaiming Dietrich Bonhoeffer: The Promise of His Theology*. New York: Oxford University Press, 1996.

Matheson, Peter, ed. *The Third Reich and the Christian Churches: A Documentary Account of Christian Resistance and Complicity During the Nazi Era*. Grand Rapids: Eerdmans, 1981.

Matthews, John W. *Anxious Souls Will Ask . . . : The Christ-Centered Spirituality of Dietrich Bonhoeffer*. Grand Rapids: Eerdmans, 2005.

Meding, Dorothee von. *Courageous Hearts: Women and the Anti-Hitler Plot of 1944*. Translated by Michael Balfour and Volker R. Berghahn. Providence, RI: Berghahn Books, 1997.

Metaxas, Eric. *Bonhoeffer: Pastor, Martyr, Prophet, Spy*. Nashville: Thomas Nelson, 2010.

Moltke, Freya von. *Memories of Kreisau and the German Resistance*. Translated by Julie M. Winter. Lincoln: University of Nebraska Press, 2003.

Moltke, Helmuth James von. *Letters to Freya, 1939–1945*. Edited and translated by Beate Ruhm von Oppen. New York: Alfred A. Knopf, 1990.

Mommsen, Hans. "The Kreisau Circle and the Future Reorganization of Germany and Europe." Chap. 4 in *Alternatives to Hitler: German Resistance under the Third Reich*. London: I. B. Tauris, 2003.

Moorhouse, Roger. *Killing Hitler: The Plots, the Assassins, and the Dictator Who Cheated Death*. New York: Bantam Books, 2006.

Morris, Kenneth E. "Bonhoeffer's Critique of Totalitarianism." *Journal of Church and State* 26 (1984): 255–72.

Moses, John A. "Dietrich Bonhoeffer's Repudiation of Protestant German War Theology." *The Journal of Religious History* 30 (2006): 354–70.

Nation, Mark. "The Politics of Compassion: A Study of Christian Nonviolent Resistance in the Third Reich." Master's thesis, Associated (Now Anabaptist) Mennonite Biblical Seminary, 1981.

———. "'A Blanket License to Commit Evil Acts?': A Fresh Examination of Bonhoeffer's Christological Framing of *Ethics*." *Perspectives in Religious Studies* 40 (2013): 143–53.

———. "'Pacifist and Enemy of the State': Bonhoeffer's 'Straight and Unbroken Course' from Costly Discipleship to Conspiracy." *Journal of Theology for Southern Africa* 77 (December 1991): 61–77.

———. "Discipleship in a World Full of Nazis: Dietrich Bonhoeffer's Polyphonic Pacifism as Social Ethics." In *The Wisdom of the Cross: Essays in Honor of John Howard Yoder*, edited by Stanley Hauerwas, Chris K. Huebner, Harry J. Huebner, and Mark Thiessen Nation, 249–77. 1999. Reprint, Eugene, OR: Wipf & Stock, 2005.

Nelson, F. Burton. "The Relationship of Jean Lasserre to Dietrich Bonhoeffer's Peace Concerns in the Struggle of Church and Culture." *Union Seminary Quarterly Review* 40 (1985): 71–84.

Niebuhr, Reinhold. *An Interpretation of Christian Ethics*. New York: Harper & Brothers, 1935.

———. *Moral Man and Immoral Society: A Study in Ethics and Politics*. 1932. Reprint, Louisville: Westminster John Knox, 2001.

Niemöller, Martin. "Bringing the Beatitudes Down to Earth." *Sojourners*, August 1981, 15–16.

———. "'What Would Jesus Say?': An Interview with Martin Niemöller." *Sojourners*, August 1981, 12–14.

Parssinen, Terry. *The Oster Conspiracy of 1938: The Unknown Story of the Military Plot to Kill Hitler and Avert World War II*. New York: HarperCollins, 2003.

Pfeifer, Hans. "Learning Faith and Ethical Commitment in the Context of Spiritual Training Groups. Consequences of Dietrich Bonhoeffer's Post Doctoral Year in New York City 1930/31." *Beiträge zur Dietrich Bonhoeffer-Forschung* 3 (2008): 251–79.

Rasmussen, Larry. *Dietrich Bonhoeffer: Reality and Resistance*. 1972. Reprint, Louisville: Westminster John Knox, 2005.

———. "The Ethics of Responsible Action." In *The Cambridge Companion to Dietrich Bonhoeffer*, edited by John W. de Gruchy, 206–25. Cambridge: Cambridge University Press, 1999.

———. "Response to Clifford Green." *Conversations in Religion and Theology* 6 (2008): 165–73.

Rasmusson, Arne. "Church and Nation-State: Karl Barth and German Public Theology in Early 20th Century." *Ned Geref Teologiese Tydskrif* 46 (2005): 511–24.

———. "Church and War in the Theology of Karl Barth." In *Living Theology*, edited by Len Hansen et al., 386–98. Wellington, South Africa: Bible Media, 2011.

Roberts, Andrew. *The Storm of War: A New History of the Second World War*. New York: Harper, 2011.

Roon, Ger van. *German Resistance to Hitler: Count von Moltke and the Kreisau Circle*. Translated by Peter Ludlow. London: Van Nostrand Reinhold, 1971.

Sax, Benjamin, and Dieter Kuntz, eds. *Inside Hitler's Germany: A Documentary History of Life in the Third Reich*. Lexington, MA: DC Heath, 1992.

Schliesser, Christine. *Everyone Who Acts Responsibly Becomes Guilty: Bonhoeffer's Concept of Accepting Guilt*. Louisville: Westminster John Knox, 2008.

Schlingensiepen, Ferdinand. *Dietrich Bonhoeffer 1906–1945: Martyr, Thinker, Man of Resistance*. Translated by Isabel Best. London: T&T Clark, 2010.

Scholder, Klaus. *Preliminary History and the Time of Illusions, 1918–1934*. Vol. 1 of *The Churches and the Third Reich*. Translated by John Bowden. Philadelphia: Fortress, 1988.

———. *The Year of Disillusionment: 1934—Barmen and Rome*. Vol. 2 of *The Churches and the Third Reich*. Translated by John Bowden. Philadelphia: Fortress, 1988.

Semelin, Jacques. *Unarmed against Hitler: Civilian Resistance in Europe, 1939–1943*. Westport, CT: Praeger, 1993.

Steigmann-Gall, Richard. *The Holy Reich: Nazi Conceptions of Christianity, 1919–1945*. Cambridge: Cambridge University Press, 2003.

Taylor, Charles. *Sources of the Self: The Making of Modern Identity*. Cambridge, MA: Harvard University Press, 1989.

Thielicke, Helmut. *Modern Faith and Thought*. Translated by Geoffrey W. Bromiley. Grand Rapids: Eerdmans, 1990.

Tödt, Heinz Eduard. "The Bonhoeffer-Dohnanyi Circle in Opposition and Resistance to Hitler's Regime of Violence: Interim Report on a Research Project." In *Authentic Faith: Bonhoeffer's Theological Ethics in Context*, edited by Ernst-Albert Scharffenorth and Glen Harold Stassen, translated by David Stassen and Ilse Tödt, 179–231. Grand Rapids: Eerdmans, 2007.

———. "Dealing with Guilt in the Church's Confession and in the Justice System after 1945." In *Authentic Faith: Bonhoeffer's Theological Ethics in Context*, edited by Ernst-Albert Scharffenorth and Glen Harold Stassen, translated by David Stassen and Ilse Tödt, 260–78. Grand Rapids: Eerdmans, 2007.

———. "Dietrich Bonhoeffer's Decisions in the Crisis Years 1929–33." *Studies in Christian Ethics* 18, no. 3 (2005): 107–23.

The Top Secret Trial of the Third Reich. Directed by Jochen Bauer. DVD. New York: First Run Features, 1979.

Valkyrie. Directed by Bryan Singer. DVD. Beverly Hills, CA: MGM, 2008.

Wartenburg, Marion Yorck von. *The Power of Solitude: My Life in the German Resistance*. Lincoln: University of Nebraska Press, 2000.

Webster, John. "Reading the Bible: The Example of Barth and Bonhoeffer." In *Word and Church: Essays in Church Dogmatics*, 87–110. Edinburgh: T&T Clark, 2001.

Wedemeyer-Weller, Maria von. "The Other Letters from Prison." In *Letters and Papers from Prison*, enlarged edition, by Dietrich Bonhoeffer, 412–19. Edited by Eberhard Bethge. New York: Macmillan, 1971.

Williams, Reggie. "Christ-Centered Empathic Resistance: The Influence of Harlem Renaissance Theology on the Incarnational Ethics of Dietrich Bonhoeffer." PhD diss., Fuller Theological Seminary, 2011.

Wind, Renate. *A Spoke in the Wheel.* Translated by John Bowden. Grand Rapids: Eerdmans, 1991.

Yoder, John Howard. *Karl Barth and the Problem of War and Other Essays on Barth.* Edited by Mark Thiessen Nation. Eugene, OR: Cascade Books, 2003.

Young III, Josiah Ulysses. *No Difference in the Fare: Dietrich Bonhoeffer and the Problem of Racism.* Grand Rapids: Eerdmans, 1998.

Zabel, James A. *Nazism and the Pastors: A Study of the Ideas of Three Deutsche Christian Groups.* Missoula, MT: Scholars Press, 1976.

Zerner, Ruth. "Dietrich Bonhoeffer's American Experiences: People, Letters, and Papers from Union Seminary." *Union Seminary Quarterly Review* 31 (1976): 261–82.

Ziegler, Philip G. "Dietrich Bonhoeffer—An Ethics of God's Apocalypse?" *Modern Theology* 23 (October 2007): 579–94.

Zimmermann, Wolf-Dieter, and Ronald Gregor Smith, eds. *I Knew Dietrich Bonhoeffer.* Translated by Käthe Gregor Smith. 1966. Reprint, London: Fontana Books, 1973.

INDEX